THE REWARDS
OF PUBLIC SERVICE

ROBERT W. HARTMAN AND ARNOLD R. WEBER

EDITORS

THE REWARDS
OF PUBLIC SERVICE

Compensating Top Federal Officials

THE BROOKINGS INSTITUTION

Washington, D.C.

Library of Congress Cataloging in Publication Data:

Main entry under title:

The Rewards of public service.

Includes bibliographical references and index.

1. Government executives—Salaries, pensions, etc.—
United States. 2. United States. Congress—Salaries,
pensions, etc. 3. Judges—Salaries, pensions, etc.
—United States. I. Hartman, Robert W. II. Weber,
Arnold Robert.

JK776.R48   353.001'2   79-24577

ISBN 0-8157-3494-8
ISBN 0-8157-3493-X pbk.

1 2 3 4 5 6 7 8 9

THE BROOKINGS INSTITUTION is an independent organization devoted to nonpartisan research, education, and publication in economics, government, foreign policy, and the social sciences generally. Its principal purposes are to aid in the development of sound public policies and to promote public understanding of issues of national importance.

The Institution was founded on December 8, 1927, to merge the activities of the Institute for Government Research, founded in 1916, the Institute of Economics, founded in 1922, and the Robert Brookings Graduate School of Economics and Government, founded in 1924.

The Board of Trustees is responsible for the general administration of the Institution, while the immediate direction of the policies, program, and staff is vested in the President, assisted by an advisory committee of the officers and staff. The by-laws of the Institution state: "It is the function of the Trustees to make possible the conduct of scientific research, and publication, under the most favorable conditions, and to safeguard the independence of the research staff in the pursuit of their studies and in the publication of the results of such studies. It is not a part of their function to determine, control, or influence the conduct of particular investigations or the conclusions reached."

The President bears final responsibility for the decision to publish a manuscript as a Brookings book. In reaching his judgment on the competence, accuracy, and objectivity of each study, the President is advised by the director of the appropriate research program and weighs the views of a panel of expert outside readers who report to him in confidence on the quality of the work. Publication of a work signifies that it is deemed a competent treatment worthy of public consideration but does not imply endorsement of conclusions or recommendations.

The Institution maintains its position of neutrality on issues of public policy in order to safeguard the intellectual freedom of the staff. Hence interpretations or conclusions in Brookings publications should be understood to be solely those of the authors and should not be attributed to the Institution, to its trustees, officers, or other staff members, or to the organizations that support its research.

Foreword

EVERYONE seems to have a strong opinion about the salaries paid to high public officials. But despite intense interest and strong views, the issue has been the subject of little research or fact-finding. This volume is an attempt to set out the relevant considerations, so that future debates over the pay of the nation's highest officials can be less heated and more constructive.

Because the considerations that ought to govern the remuneration of congressmen, federal judges, and cabinet and subcabinet officials do not fall within the purview of any one of the traditional academic disciplines, the contributors to this book were chosen from a variety of professions. The editors commissioned papers from historians, political scientists, economists, personnel specialists, and lawyers to ensure that differing views would be brought to bear on the subject. The papers were discussed at a Brookings conference on executive, legislative, and judicial compensation held in October 1978 that was attended by government officials and business representatives as well as academic experts. The introductory chapter is a summary, prepared by the editors, of the views, conclusions, and recommendations elicited at the conference.

The six commissioned papers, revised to reflect the discussion at the conference, constitute the remainder of this book. First, Louis Fisher of the Library of Congress discusses the long and rocky history of congressional salary changes. Roger H. Davidson of the University of California at Santa Barbara then reviews the role of public opinion and of political pressure on pay adjustments. Edward Lazear and Sherwin Rosen of the University of Chicago and Wesley R. Liebtag of IBM prepared the next two papers, which illustrate the contrasting approaches of economic analysis and of corporate sector executive pay practices to setting salaries. James C. Kirby, Jr., of the University of Tennessee College of Law then considers the possibilities and implications of conflicts of interest in salary determination. In the final paper Robert W. Hartman discusses the influence of top officials' pay on other federal employees, especially those participating in the new Senior Executive Service.

Robert W. Hartman is a senior fellow in the Brookings Economic Studies program. Arnold R. Weber is provost of Carnegie-Mellon University. They and the authors are grateful for the useful comments of Joel Aberbach, Hugh Heclo, Darwin G. Johnson, Norman J. Ornstein, Albert Rees, Jerome M. Rosow, and Laurence H. Silberman. The manuscript was edited by Elizabeth H. Cross. Its factual content was verified by Ellen W. Smith, and the index was prepared by Florence Robinson.

This study was sponsored jointly by Brookings and Carnegie-Mellon University. Grants from the Alfred P. Sloan Foundation to Brookings and from the Richard King Mellon Foundation to the Public Policy Institute at Carnegie-Mellon University contributed to the support of this project. The views are those of the authors, and should not be attributed to the Alfred P. Sloan Foundation, the Richard King Mellon Foundation, or Carnegie-Mellon University, to the other conference participants, or to the trustees, officers, or other staff members of the Brookings Institution.

BRUCE K. MAC LAURY
President

November 1979
Washington, D.C.

Contents

ix

Tables

Arnold R. Weber and Robert W. Hartman

The Ways and Means
of Compensating Federal Officials

THE QUESTION of what compensation is proper for top government officials touches one of the most sensitive nerves in the body politic. Although it cannot be argued that the fate of the republic hinges on the salaries of congressmen, judges, and high-level federal executives, the determination of compensation for these officials describes the kind of government Americans want and the relationship of government officials to the citizens they serve. In a sense, the compensation issue constitutes an effigy of democracy that bears the tension, if not the catcalls, evoked by the conflicting desires to have the best people lead the government but to remind them in pecuniary terms that they are no better than anyone else.

Within this general framework, the compensation of top federal officials can be analyzed at various levels. First, the issue can be considered as a special case of wage determination in a conventional labor market context. The usual economic concepts will afford the appropriate mechanisms for determining the correct level of compensation for cabinet officers as well as cabinetmakers, that is, supply and demand, the weighing of nonpecuniary satisfactions, the opportunity for accumulating "human capital," and so on.

Second, the compensation of top federal officials is part of a broader managerial system that encompasses almost 3 million government employees whose pay is directly influenced by the treatment of 2,500 congressmen, judges, and cabinet members and other high-level federal executives. If cabinet officers and senators are the nominal "executives" in the federal government, what is the proper relationship between their compensation and that of a middle manager in the Department of Labor, a field engineer in the Bureau of Reclamation, or a file clerk in the General Services Administration? To the extent that high morale and efficiency are endorsed as goals of government performance, the relationship between compensation of the executive positions and that of the rest of federal employees should be handled in a manner consistent with these objectives. The techniques of salary administration developed in the private sector may offer some guidance, but their applicability to the special circumstances of government must be tested.

Third, the compensation issue is enmeshed in political values and processes. The decision to increase congressional and executive pay is more sensitive to constituents' reactions and public opinion than to the protocols of executive compensation at IBM. Also, since public moneys are involved, both the executive branch and Congress must play an important role in compensation decisions through the authorization and appropriation process. Because they are beneficiaries of these actions, allegations of conflict of interest are inherent in the process and raise ethical questions. The ethical issue is magnified when compensation is enlarged to include outside income that appears to be related to the status and potential influence of the lawmaker or government official. The compensation issue has been used politically to confirm both the idealism of the humble public servant and the suspicion that idealism is not always a sufficient safeguard against public venality.

Last, the question of compensation for high government officials has a long historical record, if not tradition, which conditions the public's response in a contemporary setting. There has always been full recognition of the public sensitivity to the issue, particularly as it relates to congressional salaries. Similarly, there has been a pattern of experimentation with timing, the size of the increases, and the procedures used to determine salary adjustments. As in most political matters, it is impossible to start with a clean slate; rather, any proposal for modifying the current approach to the compensation of federal officials must be evaluated in the light of long-established practices. The notion that compensation in any large enterprise can be determined by rules laid down more than two hundred years ago is startling, but tradition must be taken into account every time Congress uneasily approaches this issue.

Compensation as a Historical Issue

The record reveals the ambiguities and sensitivities that have characterized the compensation issue. As Louis Fisher indicates, the Constitution provided almost no guidance for future legislative bodies in setting their own pay. The members of the Constitutional Convention cautiously circled the issue and were content with the statement, "The Senators and Representatives shall receive a Compensation for their Services, to be ascertained by Law, and paid out of the Treasury of the United States" (Article I, section 6). This established the principle that the legislators should be paid *national* officials, but beyond making this political judgment passed the buck to prospective legislators.

The other constitutional references to compensation are equally terse and affirm that the President and federal judges shall receive compensation for their services and that such compensation shall not be diminished during their terms in office. An effort was made to fuse this limited directive with contemporary inflation economics in 1976, when a group of federal judges filed a suit to force the government to raise their pay on the grounds that the failure to adjust nominal salaries for the loss in real income resulting from inflation was a diminution of compensation in the constitutional meaning of the term. The court rejected this somewhat strained, if not bizarre, argument from its brethren.[1]

The Constitution made no direct reference to the compensation of other high government officials; this detail was beyond the prescience of the convention. The standards used for determining such compensation and the methods and timing of salary adjustments were left for future deliberation. The Congress was given wide latitude for experimentation, a modus operandi that has persisted to this day. Initially, senators and representatives were paid on a per diem basis, and the remuneration of the members of the two houses was different. This gap was closed in 1796. An annual salary schedule was introduced in 1816, withdrawn one year later, and reinstated in 1856. Until 1907 Congress generally followed the practice of approving retroactive increases covering the entire term in which the raise was voted. After 1907 increases were made prospective, probably in reaction to the political controversy precipitated by the earlier policy. In 1945 Congress discovered the lump-sum expense allowance, raising effective compensation.

Before 1967, adjustments in legislative, executive, and judicial salaries were instituted through positive action by the Congress. In 1967 a new system was introduced whereby recommendations are made to the President by a commission of distinguished (and presumably disinterested)

---

1. *C. Clyde Atkins, et al.* v. *United States; Louis C. Bechtle, et al.* v. *United States; Ruggero J. Aldisert* v. *United States,* 214 Ct. Cl. 186 (1977); *Atkins, U.S. District Judge, et al.* v. *United States,* 426 U.S. 944 (1976).

citizens every four years. The President, in turn, reviews the recommendations and submits them to Congress with his modifications, if any. In the 1970s the President's proposals became law through a process of "negative legislation," that is, if neither house of Congress passed a resolution of disapproval in thirty days. In 1979 Congress reversed itself, again requiring a positive vote on the President's proposals.

Clearly, the history of top-level compensation in the federal government has been one of short-term, almost aimless experimentation. There is little evidence of a quest for or adherence to enduring principles grounded either in the Constitution or in precepts of public administration. This ad hoc method reflects the early and continuing political sensitivity of the issue. As Fisher says, "Ever since the First Congress, legislators have looked over their shoulders apprehensively, trying to anticipate how their constituents will react to a pay increase." Throughout history, legislators have suffered the outrage of their constituents in salary matters. On two occasions, in 1817 and in 1874, Congress felt obliged to rescind previous increases to mollify the public. The fact that legislative and executive salaries have been changed only eight times since 1900 testifies to the delicacy of the issue. Moreover, in recent years the public's rancor has been directed to the salaries of some high-level executives as well. Newspaper accounts of apple-cheeked presidential appointees doubling the pay they received in the private sector and of "$100,000 couples"— husband-and-wife teams that hold high executive positions in the federal government—have conflicted with egalitarian notions of public service.

The political sensitivity of the compensation issue has been deepened by the tendency of individual congressmen to demonstrate virtue to their constituents by attacking any proposed pay increase. Not every congressman would be as forthright as Ben Johnson of Kentucky, who in 1925 declared, "If my constituents should say that I am not worth $10,000 a year here, then my answer to them is, Send somebody who is."[2]

The elements of experimentalism and political hypersensitivity have given rise to tactical cunning or outright gimmicks to obscure the size of the salary adjustments or to evade direct responsibility for initiating an increase. The lump-sum expense allowance instituted in 1945 was withdrawn in 1955, when Congress raised the annual salary of its members from $12,500 to $22,500. An expense allowance was renewed in subsequent years.

2. Fisher, p. 44.

The law establishing the quadrennial commission and approval of pay increases by negative legislation was designed in part to put parliamentary distance between Congress and the compensation issue. Further, the adoption of the practice of "linkage" whereby congressional salary adjustments were coordinated with those of deputy secretaries of major federal departments and appellate judges ostensibly made congressional salary adjustments a passive expression of interoccupational equity rather than personal aggrandizement. The sizable increase in congressional pay in 1977 was mated with a code of ethics, which limited outside compensation to muffle any public outcry. Significantly, the code of ethics was pushed aggressively by the quadrennial commission, which displayed its sensitivity to the take-with-one-hand-give-with-the-other approach to compensation. After accepting the limit on outside compensation, the Senate in 1979 postponed the effective date but did not rescind the pay increase. And last, there is the current law that provides for annual adjustments—between quadrennial commissions—without a vote. This attempt to provide no-fault increases has not worked as intended.

Beyond the verification of congressional ingenuity, the historical record indicates that the question of compensation for high-level government officials has never been settled and is unlikely ever to be resolved.

The Economics of Federal Compensation

In its pure form, the issue of the proper compensation for federal executives, judges, and legislators is a subset of the general problem of wage and salary determination. Although there are institutional differences in the labor market between, say, bricklayers and cabinet officers, the same basic principles should apply in explaining the compensation for these occupations and changes in it. These principles are explicated and tested, at least intellectually, by Edward Lazear and Sherwin Rosen.

First, the compensation of top government officials should reflect rudimentary considerations of supply and demand. The supply function describes the availability of suitable candidates for the positions at various levels of compensation. The demand function reflects constitutional requirements, the current organizational needs of government, and the quality standards applied to would-be officials. At any one time, demand is fixed in the sense that the need to "hire" congressmen or cabinet officers is determined by constitutional or statutory provision rather than by wage level. For example, it would be preposterous to assert that the number of assistant secretaries in the federal government will vary with the "equilibrium wage" for this occupation.

More important—and difficult to assess—are the quality requirements. As a matter of course, we want high-quality, honest people to fill critical positions in government. A major difficulty in attaining this objective is that there are no clear, generally accepted qualification standards, except in the judiciary, where legal training and experience are expected. Even the concept of honesty becomes obscured in the complexity of conflict of interest standards. Moreover, though a little "honest graft" (to use a concept widely endorsed in Chicago) may be acceptable among legislators, standards of probity will be more stringent for judges.

Second, the concept of compensation should be subsumed in the broader notion of "net advantage," which includes both pecuniary and nonpecuniary income in the top-level positions. Nonpecuniary factors traditionally have been given substantial value in the net advantage of executive, legislative, and judicial positions. These include the satisfaction of performing public service, status, social opportunities, and the sometimes giddying participation in the determination of important national decisions. Negative factors are job insecurity, long hours of work, loss of privacy, and exposure to harsh public criticism. The calculation of the net advantage will, of course, vary from person to person and between occupational categories. For example, a federal judge with lifetime tenure obviously has greater job security than a congressman, who must run the electoral gauntlet every two years. All other considerations being the same, the judge might be expected to accept more of a discount from what he might be paid in the private sector than the congressman. Data cited by Lazear and Rosen from a study conducted for the 1976 Commission on Executive, Legislative, and Judicial Salaries (the Peterson Commission) indicate that this is the case. Similarly, James Kirby notes that congressmen with short terms of service are more likely to maintain a private law practice than legislators with seniority. Normally, newly elected congressmen are less certain of being returned to office than those who have built a large stock of political capital, so it is economically prudent for the freshman legislator to hedge his or her bet by maintaining professional visibility in private law practice.

Third, the concept of human capital places the compensation issue in the longer time frame of the individual's career and future income stream. A person will be attracted to a high-level government position not only by transient glory or immediate pecuniary gains, or both, but also because the experience will permit the acquisition of skills and knowledge that are highly valued and transferable to positions outside government. It is almost a truism to note that the federal government has played an intrusive role in the regulation of private business in the United States. While most businessmen have responded to this development with elegies for the free enterprise system, at another, less rhetorical level they have tried to cope by recruiting executives who can find their way through the government labyrinth. Even at universities, professors who can brandish government credentials as a complement to their scholarly achievements may enjoy a comparative advantage over their more monkish colleagues. If the federal government has become an octopus intruding into almost every aspect of our lives and organized economic activity, then it is also true that for many federal officials there has been a pot of gold at the end of each tentacle when they leave government.

An appreciation of the future returns from the human capital accumulated in government service can be an important element of the total compensation influencing a person's decision to seek or to accept a high-level government position. Data collected for the 1976 quadrennial commission indicate that the human capital effect is probably considerable. The respondents in a sample of those who had left government revealed that the pay for their first job after departing from Washington was an average of 87 percent higher than the compensation that they had received in federal executive positions, 84 percent higher for former judges, and 34 percent higher for former congressmen. Also, the prospects for acquiring human capital may be more enticing to those accepting executive positions since they tend to return to jobs outside government after a short period of time—two years for an assistant secretary and four years for a cabinet officer. On the other hand, few federal judges actually step down from the bench. Judges generally come to these positions after they have reached or passed their peak earnings. And their greater age implies that the present value of any future income to be derived from newly acquired human capital will be reduced because there are fewer years of professional employment remaining.

Fourth, an economic framework for assessing the proper approach to compensation should recognize segmentation within markets and differences in the market segments. Thus it is misleading to designate a single, comprehensive labor market for high-level government officials. Rather, there are significant differences in the characteristics and structure of the submarkets for cabinet officers and other federal executives, legislators, and judges. Each occupational category requires a different set of attributes and skills and encompasses a different combination of prestige, job security, and opportunities for accumulating human capital. Entry to the legislator's market is overtly political, the recruitment and selection of federal executives reflects a variable weighting of political considerations and objective standards of competence, and judges are formally held to "merit" criteria imposed by external bodies such as the American Bar Association. Recognition of these differences in both supply and demand should be taken into account in any compensation arrangement covering legislators, executives, and judges.

Undoubtedly, these economic notions contribute in a general way to the process of salary determination for top federal officials. However, the use of economic concepts in this area is analogous to Molière's *bourgeois gentilhomme,* who learned that he had been speaking prose all his life. In fact, economic considerations per se have seldom been addressed or used explicitly as policy tools in adjusting compensation. As a historical matter, it has been agreed that compensation for top government officials should be sufficiently generous to attract and retain high-quality people without making such positions the province of those who are independently wealthy. Also, some believe that salary levels should be set so as to safeguard the honesty of public officials. But it is not clear whether honesty is promoted by high or low salaries since high salaries may make misfeasance less tempting but attract people with a taste for pecuniary gains.

The most direct refutation of economic rationality in setting the compensation for high-level government officials was expressed by the approval in 1969 of the principle of linkage, whereby the salaries of executives, judges, and legislators are subject to uniform treatment by establishing identical compensation for members of Congress, level II executives (deputy secretaries), and appellate judges. This elaborate effort to deal with the compensation issue was founded on the assumption that differential market considerations are irrelevant or overwhelmed by other, noneconomic factors. When Under Secretary of Health, Education, and Welfare Hale Champion resigned his $52,500 position in mid-1979 to return to Harvard, he exclaimed, "I'm broke. I can't afford it anymore."[3] But it seems clear that no one, except perhaps his immediate family, was listening.

3. *New York Times,* May 18, 1979.

Compensation as a Management System

If economic concepts per se have had limited relevance in determining executive, legislative, and judicial pay, can more powerful tools be applied by considering the compensation of high government officials as part of a comprehensive system of management and personnel administration? With this approach, the federal government is treated as another firm, albeit one of gargantuan proportions, and cabinet officers, judges, and members of Congress are viewed as comparable to business executives. The problem of determining the appropriate compensation for top government positions can then be attacked by applying the techniques sharpened in the private sector: formal job descriptions, job evaluation, comparability studies, an objective data base, and the rank ordering of the positions in a rational salary structure.

The use of this approach should not be regarded as reflecting a witless belief in the inherent superiority of private sector methods over public sector bumbling. The techniques of formal wage and salary administration have long been used for general schedule federal employees, including the supergrades. The 2,500 people in the top executive, legislative, and judicial positions are part of a complex organizational structure in which internal relationships are perceived as dominant. Moreover, dealing with the question of compensation for high government officials as an exercise in conventional salary administration may provide a basis for systematic reference to external market factors that in the past have been ignored or downgraded. Indeed, the various quadrennial commissions have encouraged a more explicitly managerial approach to determining what a cabinet officer, a judge, or a senator is "worth" in conventional economic terms.

The applicability of the private sector approach to federal executive compensation is tested by Wesley Liebtag. The results are mixed at best. In Liebtag's judgment, the unique aspects of top government positions present an insurmountable obstacle to the detailed use of comparability with private sector executive jobs to determine the appropriate level of compensation. The notion of comparing the secretary of defense to, say, the chief executive officer of a conventional private sector firm is somewhat fanciful. Even if a relevant basis for comparison was identified—for instance, the chief executive of General Motors—the pecuniary chasm between the total compensation of the latter and what can realistically be defined as the upper limit of a cabinet officer's pay makes the comparison of no practical significance. The public and Congress would be stunned by even the hypothetical suggestion that the job responsibilities of the secretary of defense justify an annual salary of $750,000 to $1,000,000. Also, the fact that the principle of parity in compensation for all cabinet officers is firmly established despite differences in the operational responsibilities of the individual departments further weakens the appeal of comparisons with the private sector based on abstract job descriptions. If the process of executive, legislative, and judicial compensation does reach out of the federal governmental structure, Liebtag asserts that the most sensible referent or data base is the compensation of municipal and state officials.

The principle of comparability with similar jobs in the private sector is perhaps on firmer ground when applied to the *rate* of change, rather than the actual *level* of compensation. Sensitivity to the percentage change in the compensation of equivalent executive positions provides a proxy for the current strength of market forces, regardless of the absolute differences in the compensation of top government officials. Liebtag suggests that these data should be supplemented by other broad measures of economic conditions such as the consumer price index, the index of average hourly earnings, and the annual national survey of professional, administrative, technical, and clerical pay (PATC).

Private sector practice probably is more useful in helping to identify problems or anomalies in the compensation of top government officials than in providing guides to positive action. For example, the concept of linkage has no rational basis when objective position descriptions and an evaluation of job attributes reveal wide diversity among the legislative, judicial, and executive categories. Private sector experience also indicates that the pay intervals between executive level positions, which range from 5.0 percent to 9.5 percent, are too small and should be increased to reflect the hierarchy of job duties and responsibilities more accurately. The corporate world, for instance, would find it difficult to justify the fact that the director of the FBI enjoys the same executive rank (level II) as the deputy attorney general, to whom he nominally reports. A further anomaly is the modest classification (level IV) of the social security commissioner, in view of the agency's work force of 80,000 and $100 billion budget.

An analysis of the compensation system for top government officials in private sector terms is most revealing in identifying the chronic problem of compression that has arisen from the failure to coordinate the executive pay structure with adjustments in the general schedule for other government employees. As Hartman recounts, the executive pay structure is vertically linked to the general schedule by the fact that the compensation for level V executives (the bottom rung in the executive schedule) establishes the ceiling for employees in the general schedule. Because statutory provisions call for annual pay adjustments of GS employees while executive compensation is in practice adjusted infrequently, the salaries of top civil servants bump against the level V limit with demoralizing regularity. In a highly inflationary period, this compression is particularly severe, and it reaches down even below the ranks of the so-called supergrades (GS-16 to GS-18), who have been the top career civil servants.

Conversely, pressure is exerted in the overall federal pay structure to raise the pay of noncareer presidential appointees in the executive ranks in order to provide relief for the victims of compression in the general schedule. Once this step was taken, the practice of (horizontal) linkage would raise the compensation of legislators and judges without any searching inquiry into the merits of the adjustment. Whether or not the process was designed with this objective in mind, congressional salaries might become a tail on a high-flying kite with "linkage" emblazoned on one side and "equity" on the other. As Hartman says, this problem has been partially remedied by the law establishing the Senior Executive Service, which permits annual bonuses for top civil servants that can bring their total compensation up to the level of full cabinet officers. But other, more subtle problems of compression associated with the pivotal position of the pay for level IV executives under the new system will still result.

Treating the compensation of top government officials as analogous to executive compensation in the private sector will not afford a comprehensive or fully realistic basis for addressing the issue. Such an approach would offer few guides to the question of the proper level of compensation and would have limited value in comparing legislative apples with judicial oranges and cabinet-hued plums. However, private sector practice does provide some basis for filtering market trends into the federal pay system, identifying important structural problems *within* the total system, and at least casting in sharp relief decisions that are inconsistent with economic or administrative objectives.

The Politics of Federal Compensation

If economic and managerial considerations only partially explain the process of salary determination for top government officials, then political factors should be recognized as the dominant influence. From the earliest days of the republic, executive, legislative, and judicial compensation has been set by political functionaries responding to changing political values in an avowedly political setting. While economics may set the tone and management techniques may be used for fine tuning, the score is political in conception and execution.

The early view of compensation for top government officials accepted the need to attract qualified people to government service by offering adequate salaries so as not to limit the effective supply to the wealthy or the elite. "Adequacy" has been defined primarily by the economic perspectives of the ordinary citizen rather than the theoretical exigencies of supply and demand. It is difficult for an ordinary citizen who must manage on $15,000 a year to understand why a congressman should receive $57,500. In 1977 Peter G. Peterson, the chairman of the last quadrennial commission, organized the Citizens' Committee for Restoring Public Trust in Government to persuade the public that the generous increases proposed by the commission (up to a third or more) were justified by the government's "desperate need for outstanding executives."[4] Peterson conceded, however, that the task of persuading people in his home town of Kearny, Nebraska, that these claims were meritorious was a difficult one. Roger Davidson reveals that there is no evidence that the public believes in any relationship between the pay of federal officials and demonstrable competence or in the necessity for high salaries to improve the quality of government.

The general indifference to salary as a managerial tool has been further conditioned by the degree of public esteem granted high government officials. Davidson's analysis emphasizes the fact that neither legislators nor federal executives, particularly when lumped with the larger group of "government employees," enjoy the respect or confidence of the general public. Indeed, when the Peterson Commission recommended coupling proposed salary increases with a code of ethics for Congress that would restrict legislators' outside income and otherwise reassure the public that the raise was warranted, both the increase and the code were instituted; but one year later the Senate gave credence to the public's suspicions by delaying the reduction in allowable outside earnings scheduled to take effect in January 1979. The issue is further complicated by the strong belief, expressed by Kirby, that the question of appropriate ethical standards

---

4. Davidson, p. 96.

for congressmen is separable from the compensation issue and that it was a mistake to link the two as a short-term political strategy.

The political aspects of executive, legislative, and judicial compensation have been intensified by the process for reviewing and approving salary adjustments. First, for reasons of conviction or political advantage, proposed increases in the pay of top government officials generally have been considered fair game for criticism. Although these attacks have usually been directed at congressional salaries, adherence to the practice of linkage means that salary adjustments for executives and judges have also been tainted by inference. This ritual critical pelting does not build public confidence that pay changes are necessary to meet real needs.

Second, the practice of approving salary adjustments by negative legislation under the provisions of the 1967 law has helped sustain the belief that the system of compensation is a method for enriching top federal officials without clear accountability. Because negative legislation (or the legislative veto) does not require affirmative action by Congress, the legislators can claim that they have reluctantly acquiesced to a recommendation made by the impartial quadrennial commission, as reviewed and modified by the President. Fisher's discussion reveals that the question of accountability is of long standing. After the clamor provoked by the 1977 pay increase, Congress did change the rules to require an affirmative vote for the quadrennial salary adjustments.

Third, the timing of the adjustment process so that it is coincident with a presidential election ensures that the compensation of top government officials will be the topic of heated campaign oratory. Attacking proposed increases is duck soup for neopopulists and conservatives alike. In the 1976 campaign, for example, Jimmy Carter was inevitably drawn into the debate over the procedures and standards used for changing the salaries of top government officials.

The assertion that the determination of executive, legislative, and judicial compensation is highly politicized is not surprising. In truth, it is a messy political process lacking the traditional disciplines that impart some order, if not rationality, to the proceedings. Although Davidson indicates that Democrats are more likely to support pay increases than Republicans, the compensation of high government officials is not a partisan or ideological issue. Therefore, it has not been susceptible to party discipline. Also, compensation is not the kind of issue that inspires aggressive presidential leadership or involvement. As chief executive, the President nominally is the chief personnel officer for the federal government as well. But this responsibility has a low position on his agenda, except when he presses for one of the recurrent "reforms" of the civil service. Without party discipline or presidential leadership, the determination of executive, legislative, and judicial compensation has been the product of transient outbursts of congressional interest, informal lobbying by the groups that bear the weight of salary compression, and a sensitive reading of constituents' reactions. As such, the process is hardly calculated to promote consistency or rationality. Economic considerations set the broad limits of compensation for high government officials within which political factors have dictated both the actual process of determination and the outcomes.

Recommendations

This review of the background of issues in and approaches to compensation of high federal officials illuminates some of the determinants of the upper and lower bounds on pay. The amount paid to such officials should not exceed the level where the public becomes resentful, where doing public service becomes just another job sought for primarily economic rewards, or where (as with outside income) conflicts of interest become likely. On the other hand, compensation must be kept above the level where the pool of qualified talent dries up or where, as in some state and local governments, public service is a part-time sideline to some other career. Although it is beyond the scope of this review to attach dollar signs to these upper and lower bounds on federal pay for high officials, we think we have defined some central issues that can help in the future to identify appropriate levels.

Breaking Linkage

First and foremost, the linkage between the salaries of members of Congress and those of other federal officials should be severed. There never was any real justification for establishing the equivalence of congressional pay and that of appeals court judges and executive level II jobs; maintaining the linkage has become an impediment to intelligent paysetting throughout the federal government.

The considerations relating to congressional salaries differ in virtually every important respect from those for other officials. Insofar as public opinion sets a cap on federal officials' pay, the compensation of members of Congress and of cabinet officers seems to be most subject to this constraint. This may mean that the salaries of such officials will necessarily be sticky because of their visibility. But public opinion may prove to be quite different for judges and assistant secretaries in the executive branch. The compensation of these officials—for good reasons or otherwise—does not seem to arouse such extreme emotions in the general public. Thus, while it may be inevitable that the vagaries of public opinion limit salaries or affect the timing of adjustments for members of Congress (and perhaps cabinet officers), no good purpose is served by similarly constraining pay in the other sectors of federal officialdom.

External labor market considerations also militate against a rigid linkage with congressional salaries. The various occupations and their job requirements differ greatly for the three branches of government. For the judiciary, the "labor market for top lawyers" is the relevant outside indicator; federal judgeships are normally the top rungs in the career ladder. High political appointees in the executive branch are drawn from various walks of life and hold federal positions for a short time, usually enhancing their future income possibilities significantly. Top-level career officials in the executive branch are also drawn from various occupations but, like the judiciary, the federal office is a major part of the lifetime career.

Members of Congress relate to external labor markets in yet a different way. First, they too are increasingly drawn from a variety of occupations. Second, it is clear that most members mean their federal careers to be long and many succeed in that ambition. However, many members depart after a fairly short time and are able to improve their economic status significantly over that of their pregovernment days.

These differences in public opinion and the relevant labor markets suggest that salary levels and changes therein in the three branches of government should be differentiated. Judicial salaries and career positions in the executive should be closely linked (after due regard for retirement benefits) to the relevant labor market. Salaries for political positions in the executive schedule need not be so closely tied to external markets; here internal alignment with the Senior Executive Service is probably more relevant.

There are no easy answers to the determination of salaries for members of Congress. What seemed to be the apparent solution—automatically raising congressional salaries every year without a recorded vote—has failed, as history and politics would have predicted. There seems little question that when congressional pay is adjusted it will, and should, be the result of an explicit vote, and this means that all the political difficulties of facing constituents will have to be met by the legislators. While it is hard to be sanguine about the outcome, there really is no satisfactory alternative to this procedure for accountability.

The thrust of this recommendation, then, is that, whatever the difficulties of adjusting the compensation of members of Congress, it is imperative that those difficulties not be a stumbling block to the pay adjustments for executive branch and judicial officials. The only way to avoid this is to end the practice of linking congressional salaries with designated points in the executive and judicial ranks.

Data and Research

Every study of a public policy problem seems to end in a call for more research, and this one is no exception. But in dealing with the issue of compensation for high-level government officials, the need for pertinent data and research is manifest.

The first area for improving data ought to be the labor-market characteristics of people who enter and leave high-level jobs in the government. While there have been occasional special studies of before-and-after salaries, occupational classification, and demographic characteristics of jobholders, few data have been collected (and fewer analyzed) on a continuing basis to put these sporadic exercises in context. Such data are needed, if only to make changes in trends apparent.

A second area for expanded data and research is a more specific determination of public opinion regarding compensation for high-level officials. Since legislators cite public outrage over pay increases as the single most important cause for their failure to act, it is odd that such public antipathy has never been fully documented. Letters from constituents and irate editorials do not constitute documentation. Needed here are periodic surveys that probe public attitudes about different components of compensation for different groups of officials. Perhaps the public would support much higher salaries for career executives, for example. It would certainly have helped to know this before the Senior Executive Service plan for bonuses was fully implemented.

Data gathering and compilation are also sorely needed on the extra costs and existing nonsalary benefits for high federal officials. Just how much does it cost a member of Congress to maintain two homes? Is the taxpayer being scalped because a representative gets cheap haircuts? Who pays for the entertaining of and gifts to constituents? Who gets subsidized parking and what is it worth? The evaluation of the costs of public service and a full accounting of the current benefits has too often been left to people with a vested interest in the outcome; as a result, the public imagines all sorts of benefits that do not even exist (and is unaware of some that do). Beyond these pecuniary benefits, more attention should be paid to how officials evaluate the psychic rewards of their positions.

Further research on the dynamics of entry into and exit from government executive positions is crucial. Two areas in particular need to be looked at more systematically than in the past: refusals and retention rates.

Little is known, except anecdotally, about those who reject government positions. The lack of knowledge sometimes leads to incorrect inference. For example, many government reports have cited the difficulty of attracting a chief actuary as a reason for a general pay increase for federal executives. To draw such a conclusion should surely require much more information about many positions. In any event, if there is dissatisfaction with the kind of people attracted to government, the first step toward remedying the problem is to find out who is being offered jobs and why they are refusing them.

Similarly, there is only sporadic information about job tenure. Specifically, when many high officials resign at one time, this gives the impression of high turnover; on all the days when no one has resigned the evening news does not report that fact. Future salary change proposals ought to be influenced in part by an evaluation of whether turnover rates are too high or too low and what they have been for different positions. There is no better way to start on this than by ascertaining such rates.

Last, salary data for comparable positions in state and local government should be systematically collected. Although the relationship of compensation for high government officials to the external market appears to be tenuous, the salaries of other public officials provide some basis for comparability in a generalized market for "public servants." In some cases, local officials have received higher pay than federal executives in comparable jobs. Identification of these relationships can contribute to the determination of salary adjustments at the federal level. Not all public positions are big league, but they are all in the same game.

Some of the research needs discussed here can probably be completed quickly by the Office of Personnel Management, even in time for consideration by the quadrennial commission that meets in 1980. But most of the research will require a continuing commitment of people and money that is beyond currently available government resources. The Peterson Commission in 1976 recommended that an independent staff be created to undertake a research agenda similar to the one proposed here. This plan went nowhere, perhaps because the Peterson group placed more emphasis on other aspects of its proposals. It would be unfortunate if this needed information were not pursued.

Procedures for Salary Determination

The quadrennial commission, which is made up of distinguished citizens selected by the three branches of government, is the newest wrinkle in salary-setting procedures for high-level government officials. It was designed to avert many of the problems that had afflicted past efforts to adjust executive, legislative, and judicial compensation and to provide an expert objective review of the problem. Salary increases based on the commission's recommendations would be better insulated from political pressure and from criticism. And the fact that the commission would be convened every four years assured regular consideration of the compensation issue.

Few of these expectations have been fully realized. The experience with the first three quadrennial commissions indicates that some constructive changes may be in order. First, the frequency and timing of the commissions are inappropriate. Four years is too long an interval between comprehensive reviews of the compensation of top government officials, especially in highly inflationary times. Also, the fact that the appointment of each commission coincides with a presidential election year is not calculated to promote cool, apolitical consideration of the commission's recommendations. For these reasons, it would be desirable to convene the commission every two years, six months or less after each national election. Or a single commission could be appointed for the four years immediately after the presidential election and carry out a comprehensive review the first year and annual updates in subsequent years. This approach would provide the commission's deliberations with greater timeliness and continuity. It would also permit better coordination with the pay adjustments of other federal employees.

Second, some believe that representation on the quadrennial commission should be drawn from a wider range of citizen groups than has been the case in the past. Commission members are now drawn from the elite groups that have held high positions either in the federal government or in organizations that have a considerable stake in the policies of the federal government. It may not be necessary to make the commission representative of all walks of life, but a concerted effort should be made to include persons who have no established Washington connection. A broader membership would better advance the educational mission of the commission and strengthen its impartiality.

Agenda for the Next Quadrennial Commission

The next quadrennial commission will report to the President after the 1980 election. It will face all the problems discussed in this summary and in this book (and probably some new ones). Its task is complex and can perhaps be aided by some suggestions for priorities in the commission's work.

We have already discussed three essential priorities: breaking the linkage of congressional pay with that of other federal officials, designing an effective vehicle for conducting continuing research into executive-level labor markets, and modifying the procedures of the commission itself. On each of these matters past commissions have failed because of inadequate follow-through. Accordingly, the 1980 commission should devote considerable resources and political capital to overcoming the stasis of these issues.

To break the congressional pay linkage will obviously require the agreement of the leaders of Congress. It would be a mistake, to say the least, to assume that such support will arise spontaneously. Nor will it arise just because a persuasive commission report is issued. The missing element in the past has been strong and forthright presidential leadership. A newly elected president should be in a position to make the ending of linkage— and the potential improvement in the quality of public service therefrom —a major point at the start of his administration. Unless the 1980 commission lays the groundwork for such presidential support, its recommendations may enter the annals of good ideas whose time has not yet come.

Establishing a research effort in high-level labor markets unfortunately is not a matter for presidential concern. But its importance is such that the 1980 commission should obtain an early commitment from the Office of Personnel Management and other relevant agencies to help design the research effort. If detailed plans—on the substance, organization, and manpower requirements of the task—can be laid out in the commission's report, there may be some hope that the people who work on the plans will have a stake in carrying them out.

Modifying the commission's composition is within the immediate discretion of the appointing agencies; modifying its frequency would require legislative changes. In any case, the next quadrennial commission should indulge in some constructive stocktaking and consider making recommendations to Congress concerning its nature and procedures. A start was made in this direction by the Peterson Commission in 1976; this review should be extended.

Beyond these issues, there are three others that deserve high priority on the 1980 commission's agenda. The first is the growing importance of benefits and the need to consider them separately for each area of the commission's domain. With the institution of the Senior Executive Service for high-level career officials (with a new pay system distinct from the general schedule) and, it is hoped, a separation of congressional pay from that of executive and judicial leaders, it should be possible to address the question of the optimum set of benefits for each employee group. The current retirement programs, to take the most prominent benefit, for all employees of the legislative and executive branches are very similar, though not identical. It is hard to imagine that such uniformity is ideal for the range of jobs and career patterns found in the federal service. Consideration should also be given to a more varied package of fringe benefits that would be responsive to the special burdens and needs of high government officials. Here the experience of the private sector may be instructive. Fringe benefits such as moving allowances, protection against undue financial loss when changing residences, and educational allowances for children may be relatively low-cost methods of recruiting candidates who otherwise would be reluctant to accept government service because of the effect of the decision on the family economy.

Breaking the congressional pay linkage should also pave the way for the 1980 commission to review the status of the laws now governing the timing of pay adjustments and other links between pay systems. In particular, although it is clear that automatic annual adjustments, between commissions, cannot work for the salaries of members of Congress, the situation has never been assessed independently for the judicial and executive schedules. While one may have misgivings about the political practicalities of it, some consideration should be given to allowing the automatic annual increase law to continue to operate between 1980 and 1984 for all but congressional salaries to see whether such increases would take place in a decentralized salary system.

Some fine tuning may, however, be needed in the system of annual increases because of other changes in federal salary administration. One of these is that the 1978 law establishing the Senior Executive Service contained provisions that may narrow the pay range for that service if automatic increases for executives are scaled to the average general schedule increase. Another proposal that must be carefully coordinated with any revision of high-level pay is the Carter administration's 1979 proposal to adjust total compensation of general schedule workers for comparability with the nonfederal sector. This proposal raises the question of whether average general schedule salary increases or total compensation increases should be used in adjusting executive and judicial pay.

This agenda will use up all of the 1980 commission's time, money, and patience. Not recommended for study are ethical standards and limits on outside earnings by members of Congress. This area of political life is surely important, but it is a matter that should be settled specifically by conflict of interest considerations and not as part of some subtle, or not so subtle, strategy for bargaining with Congress and the public. Even if the 1980 commission should recommend a large salary increase for members of Congress and be tempted to find a quid pro quo to make the boost palatable, linkage to a new code has proved to be too controversial. Whatever the 1980 commission proposes for changing the pay of the executive, legislative, and judicial branches should be defended as necessary to provide the kind of government officials the nation wants and deserves. Only if that case can be made will the recommendations stand up to the test.

Above and beyond the immediate and pressing policy question is the larger question of restoring incentives for public service in an era when such service is scorned. We are caught in a vicious circle. The public, for a variety of reasons, concludes that its government has gone astray and its public servants are unworthy of approbation. This not only makes it more difficult politically to support monetary rewards for public service; it also undercuts the nonmonetary rewards—the feeling of well-being and the deference that all people want and that public service, ideally, offers. Under such conditions it becomes increasingly difficult to lure the "best and brightest" into government service, and this results in a kind of self-fulfilling prophecy. The public eventually gets exactly the kind of public servants it assumes it has had all along. This is not an issue that can be dealt with solely by study groups. It must be addressed by opinion leaders —scholars, journalists, commentators, statesmen—and by citizens, who have the largest stake in how it is resolved.

Part One

History and Politics

Louis Fisher

History of Pay Adjustments
for Members of Congress

AFTER reading the debates on compensation for members of Congress, starting with the Constitutional Convention and threading my way from 1789 to the present day, I find myself in sympathy with the assessment of Congressman Morris K. Udall: "I do not know why it is, but debating this subject always produces more self-righteousness and more passionate oratory and more posturing and more nonsense, if I may say so, than almost any other subject."[1] The debates are tedious, bombastic, repetitious. They do not represent Congress's finest hour. Still, they contain valuable insights into the workings of a legislative body, yield many delightful anecdotes, and provide important guidance for the questions that face us today.

Several issues define the scope of this study. What factors should be kept in mind in determining compensation for senators and representatives? Should pay increases apply only to a future Congress? To what extent should legislators suspend their individual judgment and follow public opinion, especially when "instructed" by states and constituents? What are the election risks of voting on your own pay raise? How much responsibility should be delegated to salary commissions and to the President?

Compensation takes many forms: salary, travel allowance, franking, clerks, messengers, stationery, and other supports needed for a legislator's office. Adjustment in one area often indirectly augments a member's salary. Complaints are then voiced about subterfuge in the legislative process. Pursuing such issues is worthwhile, but this paper focuses principally on salary. To treat every aspect of pay and perquisites in a study of this size would detract from the fundamental themes that deserve thorough examination.

1. *Congressional Record,* daily edition (June 29, 1977), p. H6677.

25

The Constitutional Provision

The constitutional language seems straightforward and free of duplicity: "The Senators and Representatives shall receive a Compensation for their Services, to be ascertained by Law, and paid out of the Treasury of the United States" (Article I, section 6). Yet little did the framers anticipate the embarrassment, contention, and evasion that would accompany legislative efforts to set the pay for members.

Only one compensation issue was fully resolved at the Constitutional Convention: the source of the funds used to pay members of Congress. On a motion that wages should be paid out of the national treasury, eight states voted in favor, with only three opposed.[2] The draft report of the Committee of Detail later stipulated that the members of each house were to receive a compensation "to be ascertained and paid by the State, in which they shall be chosen."[3] The convention, however, decided to vest that responsibility in the national government. Since the Articles of Confederation had enfeebled national powers, it seemed indispensable to make the new national structure independent of the state legislatures. Elbridge Gerry feared that the state legislatures might "turn out the Senators by reducing their salaries."[4]

How Much Compensation?

The Randolph Resolutions of May 29, 1787, proposed "liberal stipends" for members of both houses.[5] Benjamin Franklin disliked the word "liberal," preferring "moderate" if the delegates needed a substitute. "Liberal" was struck without further discussion.[6]

James Madison advocated a fixed compensation for members, partly because he did not want members of Congress dependent on state legislatures for their compensation. He also believed that it "was an indecent thing" to let members regulate their own wages "and might in time prove a dangerous one." Madison suggested that wheat or some other commodity could serve as a proper standard, selecting "the average price throughout

2. Max Farrand, ed., *The Records of the Federal Convention of 1787,* rev. ed. (Yale University Press, 1966), vol. 1, p. 216.
3. Ibid., vol. 2, p. 180.
4. Ibid., vol. 2, p. 291. See also vol. 1, pp. 427–28; vol. 2, pp. 282, 290–92; and vol. 3, p. 148.
5. Ibid., vol. 1, p. 20.
6. Ibid., p. 216.

a reasonable period." His motion passed, 8–3.[7] The Committee of Detail, borrowing extensively from an idea put forth earlier by Thomas Jefferson, developed a more elaborate procedure. At the beginning of every six years after the first year Congress assembled, "the supreme judiciary shall cause a special jury of the most respectable merchants and farmers to be summoned to declare what shall have been the averaged value of wheat during the last six years, in the state, where the legislature may be sitting: And for the six subsequent years, the senators shall receive per diem the averaged value of [blank] bushels of wheat."[8]

On June 22 the convention voted unanimously (11–0) to strike the words "to receive fixed stipends by which they may be compensated for the devotion of their time to public service" and to substitute therefor "to receive an adequate compensation for their services."[9] According to the notes of Robert Yates of New York, Madison said that "it is indecent that the legislature should put their hands in the public purse to convey it into their own."[10]

A motion of August 14 to set the compensation at $5 for each day of attendance and for each thirty miles of travel going to and returning from Congress was defeated, 2–9.[11] The specifics of compensation had to be decided by the First Congress.

Distinguishing between the Two Houses

On the question of setting different pay for senators and representatives, the record of the Philadelphia convention is filled with vacillation and uncertainty. On June 12 John Rutledge of South Carolina moved to strike the clause about stipends to the Senate. His motion was defeated: three states in favor, seven against, and one divided. A motion to make the stipend for the second branch of the legislature the same as the first passed.[12] On June 26 Charles Pinckney of South Carolina proposed that "no Salary should be allowed" members of the Senate. He believed that the Senate ought to be composed of persons of wealth; elimination of a

7. Ibid., pp. 215–16.

8. Farrand, *Records*, vol. 2, p. 142. This is practically word for word from Jefferson's draft constitution of 1783 (for Virginia), except that he would have averaged over a ten-year period and he specified two bushels of wheat. *The Papers of Thomas Jefferson*, Julian P. Boyd, ed., vol. 6: *May 21, 1781 to March 1, 1784* (Princeton University Press, 1952), p. 297.

9. Farrand, *Records*, vol. 1, pp. 369, 374.

10. Ibid., p. 378.

11. Farrand, *Records*, vol. 2, pp. 282, 291–93.

12. Ibid., vol. 1, pp. 211, 219.

salary would be the best means of securing that end. After Benjamin Franklin seconded the motion, it lost, 5-6.[13]

Some delegates thought that the salary of senators should be larger than that of representatives. Nathaniel Gorham of Massachusetts insisted on extra compensation for senators:

> The Senate will be detained longer from home, will be obliged to remove their families, and in time of war perhaps to sit constantly. Their allowance should certainly be higher. The members of the Senates in the States are allowed more, than those of the other house.[14]

The language in the Constitution was neutral on this issue. Members of the First Congress also considered setting the pay of senators somewhat higher than that of representatives. Theodore Sedgwick of Massachusetts proposed $6 a day for senators and $5 for members of the House of Representatives. Longevity, as understood in the eighteenth century, was uppermost in his mind:

> The Senators are required to be of an advanced age, and are elected for six years. Now this term taken out of the life of a man, passed the middle stage, may be fairly deemed equal to a whole life; for it was to be expected, that few, if any, of the Senators could return to their former occupations, when the period for retirement arrived; indeed, after six years spent in other pursuits, it may be questioned whether a man would be qualified to return with any prospect of success.[15]

Richard Bland Lee of Virginia favored the motion for discrimination between the Senate and the House. The qualifications of senators were superior: "a Senator must be a man advanced in life, and have been nine years a citizen of the United States; while a younger man, who has been but seven years a citizen, may obtain a seat in this House."[16] Madison also wanted a distinction. To him, the Constitution anticipated "that men of abilities and firm principles, whom the love and custom of a retired life might render averse to the fatigues of a public one, may be induced to devote the experience of years, and the acquisitions of study, to the service of their country."[17] Notwithstanding such support, Sedgwick's motion lost by a "considerable majority."[18]

13. Ibid., pp. 426–27.

14. Farrand, *Records,* vol. 2, p. 293.

15. *The Debates and Proceedings in the Congress of the United States, with an Appendix,* Joseph Gales, Sr., comp., vol. 1: *March 3, 1789–March 3, 1791* (Gales and Seaton, 1834), p. 677 (July 15, 1789). Also known, and hereafter cited, as *Annals of Congress.*

16. Ibid., p. 678.

17. Ibid., p. 679.

18. Ibid., p. 684.

On August 4, 1789, a House committee recommended a sum of $6 a day as compensation for each member of the Senate and the House. The next day John Page of Virginia supported a difference in pay for senators and congressmen, believing that the services of senators required greater compensation. A motion by Madison, to differentiate between the two houses, lost on a voice vote.[19]

The Senate voted in favor of a different compensation for senators and representatives. The idea was to give members of the two houses $6 a day until March 4, 1795, at which time senators would receive $7 a day.[20] House conferees went along with that compromise.[21] When George Washington heard of the settlement, he confided to Madison: "Being clearly of opinion that there ought to be a difference in the wages of the members of the two branches of the Legislature would it be politic or prudent in the President when the Bill comes to him to send it back with his reasons for non-concurring?"[22] But Washington did not exercise his veto power. He signed the bill, establishing the compensation of senators and representatives at $6 for each day of attendance until March 4, 1795, after which the compensation for senators would be raised to $7 a day.[23]

The issue had to be faced again in 1796. A motion to continue the Senate rate at $7 failed on the House side.[24] As enacted into law, the bill adopted $6 for every day of attendance as the compensation for both senators and representatives.[25]

Conflict of Interest?

Members of Congress often complain about the "delicate" task of setting their own pay levels. Many find it burdensome and embarrassing to act as judges in their own cause. To Elbridge Gerry, however, the Consti-

19. Ibid. (August 5, 1789), pp. 701–05.
20. *Journal of the First Session of the Senate of the United States*, 1 Cong. 1 sess.; reprinted as *Documentary History of the First Federal Congress of the United States of America, March 4, 1789–March 3, 1791*, vol. 1: *Senate Legislative Journal*, Linda Grant De Pauw, ed. (Johns Hopkins University Press, 1972), pp. 138–44. See also *The Journal of William Maclay, 1789–1791* (Frederick Ungar, 1965), pp. 131–40.
21. *Annals of Congress* (September 10, 1789), vol. 1, p. 923.
22. John C. Fitzpatrick, ed., *The Writings of George Washington from the Original Manuscript Sources, 1745–1799*, vol. 30: *June 20, 1788–January 21, 1790* (Government Printing Office, 1939), p. 394.
23. 1 Stat. 70-71 (1789).
24. *Annals of Congress* (February 26, 1796), 4 Cong. 1 sess. (Gales and Seaton, 1849), p. 378.
25. 1 Stat. 448-49 (1796).

tution of 1789 spoke in plain terms, placing upon legislators a duty they could not, in conscience, evade:

It seems, from such sentiments, as if we were afraid to administer a constitution which we are bound to administer. How are those sentiments reconcilable to the oath we have taken? The constitution requires that we shall, by law, compensate the services of the members of both Houses.[26]

According to a House rule that dates back to 1789, members shall vote on each question put "unless he has a direct or pecuniary interest in the event of such question." That injunction survives today as House Rule VIII.[27] Section 376 of *Jefferson's Manual of Parliamentary Practice* elaborates on the principle:

Where the private interests of a Member are concerned in a bill or question he is to withdraw. And where such an interest has appeared, his voice has been disallowed, even after a division. In a case so contrary, not only to the laws of decency, but to the fundamental principle of the social compact, which denies to any man to be a judge in his own cause, it is for the honor of the House that this rule of immemorial observance should be strictly adhered to.

In 1925 Joseph W. Byrns, a Democrat from Tennessee, argued that members could not vote on their own pay without directly and specifically violating the spirit of House Rule VIII.[28] In that same year Clarence Cannon, Democrat from Missouri, made a point of order under Rule VIII that any member of the House who stood to benefit from a salary increase was not entitled to vote on the proposition. To Cannon, that rule applied to members-elect of the next Congress, when an increase would become effective. The Speaker overruled the point of order, observing that the House rule conflicted with the provision in the Constitution stating that the House shall fix its own salaries: "the universal practice has been to hold it in order."[29]

Deciding What Is Adequate Compensation

From 1789 to the present day, members of Congress have repeated a theme that by now is threadbare with use. Compensation should be neither

26. *Annals of Congress* (August 6, 1789), vol. 1, p. 709.
27. House rules stated in 1789: "No member shall vote on any question, in the event of which he is immediately and particularly interested"; *Annals of Congress* (April 7, 1789), vol. 1, p. 104.
28. *Congressional Record,* vol. 66 (1925), p. 4262.
29. Ibid., p. 4266.

too high (to attract profit-seekers) nor too low (allowing only the wealthy to serve). Finding a satisfactory course between those two extremes has been painful and frustrating.

The Proper Incentive

John Page told his colleagues in 1789 that in matters of legislative pay he "dreaded the abuse of economy": a "parsimonious provision, would throw the Government into the hands of bad men, by which the people might lose every thing they now held dear." No one who served his country should "receive less than will defray the expenses he incurs by performing his duty." Otherwise, public affairs "will get exclusively into the hands of nabobs and aspiring men, who will lay the foundation of aristocracy, and reduce their equals to the capacity of menial servants or slaves."[30] Another member of the First Congress, Elbridge Gerry, warned that inadequate pay would expose the legislative branch to corruption.[31] Danger could come from two sources: the private sector and the executive branch.

In 1816, when Congress considered changing the pay from $6 a day to $1,500 a session, Benjamin Huger of South Carolina trembled to think of the quality of citizen who might be attracted to public office. The proposed salary, he predicted,

was about sufficient to tempt the cupidity and excite the avarice of the second or third rate county court lawyer, the idle and noisy demagogue, or the lowest grade of political brawlers, who haunted the taverns and tippling houses, and stunned the ears of the peaceable citizens with their devotion to republicanism, their love of the people, and their exclusive patriotism.[32]

At the end of the year a House select committee, created to review the merits of a $1,500 annual salary, compared the regular increases granted members of the executive and judicial branches with the pay restrictions imposed on Congress. Without adequate provision for legislators, the committee warned, the office would fall into the hands of two classes of people: "either of the most affluent of the country only, who can bear the charges of it without any compensation; or of those who would accept it, not for the compensation legally belonging to it, but from the hope of turning it to account by other means."[33] Other members claimed that the

---

30. *Annals of Congress* (August 5, 1789), vol. 1, p. 703.
31. Ibid. (August 6, 1789), vol. 1, p. 706.
32. *Annals of Congress* (1816), 14 Cong. 1 sess., p. 1164.
33. Ibid. (1816), 14 Cong. 2 sess. (Gales and Seaton, 1854), p. 318.

House of Representatives had been degraded by pay restrictions. Seats in Congress had been "placed below some thousand of mere ministerial offices in the gift of the Executive, which demand little more than common honesty and a knowledge of accounts." Members had left the House to accept "not foreign missions, not seats in the Cabinet, or on the bench, not any of the high and responsible officers in the Government, not even to be accountants and auditors, and comptrollers, but to take clerkships, collectorships, postmasterships, and [positions in] Indian agencies."[34]

So great was the fear of appearing to profit from office that members regularly opted for a modest compensation. When pressed to justify their low salary, they reasoned that the honor of the office conferred a kind of psychic income. Said Joseph Desha, Democrat from Kentucky, in 1817, when Congress was debating the repeal of a pay increase: "We are the immediate representatives of thirty-five thousand free people. What can be more honorable? And is it fair to contrast such situations with places that have only pecuniary reward, as an inducement to acceptance?"[35] To other legislators the emphasis on honor seemed tedious and insubstantial. Complained John W. Hulbert, a Federalist from Massachusetts:

Honor, sir! are we chamelions, that we can live on air? I must acknowledge that I fear we shall prove ourselves rather too much like those strange animals; for if we now repeal this law, we shall prove at least that we can change our opinions quite as easily as they can change their colors.[36]

Hulbert's plea was unavailing. The Fourteenth Congress repealed the compensation law that had been passed in 1816. Even so, there appeared to be broad agreement that legislative pay was inadequate. The Fourteenth Congress returned to the $6 a day because of pressure from constituents. Members, though they knew that this was insufficient, dared not take more. "Now, if this be the fact," said Peter H. Wendover of New York, "and we must obey, we may be compared to galley slaves, rowing one way but looking another."[37]

Per Diem versus Annual Salary

After experimenting with a fixed daily amount of compensation, some members of Congress concluded that the system had an unhealthy effect on attendance. It was thought that members dawdled in order to receive

34. Ibid., p. 604; statement by Richard H. Wilde (Democrat, Georgia).
35. *Annals of Congress* (1816), 14 Cong. 1 sess., p. 491.
36. Ibid., p. 551.
37. Ibid., p. 667.

additional pay. When the House of Representatives met on February 8, 1796, they considered a bill that proposed paying each member an annual salary of $1,000 instead of the prevailing daily $6. Congressman Benjamin Goodhue of Massachusetts explained that members, if they received an annual payment, "might be induced to greater dispatch in business, and to do away an idea which had gone abroad amongst many people, that, being paid by the day, the members of that House protracted their session to an unreasonable length." William B. Giles of Virginia opposed the motion, primarily because he thought it a poor idea to encourage members to push business forward too rapidly: "It would be a constant temptation to members to neglect their duty; it would tend to embarrass all their deliberations."[38]

Other legislators also had misgivings about an annual payment. The greatest difficulty at the end of a session, William Findley of Pennsylvania said, "was to keep members together," implying that a per diem allowance would achieve that purpose better than an annual salary. John Williams of New York made the point more explicitly: "If members were paid by the year instead of by the day, all those whose business was not completed would be ready to say that members were hastened away to enjoy their salary at home."[39] A motion to strike the word "annually" was passed by voice vote. The public law that year continued the per diem allowance.[40]

In 1816 Congress changed the mode of compensation from $6 a day to $1,500 a session. The principal motivation remained the same: "despatch of public business."[41] But a year later Congress repealed the act after a storm of protest swept the country, forcing legislators into an unseemly retreat. The intensity behind the public uproar was acknowledged even by those who had supported the annual payment. Precisely what brought on the pandemonium became the topic of much speculation and theorizing, but certainly the switch to a "salary" did not sit well.

Some legislators tried to argue that it was immaterial whether members received a flat annual sum or a fixed daily amount. Said Richard M. Johnson of Kentucky:

But the mode makes us salary officers. Indeed! and what magic is there in the name of salary officers? The only difference between a salary officer and a per

38. *Annals of Congress* (February 8, 1796), 4 Cong. 1 sess., p. 304.
39. Ibid., p. 305.
40. 1 Stat. 448-49 (1796).
41. *Annals of Congress* (1816), 14 Cong. 1 sess., p. 1158.

diem, is simply in the mode of payment, and not in the amount. It is immaterial whether you give the President his sixty-eight dollars per day, or whether he draws his $25,000 quarter-yearly. The same may be said of the Military, and the Executive, and the Judicial departments.[42]

Johnson glossed over some important differences between the branches. The positions of executive and judicial officers were regarded as full time, eliminating any opportunity for outside employment or supplementary income. Legislators, on the other hand, were not expected to be in session throughout the year. They could more easily carry on a second occupation at home, especially during the "short session" (the second session), which lasted only three or four months.

Congress raised the per diem to $8 in 1818. Not until 1856 did it adopt a permanent salary schedule, fixing the amount at $3,000 a year. Much of the debate centered not on the salary issue but on the mileage allowance and payment for books for members.

Throughout this period it was common practice to keep salaries below actual expenses. Members compensated for this by maintaining an auxiliary source of income. As John W. Gaines of Tennessee explained in 1906:

Members living near here I know practice law regularly at home when they ought to be here attending to the public business, and I dare say if all the lawyers lived near enough that they would all more or less practice law at home while Congress is in session. And why? Simply because the man has to run the mill at home in order to have something left when the people, justly or unjustly, turn him out of Congress at the end of two or more terms.[43]

Gaines remarked that the lawyer was not alone in doing work "on the side." The banker went home to tend to his business. So did the farmer, "and the coal king and the cattle king, no matter how rich they are, must go back home to look after their business."[44]

The same perspective was offered by Oscar W. Underwood, a Democrat from Alabama who served two decades in the House (1895–1915) before joining the Senate for two terms. Despite his many years in office, Underwood estimated that the average member of the House did not serve as long as two terms. A legislator did not come to Washington "to make his living, as the judge goes to the Federal bench, to stay there for a lifetime and support himself from his salary and lay aside something for

42. *Annals of Congress* (1816), 14 Cong. 2 sess., pp. 240–41.

43. *Congressional Record*, vol. 41 (1906), p. 285. Congress waited until 1946 to initiate a retirement program for members.

44. Ibid.

his family."[45] The twentieth century gradually pushed legislators into the same full-time mold as other federal officials. By 1925 John Q. Tilson, a Republican from Connecticut, could say: "The average period of actual service in Washington, with its additional expense, has increased from about 10 months in 2 years to about 18 or 20 months in 2 years, so that it has become practically impossible to carry on any business whatever at home."[46]

The Timing of a Pay Raise

Many legislators, uncomfortable because they have to vote on their own salary, prefer to make pay increases effective for the following Congress. In 1977, for example, the House considered the congressional salary deferral bill, which stated that adjustments in the rates of pay for members of Congress should take effect at the beginning of the Congress following the Congress in which they were approved.[47] While such proposals are widely accepted today, they are greatly at odds with the historical record.

A Proposed Constitutional Amendment

As part of the original Bill of Rights, Madison offered the following addition to Article I: "but no law varying the compensation last ascertained shall operate before the next ensuing election of Representatives." He elaborated on his proposition:

That article which leaves it in the power of the Legislature to ascertain its own emolument, is one to which I allude. I do not believe this is a power which, in the ordinary course of Government, is likely to be abused. Perhaps of all the powers granted, it is least likely to abuse; but there is a seeming impropriety in leaving any set of men without control to put their hand into the public coffers, to take out money to put in their pockets; there is a seeming indecorum in such power. . . . I have gone, therefore, so far as to fix it, that no law, varying the compensation, shall operate until there is a change in the Legislature; in which case it cannot be for the particular benefit of those who are concerned in determining the value of the service.[48]

45. Ibid., p. 379.
46. *Congressional Record,* vol. 66 (1925), p. 4264.
47. H.R. 9282, brought up under suspension of the rules on November 1, 1977, failed to obtain a second; *Congressional Record,* daily edition (November 1, 1977), pp. H11937–41.
48. *Annals of Congress* (June 8, 1789), vol. 1, pp. 451, 457–58.

Congress established a committee to report a list of amendments to the Constitution. These words were to be added to Article I, section 6: "but no law varying the compensation shall take effect, until an election of representatives shall have intervened."[49] Theodore Sedgwick thought "much inconvenience" and "very little good" would result from this amendment. It might, he said, serve

as a tool for designing men; they might reduce the wages very low, much lower than it was possible for any gentleman to serve without injury to his private affairs, in order to procure popularity at home, provided a diminution of pay was looked upon as a desirable thing. It might also be done in order to prevent men of shining and disinterested abilities, but of indigent circumstances, from rendering their fellow-citizens those services they are well able to perform, and render a seat in this House less eligible than it ought to be.[50]

John Vining of Delaware, a member of the committee responsible for the proposed amendments, said that there was a "disagreeable sensation occasioned by leaving it in the breast of any man to set a value on his own work." While the First Congress was forced to act on the compensation question, and to make the pay immediately applicable, such votes "ought to be avoided in future." The proposition carried by the vote of 27–20.[51] On September 9, 1789, the Senate passed a similar provision: "No law, varying the compensation for the services of the Senators and Representatives, shall take effect, until an election of Representatives shall have intervened."[52] The identical language, proposed by Congress to the states as one of twelve constitutional amendments, was never ratified.[53]

The Salary Act of 1816

In 1816 members of Congress confronted the troublesome issue of raising their own salaries in a current Congress. On March 6, 1816, toward the end of the first session of the Fourteenth Congress, a House select committee reported a bill changing compensation from $6 a day to $1,500 a session. The new salary was made retrospective, covering the entire first session. John Randolph moved to divest the measure of "its

49. Ibid. (August 14, 1789), p. 756.
50. Ibid.
51. Ibid., p. 757.
52. Edward Dumbauld, *The Bill of Rights and What It Means Today* (University of Oklahoma Press, 1957), p. 217.
53. Ibid., p. 220.

only odious consideration" by delaying it until the following March 4, so it would not take effect during the Fourteenth Congress.

Several members spoke in opposition to the Randolph amendment. Richard Johnson, chairman of the select committee on compensation, thought that if the bill was necessary at all "it was as proper for the present Congress as a future one." Thomas P. Grosvenor, a Federalist of New York, agreed:

If it be necessary, is it not so at this, as the next session? On what principle . . . was it necessary to postpone the effect of the bill? It would be viewed only as a little attempt to evade the imputation of regarding their own particular interest.[54]

Those opposed to the amendment had some logic on their side. If an increase seemed necessary, it was appropriate to make it now rather than later. But Congress invited trouble by making the increase retrospective for a session of Congress nearly complete. Also, as Benjamin Huger noted, the increase came "at the close of a bloody and expensive war" with England. Taxes had been high, as had duties on foreign imports. Huger could not find it in his conscience to ask taxpayers to finance a pay raise for Congress.[55] On the question of computing salaries under the two modes of compensation, Johnson estimated that he had received $1,500 for one session under the previous system of $6 a day, and that a nine-month session would have yielded each member $1,620 under the old system.[56] However, the second session of a Congress averaged only three or four months.[57]

Henry Clay, Speaker of the House, gave his support to Johnson's bill. He saw no merit in deferring a pay raise until the next Congress. It was more respectful, he said, to let a future Congress decide for itself the just measure of indemnity for expenses.[58] It was also pointed out that many of the members of the Fourteenth Congress would be reelected, "so that the veil of delicacy would be too thin to conceal the views of members to provide for themselves, though in future."[59] And since only one-third of the senators were up for election every two years, the members of that body could avoid a conflict of interest only by postponing a pay raise for at least six years.

54. *Annals of Congress* (1816), 14 Cong. 1 sess., p. 1159.
55. Ibid., p. 1161.
56. Ibid., p. 1172.
57. *Congressional Directory, 1977,* 95 Cong. 1 sess. (GPO, 1977), pp. 394–95.
58. *Annals of Congress* (1816), 14 Cong. 1 sess., p. 1174.
59. Ibid., p. 1181.

Randolph's motion to suspend the pay increase until the next Congress was defeated "by a large majority."[60] Johnson's bill, setting compensation at $1,500 for each session of the Fourteenth Congress and for future Congresses, passed on a roll-call vote of 81–67.[61]

The Outcry for Repeal

After the elections of 1816, the Fourteenth Congress repealed the new salary of $1,500 for each session, returning to the former standard of $6 a day. That there was great agitation for repeal is borne out by the remarks of Richard Johnson, who had provided the leadership for the change in compensation. Some of his constituents favored the change. Others, though not totally hostile, had various misgivings. Johnson concluded that they would "all either unite or acquiesce in a repeal of the statute; that the public mind might be tranquillized; that the great mass of inflammable matter which was afloat might be decomposed and rendered harmless; that hobby riders may be dismounted, and popularity-traps put flat on the surface." Johnson recognized the violent temper of the country. He said that the compensation bill had excited more discontent than the Alien and Sedition Acts, the quasi-war with France, the internal taxes of 1798, Jefferson's embargo, the War of 1812, the Treaty of Ghent, "or any one measure of the Government, from its existence." As he noted with some bitterness, all manner of accusations had been thrown at Congress:

Odious as this measure was supposed to be, some were not satisfied with magnifying every feature into a Gorgon's head; but, what was the unkindest cut of all, it was represented that, while we were providing for ourselves, we had neglected to provide for the widow, the orphan, the wounded soldier, the discharge of the national debt, the volunteer who had lost his arms or his horse in the public service, and other claimants; that we had been loading the people with heavy taxes, when the session was taken up in reducing and repealing the taxes.[62]

Bowing to the force of this public pressure, Johnson submitted a resolution to create a committee to inquire into the expediency of repealing or modifying the compensation law of 1816. Johnson and six other members of the House were appointed to the committee. Two weeks later the committee issued its report, recommending a repeal of the $1,500 annual

60. Ibid., p. 1176.
61. Ibid., p. 1188. See 3 Stat. 257 (1816).
62. *Annals of Congress* (1816), 14 Cong. 2 sess., pp. 236, 237, 243.

salary and a return to a set amount (to be decided) for each day of attendance. Although backtracking on the salary issue, the committee endorsed the general thrust of the statute of 1816:

The power, vested in Congress by the Constitution, of providing for the pay of its own members, is, doubtless, a delicate trust; and it might have been apprehended, as well from the nature of the subject, as from former experience, that the most judicious exercise of that trust would not [be] exempt from some degree of public animadversion. The committee, however, cannot perceive, either in the increase of compensation provided by the late act, or in the mode of making that compensation, cause of excitement or alarm, adequate to the effects which are understood to have been produced.[63]

Part of the opposition was to the haste with which the law of 1816 had sailed through Congress. The bill was reported in the House on March 6 and adopted two days later.[64] Lewis Condict of New Jersey prepared a penetrating analysis of the political forces for repeal:

The tranquillity of the public mind at that season [in 1816] was highly favorable for the views of the demagogues of faction and noise. An universal calm pervaded every section. Party animosity had subsided. Political distinctions had nearly ceased. The Federal copartnership was dissolved. The Hartford Convention had dispersed. Bonaparte in St. Helena. No embargo. No war. Newspaper editors were in danger of starvation, and, for want of other prey, they pounced upon the compensation law, and, like Peter's brown loaf, it has served them for beef and mutton, custard, and plumb-pudding. It was a standing dish for months, and was served up in every possible shape, boiled and roasted, stewed and fricaseed. Devoured by the demagogues of faction, it has been reissued from their pestiferous jaws at the tippling houses and dram shops, highly seasoned with falsehood and misrepresentation. And this is called "public sentiment," and "public opinion." This is "instruction from our constituents," which the Representative is bound to obey.[65]

Condict's sophisticated interpretation is more persuasive than explanations that hinge on the backdating charge. Within a year, in fact, after the dust had settled from the 1816 elections, Congress had increased the compensation for members from $6 to $8 for each day of attendance. The increase, enacted on January 22, 1818, became effective as of March 3, 1817. The debate was brief and noncontroversial.[66] When Congress

63. Ibid., p. 312.
64. See the critique of Joseph Desha, in *Annals of Congress* (1817), 14 Cong. 2 sess., p. 493.
65. *Annals of Congress* (1817), 14 Cong. 2 sess., p. 682.
66. *Annals of Congress* (1818), 15 Cong. 1 sess., pp. 567–79, 583–90; 3 Stat. 404 (1818).

next increased its compensation, in 1856, the new $3,000 annual salary was backdated some eleven months.[67] Ten years later the salary was increased to $5,000 a year and backdated once again, this time by sixteen months.[68]

The "Salary Grab" of 1873

The ultimate in backdating occurred on March 3, 1873, the day before the Forty-second Congress adjourned. On that day the Congress raised the annual salary to $7,500 and made the salary increase applicable to the whole of the Forty-second Congress. Each member received, in effect, a $5,000 bonus or windfall for the two-year period.[69] Most of the debate took place on the last day of February and the first three days of March. Moreover, the increase had been added as a rider to an appropriation bill instead of following the traditional (at that time) route of a legislative bill.

Within a year Congress acted to repeal this pay increase. The debate was of enormous length, occupying almost two hundred pages of the *Congressional Record*. James A. Garfield of Ohio, hoping to avert a prolonged discussion, said that the debate of 1817 (repealing the salary increase of the previous year) "was, perhaps, as fruitless and valueless as any debate recorded in the annals of Congress."[70] But restraints could not be placed on members eager to castigate the action of the Forty-second Congress. The Democratic Convention held in New York in October 1873 adopted a resolution containing this language: "We condemn and denounce the salary grab, and all Congressmen, democratic or republican, who voted for it, or who have not renounced all share in plunder seized for a service already done and paid for."[71] Samuel S. Cox, Democrat of New York, believed that the public clamor arose not so much from the pay increase as from the "back pay" provision.[72] William Lawrence, Republican of Ohio, identified the three events of the previous twenty years

67. Act of August 16, 1856, 11 Stat. 48, applying to the Thirty-fourth Congress, which began March 4, 1855. Although the increase was backdated to March, the Congress did not actually meet until December 3, 1855.

68. Act of July 28, 1866, 14 Stat. 323, applying to the first day of the Thirty-ninth Congress, which began March 4, 1865. Again, the Congress did not meet until December 4, 1865.

69. 17 Stat. 486 (1873).

70. *Congressional Record*, vol. 2 (1873), p. 94.

71. Ibid., p. 110.

72. Ibid., p. 111.

that had most excited public indignation: the repeal of the Missouri Compromise, the attack on Fort Sumter, and the salary bill of March 3, 1873. He referred to these words adopted by the Ohio Republican Convention:

That when retrenchment is required to lighten the burden of taxation and to continue the reduction of the public debt, the increase of salaries is unwise; that we condemn, without reserve, the voting for or receiving increased pay for services already rendered; and we demand that the provisions of the late act of Congress, by which salaries were increased, shall be promptly and unconditionally repealed.[73]

Despite the efforts of some legislators to defend the act of 1873, the forces for repeal swept on to victory. In addition to repealing the law (except for the compensation of the President and Supreme Court justices, whose salaries may not be diminished), Congress tried to recoup some of the funds given to legislators. The new act stated that all moneys appropriated as compensation to the members of the Forty-second Congress, in excess of the mileage and allowances fixed by law at the start of that Congress, "and which shall not have been drawn by the members of said Congress respectively, or which having been drawn, have been returned in any form to the United States, are hereby covered into the Treasury of the United States, and are declared to be the moneys of the United States absolutely, the same as if they had never been appropriated as aforesaid."[74]

Shifting from Retroactivity

When Congress raised compensation in 1907 to $7,500 a year, it specifically made the increase effective at the start of the next Congress.[75] The next pay increase was also prospective. The Sixty-eighth Congress, which adjourned on March 3, 1925, increased the annual salary to $10,000 and made it effective on and after March 4, 1925.[76]

As part of a general economy move during the Great Depression, Congress cut its salary by 10 percent in 1932 (from $10,000 to $9,000) and by another 5 percent a year later (from $9,000 to $8,500). The first cut was enacted on June 30, 1932, and applied to the fiscal year beginning the

73. Ibid.
74. 18 Stat. 4 (1874).
75. 34 Stat. 993.
76. 43 Stat. 1301.

following day. The second cut, enacted on March 20, 1933, was made effective April 1, 1933.[77]

The $10,000 salary was restored by two statutes. On March 28, 1934, Congress reduced the 15 percent cut to 10 percent for the period from February 1 to June 30, 1934. For fiscal 1935, beginning July 1, 1934, the cut was reduced still further to 5 percent (resulting in a salary of $9,500). The second statute, enacted February 13, 1935 (halfway through fiscal 1935), brought the salary back up to $10,000 after March 31, 1935.[78]

Backdating reappeared in 1945 when the House of Representatives voted itself an annual allowance of $2,500 for the expenses of official duties. It had been the practice of the Senate, though not the House, to cover such expenses by drawing on the contingent fund or other sums included in the legislative branch appropriation act.[79]

The statute providing an expense allowance for members of the House, enacted June 13, 1945, was made retroactive to January 2, 1945.[80] Legislators, complaining that they were spending their own money to purchase books for constituents and for other expenses related to official duties, wanted the government to pick up those expenses.[81] Clarence J. Brown of Ohio estimated that the $10,000 salary was largely exhausted by two demands: "We pay five thousand of it out for expenses we would not have if not in Congress, and about two thousand of it for taxes."[82] Walter C. Ploeser, Republican from Missouri, said that members had to pay for every long-distance phone call, pay rent for second offices in their hometowns, and cover about two-thirds of the cost of telegrams and the full cost of printing.[83]

Whatever the merits of the increase, to some members it smacked of chicanery. They disliked indirect means of augmenting a legislator's salary.[84] Strong objections were registered against the use of an appropriation bill to change a member's compensation:

77. 47 Stat. 401 (1932); 48 Stat. 14 (1933).
78. 48 Stat. 521 (1934); 49 Stat. 24 (1935).
79. *Congressional Record,* vol. 91 (1945), p. 5725; statement by Clarence J. Brown (Republican, Ohio).
80. 59 Stat. 244.
81. *Congressional Record,* vol. 91 (1945), p. 4425; statement by George H. Bender (Republican, Ohio).
82. *Congressional Record,* vol. 91, p. 4432.
83. Ibid., p. 4438.
84. Ibid., p. 4426; statement by Alfred L. Bulwinkel (Democrat, North Carolina).

there is no law authorizing the payment of expenses in any amount of Members of Congress. No appropriation should be made for such purpose until and unless a bill is introduced in the Congress, passed and signed by the President. Your Appropriations Committee is not a legislative committee.[85]

The Legislative Reorganization Act of 1946 provided specific authority for an annual expense allowance of $2,500 for each member of Congress "to assist in defraying expenses relating to, or resulting from the discharge of his official duties, for which no tax liability shall incur, or accounting be made."[86] Enacted on August 2, 1946, the statute made the payment effective on the first day of the Eightieth Congress (January 3, 1947). The statute also raised the annual salary to $12,500 (again effective with the Eightieth Congress) and permitted members of Congress to join the federal retirement system on a contributory basis.

In 1955 Congress raised the annual salary from $12,500 to $22,500 and repealed the $2,500 expense allowance. Enacted on March 2, 1955, during the first session of the Eighty-fourth Congress, the increase became effective on March 1, 1955.[87] To those who wanted to postpone the increase to a future time, Emanuel Celler, Democrat of New York, offered this rejoinder:

I remember the story told about Alice in Wonderland. Alice, you may remember, attended the Mad Hatter's tea party. Alice asked the White Queen for some jam. The White Queen stated: "Jam? Jam yesterday, jam tomorrow, but never jam today."

So it is with the objectors to this bill. They want to give us a salary increase tomorrow, they want to give it to us yesterday, but they never want to give it to us today. Well, we want it today.[88]

Monitoring the Moods of Constituents

Ever since the First Congress, legislators have looked over their shoulders apprehensively, trying to anticipate how their constituents will react to a pay increase. Some members, fearing the voters' wrath, vote for low compensation and infrequent increases. Others, at the risk of losing office, push for salary levels that seem to them fair and in keeping with

85. *Congressional Record,* vol. 91, p. 4428; statement by William F. Norrell (Democrat, Arkansas).

86. 60 Stat. 850.

87. 69 Stat. 11.

88. *Congressional Record,* vol. 101 (1955), p. 1564.

a representative assembly. The latter school was represented by Elbridge Gerry in 1789, during debate on the compensation issue:

If gentlemen say it is justice to their constituents, I am willing to appeal to their tribunal; let them know the reason upon which we act, and I will abide by their determination; but I am against being influenced by an apprehension that the people will disapprove our conduct. I am not afraid of being left out, even if it were thought a disgrace to be left out. I would risk that disgrace rather than agree to an establishment which I am convinced would end in the ruin of the liberties of my fellow-citizens. It would give my heart more satisfaction to fall the victim of popular resentment, than to establish my popularity at the expense of their dearest interest.[89]

In this forthright tradition stood Henry Clay: "With regard to the supposed indelicacy of our fixing upon our own compensation, let the Constitution, let the necessity of the case, be reproached for that, not us."[90] And Ben Johnson, Democrat of Kentucky, made this declaration in 1925 while advocating a salary increase: "If my constituents should say that I am not worth $10,000 a year here, then my answer to them is, Send somebody who is."[91]

The Doctrine of Instruction

As one reason for voting against pay increases, some members of Congress have relied on "instructions" from their constituents and states. Other legislators are violently opposed to the idea of a binding instruction; they regard it as hostile to representative government. When the Fourteenth Congress voted to repeal a pay raise of the previous year, John C. Calhoun of South Carolina denounced the doctrine of instruction. He said that the ear of the House, on the repeal vote, had been sealed against truth and reason: "What has produced this magic spell? Instructions! Well, then, has it come to this? Have the people of this country snatched the power of deliberation from this body?" Calhoun declared that he had been instructed only by the Constitution: "Written by the hand of the people, stamped with their authority, it admits of no doubt as to its obligation."[92]

An effort had been made in the First Congress to include the doctrine of instruction in the Bill of Rights. Thomas T. Tucker of South Carolina

89. *Annals of Congress* (August 6, 1789), vol. 1, p. 707.
90. *Annals of Congress* (1816), 14 Cong. 1 sess., p. 1174; but see also his views a year later, in *Annals of Congress,* 14 Cong. 2 sess., pp. 495–96.
91. *Congressional Record,* vol. 66 (1925), p. 4265.
92. *Annals of Congress* (1817), 14 Cong. 2 sess., pp. 576, 578.

moved to add "to instruct their Representatives" to draft language that already contained "the right of the people peaceably to assemble and consult for their common good, and to apply to the Government for redress of grievances." To supplement those advisory forms of communication, Tucker wanted a mandatory voice for the people.[93]

Thomas Hartley of Pennsylvania opposed the motion on the ground that, "according to the principles laid down in the Constitution, it is presumable that the persons elected know the interests and the circumstances of their constituents, and being checked in their determinations by a division of the Legislative power into two branches, there is little danger of error." If legislators forfeited the confidence of the people, their constituents were empowered to vote them out of office. But during the period for which they were elected, members of Congress ought to be entrusted with responsibility for their actions. Hartley continued:

Representation is the principle of our Government; the people ought to have confidence in the honor and integrity of those they send forward to transact their business; their right to instruct them is a problematical subject. We have seen it attended with bad consequences, both in England and America. When the passions of the people are excited, instructions have been resorted to and obtained, to answer party purposes; and although the public opinion is generally respectable, yet at such moments it has been known to be often wrong; and happy is that Government composed of men of firmness and wisdom to discover, and resist popular error.[94]

Hartley reasoned that the principle of representation was "distinct from any agency, which may require written instructions." Instructions that necessarily embody a local or partial view could never be assimilated to form a national policy: "Were all the members to take their seats in order to obey instructions, and those instructions were as various as it is probable they would be, what possibility would there exist of so accommodating each to the other as to produce any act whatever?"[95]

John Page of Virginia argued that instruction and representation in a republic were not only compatible but inseparable: "Under a democracy, whose great end is to form a code of laws congenial with the public sentiment, the popular opinion ought to be collected and attended to."[96] Here Page confused a republic, which operates through elected representatives, with a democracy, where people rule directly. If instructed, members of Congress could find themselves torn between the voice of their constitu-

---

93. *Annals of Congress,* vol. 1 (August 15, 1789), p. 760.
94. Ibid., p. 761.
95. Ibid., p. 762.
96. Ibid.

ents and their oath to uphold the Constitution. As James Jackson of Georgia noted: "What may be the consequence of binding a man to vote in all cases according to the will of others? He is to decide upon a Constitutional point, and on this question his conscience is bound by the obligation of a solemn oath; you now involve him in a serious dilemma."[97] The House voted against the Tucker motion to add the doctrine of instruction to the Bill of Rights; 10 favored it and 41 were opposed.[98]

The doctrine reappears from time to time, illustrating how members differ in their willingness to exercise individual judgment. Said John Randolph in 1816 during debate on a salary increase for legislators: "The gentleman had advised us to go home and consult our constituents. Consult them for what? For four-pence-halfpenny?" Instead of receiving instructions from constituents on the subject, Randolph thought it more appropriate for him to instruct the constituents.[99] Thomas Grosvenor regarded the office of representative as wholly incompatible with the doctrine of instruction: "The members of this House and the Senate are 'instructed' to make the laws; the judges are 'instructed' to interpret, and the President to execute them. Does not the power of legislation imply, of necessity, volition, free agency—the right to make the law, or not to make it, as the legislator shall deem expedient?" Grosvenor repudiated the idea of accepting instructions from popular conventions:

I have seen one orator mount the table, and, as he developed his political opinions and conduct, I have seen the hats, and the caps, and the shouts of approbation fill the very heavens. I have seen another succeed him; and, as he developed opinions and conduct exactly opposite, again I have seen the hats and the caps blacken the air, and the earth shake with thunders of applause.[100]

Elijah H. Mills of Massachusetts brought within his gunsight the revered maxim "vox populi, vox Dei"—the voice of the people is the voice of God. Mills could equate the two, but only in the sense that they both unleashed a terrible and destructive power:

It is the voice which speaks in the thunder, the earthquake, the tornado. It carries ruin, and havoc, and desolation in its train. It sometimes subverts the deep foundations on which the great pillars of morality and order are erected, and introduces universal anarchy and confusion, the reign "of chaos and old night," in their stead.[101]

97. Ibid., p. 764.
98. Ibid., p. 776.
99. *Annals of Congress* (1816), 14 Cong. 1 sess., p. 1183.
100. *Annals of Congress* (1817), 14 Cong. 2 sess., pp. 626, 631.
101. Ibid., p. 663. See also, on p. 648, the comments by Thomas Clayton of Delaware: the framers "meant that the people of this country should elect the wisest and best men to enact their laws; men who could discern the public good, and discerning

Reelection Jitters

After the elections of 1816, Congress repealed a compensation law that had been on the books less than a year. Some writers have suggested that most of the members who had supported the pay increase were promptly voted out of office by outraged constituents. Wrote Neil Mac-Neil: "The furious outcry across the land caused the defeat of many Representatives. All the members from Ohio, Delaware, and Vermont were defeated, and so were most of the members from Georgia, Maryland, and South Carolina."[102] MacNeil does not document his statement, but he probably relied on the following passage from a work by Robert Luce:

That some grumbling and complaint would be called forth [after the 1816 salary increase] was fully expected. But that every man who voted for it would be denounced from one end of the country to the other was not expected. . . . In the elections next following, from Ohio, Delaware, and Vermont not one member was returned. Georgia sent back but one of the old members, South Carolina but three out of nine, Maryland but four out of nine, and Pennsylvania thirteen out of twenty-three.[103]

Luce simply says that most of the members were not returned, although he implies a relationship between support for the compensation bill and the heavy turnover of membership. Yet compensation bill or not, turnover was always heavy in those days. Luce himself drew attention to the marked decline in the percentage of members reelected. From highs of 63.7 percent in 1790 and 54.0 percent in 1800, the proportion fell steadily over the following decades, dropping to 41.7 percent in 1810, 26.0 percent in 1820, 22.6 percent in 1830, and 12.7 percent in 1840.[104] Few legislators regarded their position in Congress as a career. Members stayed in Congress an average of four to five years.[105] The fact that few

---

it would steadily pursue it, regardless of any temporary excitement which might be produced by mistaken notions of the subject. Of what avail is it that we are here assembled, and gravely deliberate upon and discuss subjects, if we are not to act according to our own judgments? It is a waste of time. Wisdom, talents, and integrity are useless."

102. Neil MacNeil, *Forge of Democracy: The House of Representatives* (David McKay, 1963), pp. 144–45. MacNeil's story is repeated in *Congress and the Public Trust*, Report of the Association of the Bar of the City of New York, Special Committee on Congressional Ethics (Atheneum, 1970), p. 156.

103. Robert Luce, *Legislative Assemblies: Their Framework, Make-Up, Character, Characteristics, Habits, and Manners* (Houghton Mifflin, 1924), pp. 541–42.

104. Ibid., p. 356.

105. Nelson W. Polsby, "The Institutionalization of the U.S. House of Representatives," *American Political Science Review*, vol. 62 (March 1968), p. 146, table 2.

were returned to Congress does not necessarily link the vote on the salary bill to voter sentiment. Those who voted against the salary increase seemed to fare no better than those who voted for it. According to a contemporary legislator: "As far as the result of the election is known, I believe more members are returned to the next Congress who were in favor of the law, than of those who were against it."[106]

If attention is limited to the seven states mentioned in Luce's analysis, of the forty-eight members who voted on the compensation bill, only fourteen returned to the Fourteenth Congress. Of those fourteen, five voted for the pay increase and nine voted against it. A look at each state provides a deeper understanding.

Of the six members in the Ohio delegation, only four voted on the pay increase—all in favor. None returned to the Fifteenth Congress, but John Alexander was the only unsuccessful candidate for the House that I know of.[107] John McLean resigned in 1816. William Creighton failed in his bid for the Senate, but he later served in the Twentieth, Twenty-first, and Twenty-second Congresses, so it does not appear that his support for the 1816 pay raise alienated his constituents. I do not know if the fourth member, David Clendenin, sought reelection.

In the Delaware delegation, Thomas Clayton voted for the pay increase; Thomas Cooper did not vote on the bill. Clayton went on to serve in the state senate in 1821 and in the U.S. Senate from 1824 to 1827 and from 1837 to 1847. Again, his vote apparently did not hurt him politically.

For those from Vermont, Chauncey Langdon voted against the pay raise but was not a candidate for renomination. Asa Lyon voted against it; whether he sought reelection is uncertain from available sources. Daniel Chipman, who voted for the pay increase, resigned his seat several months later. Luther Jewett, Charles Marsh, and John Noyes voted in favor of the pay increase. I have no information that they sought reelection.

The record for other states is also mixed. Georgia sent back John Forsyth, who voted against the pay raise. The other members of the Georgia delegation also voted against the increase. Albert Cuthbert, one of the

106. *Annals of Congress* (1817), 14 Cong. 2 sess., p. 681; statement of Lewis Condict of New Jersey.

107. Information on individual members comes from *Biographical Directory of the American Congress: 1774–1949*, H. Doc. 607 (GPO, 1950). *Guide to U.S. Elections* (Congressional Quarterly, 1975) contains statistics on House elections beginning only with 1824.

five, resigned his seat on November 9, 1816, and was replaced by Zadock Cook. Richard Henry Wilde was an unsuccessful candidate for the Fifteenth Congress. Whether the other three (Bolling Hall, Wilson Lumpkin, and Thomas Telfair) sought reelection is something I cannot determine from available sources.

Of the three South Carolina members who voted on the measure and returned to the Fifteenth Congress, John Calhoun and Henry Middleton voted for the pay increase and William Lowndes voted against it. William Mayrant voted for it but resigned his office on October 21, 1816. John Taylor, after voting for the pay increase, was an unsuccessful candidate for the Fifteenth Congress. That leaves four other members who did not return: Benjamin Huger, who opposed the increase, and John J. Chappell, Thomas Moore, and William Woodward, who favored it.

Five members of the Maryland delegation voted on the compensation bill. Two were reelected to the Fifteenth Congress: John C. Herbert (opposed to the increase) and Samuel Smith (in favor). Robert Wright, also in favor, was an unsuccessful candidate for reelection to the House. Charles Goldsborough, who voted against the pay increase, became governor of Maryland in 1818 and 1819. George Baer, Jr., opposed to the salary raise, became mayor of Frederick, Maryland, in 1820.

Of the members of the Pennsylvania delegation who were present for the vote on the salary bill, nine (not thirteen) returned to the Fifteenth Congress. Two voted for the pay raise and six against; one did not vote.

An anecdote about Henry Clay suggests that constituents judged a legislator not on the basis of a solitary vote but on his general record in office. An old friend and neighbor told Clay that he could no longer support him for Congress because Clay had backed the pay increase in 1816:

Mr. Clay said to him, "You have a rifle which you think a great deal of; it has brought you down many fine bucks in the woods." "Yes, sir." "Well," said Mr. Clay, "if you were to raise it up and take aim for a fine chance and it was to snap, what would you do with it? Would you break it against the first tree?" "No, sir," was the reply. "I would pick the flint and try it again; and I will vote for you again, Harry."[108]

Legislators who supported "back pay" provisions not only survived politically but advanced to higher stations of public office:

The people afterward repeatedly honored Mr. Clay with their confidence, and a great national party gave him a most enthusiastic support as a candidate for

108. *Congressional Globe*, 42 Cong. 3 sess. (1873), pt. 3, p. 2045.

the Presidency. Mr. Calhoun afterward became Senator, Cabinet officer, and was elected Vice-President by the people. Mr. R. M. Johnson, author of the bill of 1816, was afterward elected Vice-President by the people. Mr. McLean was afterward made one of the supreme judges, and he was warmly solicited to become a candidate for the Presidency in 1832, but he declined. Mr. Webster was afterward repeatedly in the Senate, in the Cabinet, supported by many warm friends as a candidate for the Presidency, and became illustrious as the greatest constitutional expounder of his age. James Clark was afterward elected governor of Kentucky. To single out a few who received back pay under the act of 1856: Stephen A. Douglas and John Bell were indorsed by their respective parties as candidates for the Presidency when the times were "big with danger." John Bell carried the State of Tennessee. Lewis Cass afterward became a Cabinet officer, and Lyman Trumbull and John J. Crittenden were sent to the Senate.[109]

With some amusement, Alben W. Barkley of Kentucky recalled his experience in 1925 after opposing a salary increase to $10,000. Upon returning to his district, he expected to hear ringing words of praise for his protection of the Treasury, that he would be a hero in his hometown. For a week he waited for congratulations and compliments, but the subject never came up. Finally a farmer, a close friend of Barkley's for many years, engaged him in conversation for about an hour and eventually turned to the compensation issue: "Well, I see you fellows increased your salaries up there." Barkley said they had, but he had voted against it. The farmer looked at Barkley for about two minutes before saying: "Well, you are just a damned fool." Barkley took this as evidence that members often underestimate the intelligence of their constituents and that "we sometimes magnify our timidity in dealing with our own problems."[110]

Conclusions

Members of Congress can find some solace (though perhaps not much) in the distress with which previous members of the House and the Senate faced the pay issue. The major lesson to be drawn from this historical account, I think, is that a vote on a pay raise is uncomfortable and was meant to be uncomfortable. No amount of delegation, creation of study commissions, techniques for receiving automatic raises (the "I had nothing to do with it" approach), or other artifices will eliminate the discom-

109. *Congressional Record*, vol. 2 (1873), p. 113; statement by Charles Kendall of Nevada, quoting John M. Bright of Tennessee.
110. *Congressional Record*, vol. 91 (1945), p. 4963.

fort. There is no substitute for a member's willingness to tell constituents in plain terms why a pay raise is needed.

What is so horrendous about legislators voting themselves a pay raise? James Madison, it is true, had grave reservations about letting Congress set its own salaries. There was a "seeming impropriety," he said, in allowing legislators "without control to put their hand[s] into the public coffers, to take out money to put in their pockets." But the views of Madison, so crucial in interpreting other constitutional issues, are less reliable on the compensation question. He tried unsuccessfully to attach pay to the value of wheat, to distinguish between the pay of senators and representatives, and to incorporate into the Bill of Rights a requirement that compensation laws take effect after the election of representatives.

There is nothing improper about legislators setting their own pay and making the change effective for a current Congress. The Constitution charges them with the responsibility for deciding their compensation; custom strongly supports their right to make an increase in salary effective during their term in office. No doubt members of Congress are caught in a conflict of interest, but that conflict is created by the Constitution, not by the members.

The actions of members are controlled provided they remain accountable to the voters. Failure to take a roll-call vote on a compensation bill destroys that control. Throughout the years, legislators have diluted political responsibility by one means or another. They have attached pay increases in the form of riders to general appropriation bills. In 1955 they combined a legislative pay raise with a salary increase for federal judges and U.S. attorneys. In 1953 the Senate passed a bill, without any debate, that authorized the establishment of a commission to actually determine the salaries to be paid to members of the legislative and judicial branches. The House refused to go along with this delegation of responsibility. The law limited the commission to recommending rather than establishing salary rates.[111] Other efforts at subterfuge include tax-free expense allowances and changes in perquisites in lieu of salary adjustments.

Yet another way of defusing the issue was to create the Commission on Executive, Legislative, and Judicial Salaries (the quadrennial commission) in 1967, authorizing it to recommend every four years the rates of compensation to be paid to members of Congress, justices of the Supreme Court, federal judges, and certain high-ranking government officials. The

111. 67 Stat. 485.

President, after receiving those recommendations, submits to Congress his own proposals for salaries. The President's plan takes effect within thirty days unless disapproved by either house or replaced by a different salary schedule enacted into law. No vote by Congress is necessary for a salary increase to take effect.

I disagree with the position of the Justice Department that the procedure of the salary act of 1967 satisfies the framers' intent: "Congress remains accountable for compensation paid pursuant to statutes that it has enacted and can revise."[112] Delegating responsibility for salaries to a commission, followed by a presidential recommendation and inaction by Congress, does not make Congress accountable to the voters. Nor is there any accountability when hastily arranged hearings allow members (as in 1977) to testify on a pay raise that took effect without a recorded vote.[113] A report from a study commission is consistent with the constitutional mandate only when the study is advisory. It is inconsistent when the responsibility for changing legislative salaries is in any way shared with or delegated to the commission and the President.

Responsibility requires members to vote directly and openly on salary changes. This procedure is uncomfortable for legislators, as it was designed to be. It is to the credit of Congress that it passed legislation in 1977 requiring roll-call votes in both the House and the Senate on future pay raises for members of Congress, federal judges, and senior federal officials as recommended by the quadrennial commission.[114] Congress has consistently set its pay with an eye to executive and judicial salaries, but it would be preferable to sever the present statutory linkage, for it often becomes just one more technique of obscuring congressional responsibility.

Responsibility requires members to explain to their constituents why a salary raise is necessary. While legislators are not supposed to run for office for the sake of profit, neither should they have to dip into savings or fall into debt to make ends meet. Constituents can be instructed in such matters provided members of Congress are forthright on the issue and trust in the basic goodwill and common sense of the people who put them in office.

112. Brief for Defendant at 10, *Pressler, Member, U.S. House of Representatives* v. *Blumenthal, Secretary of the Treasury, et al.,* 431 U.S. 169 (1977).

113. *Presidential Pay Recommendations,* Hearings before the Ad Hoc Subcommittee on Presidential Pay Recommendations of the House Committee on Post Office and Civil Service, 95 Cong. 1 sess. (GPO, 1977).

114. Title IV of Public Law 95-19.

Roger H. Davidson

The Politics of Executive, Legislative, and Judicial Compensation

> A democratic State is most parsimonious towards its principal agents. In America the secondary officers are much better paid, and the dignitaries of the administration much worse, than they are elsewhere.
>
> These opposite effects result from the same cause; the people fix the salaries of the public officers in both cases; and the scale of remuneration is determined by the consideration of its own wants.
>
> Alexis de Tocqueville, *Democracy in America* (1835)

ATTRACTING our ablest citizens into the federal government's policy-making echelon is a vexing problem. These jobs are few—by the most restrictive definition, about 2,500 men and women in the three branches. In the executive branch, these include those in the so-called executive schedule; in the legislative branch are, of course, senators and representatives, delegates, and a resident commissioner; in the judiciary, federal district and circuit judges. Even if the leadership echelon is broadened to include civil service "supergrades" and comparable levels of other civilian and military schedules, it numbers about 15,000—only a tiny fraction of the federal government's 2.8 million civilian and 1.8 million military employees.

Everyone acknowledges that these people exert far more influence on government performance than their numbers suggest. Achieving a marriage of talent and leadership is, of course, a challenge as old as human society. The first great book of politics, Plato's *Republic,* addresses this issue. A decade ago the President's first Commission on Executive, Legislative, and Judicial Salaries rephrased the problem: "The ability of our nation to meet the challenges of these troubled times depends on the leadership of those who place their talents and energies at the service of their country."[1]

---

1. U.S. Commission on Executive, Legislative, and Judicial Salaries, *Report of the Commission on Executive, Legislative, and Judicial Salaries, December 1968* (Government Printing Office, 1968), p. 1.

The apparently diminishing attractiveness of federal service is a matter for concern. Scattered but unmistakable evidence indicates that high-level federal assignments are losing their appeal. Frequently, potential appointees or candidates refuse to be recruited for high-level posts. Those who are recruited tend to have short careers, leaving prematurely for other pursuits that presumably promise greater satisfaction.

Part of the problem is the level of federal compensation. Although it is open to question whether compensation is the leading factor, it is the one that is in theory the most readily manipulated, that provokes the most animated debate, and that best exemplifies the current difficulty of attracting talented people into government service.

Government compensation is both an economic and a political issue. To fill key jobs, the federal government must compete for talent with other levels of government and the private sector. In theory, federal service should offer sufficient rewards, economic and otherwise, to attract its share of the most talented and experienced leaders in their professions. Yet to keep faith with its "shareholders," the taxpaying public, the federal government must pursue strict economy in staffing, avoiding overpayment even at top management levels. If the marketplaces in which the federal government must compete were used as a basis for comparison, it might even be possible to calculate optimal levels of compensation with reasonable accuracy.

Other marketplaces also influence the level of compensation for federal officials. These are the political marketplaces, which are at least as powerful as economic marketplaces in determining what top federal workers are actually paid.

While top-echelon officers in the private sector are relatively shielded from public view, and their compensation levels a mystery to most Americans (and even to many of their employees), such is not the case with government managers. Compensation levels are, and should be, a matter of public record. Raw numbers—salaries, perquisites, or pensions—may convey an imperfect or even misleading impression, yet they are hard to mask from public view; and the higher the numbers, the more attention they will receive. As such, they are a political commodity, exposed to pressure not only from the officials themselves, but from lobbyists, the media, and even the general public.

Political factors permeate the issue of compensation in more subtle ways. It would be a mistake to assess the attractions or drawbacks of federal service in money alone. For those who enter the federal management echelon—who accept top posts in the executive branch, who assume federal judgeships, or who run for the House or Senate—other factors are often as important as salaries and perquisites, if not more so. Occupying high-level federal posts can enhance reputations, widen circles of contacts, feed self-esteem, and facilitate subsequent career advancement. And of course such posts can satisfy the desire to influence policy and perform civic service. On the other hand, many drawbacks of federal service also have nothing to do with money—for example, on-the-job restrictions, the inconvenience of moving to a new locale, or the effects of the job's schedule on incumbents and their families. The political environment influences candidates' weighing of the advantages and drawbacks of federal service. The government's standing or reputation, the urgency of its initiatives and programs, the feeling that significant work can be done—such intangible factors influence decisions to seek or reject federal service.

This paper is concerned with these political marketplaces. Since they depend on the content and role of public opinion, their workings are not fully understood. Nor do they always yield optimal, or even rational, results—like economic marketplaces, political marketplaces may not put a fair value on the "worth" of a person. Nonetheless, political forces must be understood if policymakers and interested outsiders are to grapple with the problem of recruiting leaders for the federal government.

The People's View

Decisions about federal compensation levels are not, of course, determined by popular vote. Nor is the matter of compensation a burning issue —such as inflation, busing, abortion, or gun control—with most citizens. Yet though the public is not directly charged with making decisions on such matters, its agents cannot escape this responsibility, and they are keenly aware of voters' predispositions and prejudices. The public harbors a series of attitudes, both general and specific, that set definite limits on what policymakers can practically recommend or ratify.

A Vote of No Confidence

No one today needs to be reminded that the American public expresses widespread cynicism about government and its agents. Nearly every year, Louis Harris and Associates (among other survey firms) asks a national

TABLE 1. *The American Public's Confidence in the Leadership of Major Institutions, 1966 and 1971–77*

Percent

Institution	1966	1971	1972	1973	1974	1975	1976	1977
Medicine	72	61	48	57	49	43	42	55
Higher education	61	37	33	44	40	36	31	41
Organized religion	41	27	30	36	32	32	24	34
U.S. Supreme Court	51	23	28	33	34	28	22	31
The military	62	27	35	40	29	24	23	31
Television news[a]	25	22	17	41	32	35	28	30
White House	[b]	[b]	[b]	18	18	[b]	18	26
Large companies	55	27	27	29	15	19	16	23
Executive branch of federal government	41	23	27	19	18	13	11	23
Local government	[b]	[b]	[b]	28	[b]	[b]	19	21
State government	[b]	[b]	[b]	24	[b]	[b]	16	19
The press	29	18	18	30	25	26	20	19
Law firms	[b]	[b]	[b]	24	17	[b]	12	16
Congress	42	19	21	29	16	13	9	15
Organized labor	22	14	15	20	18	14	10	15
Advertising agencies	21	13	12	[b]	[b]	[b]	7	11
Average, all institutions	43	26	26	31	26	26	19	26

Sources: Louis Harris, "Public Confidence in Institutions Remains Low," *Harris Survey*, November 13, 1972; Harris, "Confidence in Institutions," *Harris Survey*, January 5, 1978; Harris, "Confidence in Most Institutions Down," *ABC News–Harris Survey*, vol. 1 (March 5, 1979). The question was: "As far as people in charge of running (READ LIST) are concerned, would you say you have a great deal of confidence, only some confidence, or hardly any confidence at all in them?" Percentages are of those expressing "a great deal of confidence."
a. Before 1973, respondents were asked about "television."
b. Not asked that year.

sample of respondents to indicate their level of confidence in leaders of various social institutions, private as well as public. Because the questions focus on the *leadership* of institutions, rather than on the institutions themselves, they are an ideal indicator for the purposes of this paper.

The results of these surveys are given in table 1, which shows the percentages of people expressing "a great deal of confidence" in leaders of these institutions. Confidence levels plummeted between 1966 and 1971 (the questions were not asked between these two dates). This decline continued until 1976, when there was an all-time low of public confidence. A perceptible recovery is indicated by the 1977 findings; but confidence levels were still far below 1966 levels. Citizens were especially suspicious of public agencies such as Congress and the executive branch. Only a distinct minority of Americans, it seems, now claim "a great deal of confidence" in the leadership of major institutions.

TABLE 2. *The American Public's Lack of Confidence in the Leadership of Major Institutions, 1966 and 1971–76*

Percent

Institution	1966	1971	1973	1974	1975	1976
Medicine	2	6	10	7	12	11
Organized religion	9	25	22	24	20	25
The military	4	20	19	17	25	21
The press	14	26	21	23	19	25
Large companies	4	15	20	21	26	25
Executive branch of federal government	8	18	34	14	33	26
Congress	6	19	17	20	30	33
Average, all institutions	7	18	20	18	24	24

Source: Louis Harris and Associates, in Everett Carll Ladd, Jr., "The Polls: The Question of Confidence," *Public Opinion Quarterly*, vol. 40 (Winter 1976–77), pp. 545–46. The question was: "As far as the people in charge of running (READ LIST) are concerned, would you say you have a great deal of confidence, only some confidence, or hardly any confidence at all in them?" Percentages are of those expressing "hardly any confidence at all."

If few citizens express great confidence in their leaders, is it also true that a large proportion of them have little or no confidence in these same leaders? This question is harder to answer, because figures on these responses are not normally released. However, table 2 presents the percentages of respondents who stated that they had "hardly any confidence at all" in the leaders of certain institutions. Significant numbers of Americans lacked faith—again, especially in Congress and the executive branch. Fully one-third of the public had no confidence in Congress, and more than a quarter had none in the executive branch.

The proportion of the American public lacking confidence in several institutions' leadership sharply increased between 1966 and 1971. Since then, the erosion of confidence has slowed. The executive branch apparently bottomed out with President Nixon's resignation in 1974, whereas confidence in Congress continues to weaken. Other institutions display inconsistent patterns.

In view of the disquieting events of the past decade—including Vietnam, Watergate, "stagflation," and lack of policy coherence—it is perhaps remarkable that people are not more alienated than they are. Yet it is clear that top-level managers in a variety of institutions simply have no reserve of public goodwill.

These popular attitudes have sometimes been characterized as signaling a "crisis of confidence." Whether or not this is true, cynicism is surely abroad in the land. Sixty-two percent of the populace think, for example,

TABLE 3. *Public Attitudes toward Government Leaders: Selected Responses, 1974 and 1976*

"Do you think quite a few of the people running the government in Washington are a little crooked, not very many are, or do you think that hardly any of them are crooked at all?" (Peter Hart and Associates, July 1976)

Quite a few	61 percent
Not many	24
Hardly any	6
Don't know	9

"Would you say that the government in Washington is pretty much run by a few big interests or that it is pretty much run for the benefit of all people?" (Peter Hart and Associates, July 1976)

By a few big interests	62 percent
For all people	22
Other/depends (volunteered)	6
Don't know	10

"Do you think that people in the government waste a lot of money we pay in taxes, waste some of it, or don't waste very much of it?" (Survey Research Center, University of Michigan, Fall 1974)

Not much	1 percent
Some	22
A lot	74
Don't know	2

"Do you think quite a few of the people running the government are a little crooked, not very many are, or do you think hardly any of them are crooked at all?" (Survey Research Center, University of Michigan, Fall 1974)

Quite a lot	45 percent
Not many	42
Hardly any	10
Don't know	3

Source: Ladd, "The Polls," pp. 549–50.

that the national government is run on behalf of a few big interests, and 61 percent think that "quite a few" of its leaders are crooked. Four out of every five respondents profess to think that the system is arranged so that the rich fatten while the poor suffer. Three-quarters maintain that the country is on the wrong track, and the same proportion believe their government wastes a lot of money. (Some of the questions and the responses are shown in table 3.)

The reasons for this lack of public confidence are no mystery to anyone. A survey taken for the U.S. Senate (by Louis Harris and Associates) at the time of the Watergate controversy in 1973—probably the most exhaustive study of public confidence in government ever undertaken—revealed, to no one's surprise, that citizens were worried about corruption, deception, unresponsiveness, and red tape.[2] They also believed that pressing problems were not being solved and that public officials were to blame for such things as inflation, high taxes, government spending, and the declining dollar. While subsequent surveys do not yield as comprehensive a portrait of public attitudes, it would be a mistake to assume that Watergate-era cynicism has dissipated. Continuing revelations of alleged improprieties— for example, "Koreagate," the Bert Lance affair, and the General Services Administration scandal—provide fuel for public criticism; hosts of unresolved social and economic problems seem to confirm impressions of leaders' incompetence or impotence.

Whether this much distrust is normal is not known. Modern survey techniques extend systematic knowledge of public attitudes only as far back as the 1930s; beyond that, more impressionistic measures must be used. However, Americans have always displayed a deep-seated ambivalence toward political authority, a fact demonstrated by generations of irreverent humor aimed at officialdom—from Petroleum V. Nasby and Finley Peter Dunne through Will Rogers and H. L. Mencken to Johnny Carson and Garry Trudeau.

Public confidence in leadership fluctuates with the perceived effectiveness and integrity of incumbent leaders. It is known that confidence has plummeted since the mid-1960s, but the survey instruments currently in use go back no further. Earlier surveys suggest that present-day levels of distrust may have been matched in the late 1930s and the last years of the Truman administration. By contrast, the Eisenhower, Kennedy, and early Johnson administrations were, with a few exceptions, years of relatively high public confidence.[3] No doubt a detailed "fever chart" of confidence could be drawn for all of American history if only public opinion surveys had been available to take the public pulse.

Nor can it be said that Americans are disenchanted with basic social and political institutions. The surveys, though recording widespread disappointment with leaders' stewardship, at the same time reflect a tena-

2. *Confidence and Concern: Citizens View American Government, A Survey of Public Attitudes,* Committee Print, Subcommittee on Intergovernmental Relations of the Senate Committee on Government Operations, 93 Cong. 1 sess. (GPO, 1973), pt. 1, p. 223.

3. Hazel Erskine, "The Polls: Corruption in Government," *Public Opinion Quarterly,* vol. 37 (Winter 1973–74), pp. 628–44.

cious confidence in the virtues of American life and the inherent qualities of its institutions. In fact, looking at these survey results leads to the conclusion that the public has reacted predictably to the turmoil and disappointments of the past decade. Only the indifferent or uninformed, after all, could fail to be upset by recent events. But while exhibiting cynicism and even a sense of betrayal, people believe that institutions will work properly under the right circumstances and with the right leaders. A crisis of confidence, yes; but not, at least not yet, a crisis of legitimacy for the system as a whole.

What Kind of Leaders?

Although citizens are disenchanted with their leaders' performance, their assessments result more from general dissatisfaction than from the performance of specific officeholders. The average citizen has at best only a hazy idea of who the government's managers are or what they do. The President, of course, is the nation's best-known figure; for many people, he symbolizes the government's entire range of activities. Other executive-branch leaders are distinctly secondary to the President in the public's awareness. A few cabinet members may be widely known (Henry Kissinger comes to mind); beyond that, the seven hundred or so political managers in the executive branch are unknown to the general public. Their tasks are a mystery to the average taxpayer, far less comprehensible than the work of, say, mail carriers or air flight controllers.

Citizens' perception of legislators and judges is probably more precise than their perception of executive-branch managers. Judges play a highly recognizable role in society. People have a clear picture of what judges do, even though they know little about the preparation and labor that underpin the performance of judicial tasks. Legislators, too, perform readily recognizable functions. One out of every two citizens can name his congressman; three out of five can name at least one of their senators. Moreover, people have firm convictions about legislators' duty to represent local interests and communicate with constituents.[4]

Since citizens are unhappy with current leadership, what qualities would they like to see in their leaders? At the moment, people appear to place

---

4. *Confidence and Concern*, pt. 1, pp. 75–77; *Final Report of the Commission on Administrative Review*, H. Doc. 95-272, 95 Cong. 1 sess. (GPO, 1977), vol. 2, pp. 814–29.

honesty and integrity above all other attributes, including experience, intelligence, and ability. When a national sample of respondents in the Senate survey were asked to describe their standards for the "kind of people who *should* work in government," two-thirds cited honesty, 56 percent dedication to hard work, and 51 percent the desire to help people. Forty-one percent of the respondents mentioned intelligence, 35 percent courage, and 24 percent efficiency. Creativity and imagination were rarely mentioned (12 percent), although fully half of a subsample of 274 public officials mentioned them.[5]

Special strata of the public differ somewhat in the qualities they admire in the model public official and in how they respond. Elite groups, for example, are precise about what they want in government officials. In the 1973 Senate survey, the subsample of public officials mentioned more characteristics of ideal leaders than did the general public. Elite groups tend to stress competence more than the general public does. But as a general rule, the description of the ideal public servant is remarkably similar across the social and economic spectrum, although intelligence and creativity are stressed proportionately more by professionals, executives, college-educated high-income people, and public officials themselves.[6]

Citizens place less faith in leaders' personal qualities than in formal restraints on leaders' misdeeds. This tendency is understandable in light of the public's current low opinion of leadership and seeming preference for honesty over competence. It also flows from two enduring streams in American culture: egalitarianism and a faith in formal arrangements rather than in individuals.

In cultures with a tradition of deference toward various elite groups, more attention is presumably devoted to desirable qualities in leaders, and more leeway accorded leaders thought to possess such qualities. American culture, however, places little emphasis on the recruitment of talented leaders. In fact, it is widely believed that leadership qualities are disseminated throughout the population. Hence the general public leans toward an open recruitment system with tight checks on leaders instead of a system that awards leadership posts to the "right" people and then allows them to manage things with the help of experts. Leaders themselves tend to favor latitude rather than checks.[7]

5. *Confidence and Concern*, pt. 1, pp. 138–40, 306.
6. Ibid., pt. 2, pp. 369–72.
7. *Confidence and Concern*, pt. 1, pp. 146–50.

How Urgent Is the Problem?

As a consequence of these attitudes and cultural preferences, Americans do not give high priority to recruiting government leaders. Although unhappy with government performance, they rarely express the view that lack of leadership ability or experience is the crux of the problem—indeed, by a small majority, they believe that government leaders generally "know what they are doing."[8] When asked to state their reasons for assessing government performance so negatively, people criticize leaders' honesty and integrity rather than their substantive abilities.

The challenge of recruiting for government service does not seem urgent even to elite groups. In the 1973 Senate study a questionnaire similar to that given the national sample of the general public was administered to a subsample of 274 state and local officials. They were asked to discuss the factors that hamper government officials in doing their jobs. Although the questionnaire was not focused specifically on the problems of top-level officials, it nonetheless offers clues to the drawbacks of public jobs, as seen by those already in such jobs, some of whom would someday be candidates for federal posts. The results, shown in table 4, suggest the frustrations of contemporary public life.

Bureaucratic red tape, lack of time, restrictions imposed by other levels of government, lack of funds, failure of communications, public indifference or misunderstanding—all were mentioned as barriers to government officials' performance. Unqualified officials or personnel ranked seventh among the barriers cited by the respondents, mentioned by only one in ten. One in eight respondents declared there were no impediments to performance of government jobs. The answers are revealing, in part because they constitute a familiar catalog of on-the-job frustrations that may in fact make high-level government service unattractive. It is equally revealing that the respondents did not directly mention inadequate incentives, financial or otherwise, for government service.

The general public seems unconvinced that working for the government needs to be made more attractive or even that greater incentives should be given to ensure high-level performance. In the Senate survey, the national sample of respondents was asked what could be done "to

8. Unpublished data, Center for Political Studies of the Institute for Social Research, University of Michigan, November 1973.

TABLE 4. *Responses of State and Local Officials to Questions about Impediments to the Performance of Government Jobs, 1973*

Response	Percent
Closed-ended	
Intergovernmental red tape	51
Fragmentation of government authority	46
Inadequate tax base	34
Too many special interests	30
Inadequate staff	26
Inability to recruit good people	25
Underpaid staff	19
Harassment by the media	16
Apathetic public	34
Volunteered	
Restricted by higher level of government, impounding of funds, passing of laws without knowledge of local problems	23
Not enough time to do a good job	17
Bureaucracy, red tape, inertia, paperwork	15
Lack of money, resources, tax base	13
Division, suspicion, lack of communication	13
None, no impediments	12
Unqualified, intellectually inept government officials, personnel	10
Corrupt politicians, officials; politically motivated, work for own gain	9
Lack of public understanding of government	8
Special interest groups exert too much influence, pressure	7
Public is apathetic, resistant to change	6
Need more staff, help	4
People only concerned with single issues affecting them directly	4
Hard to keep up with changes in laws, regulations	3
Lack of accurate, timely information	3
Inadequate, inaccurate reporting to media	3
Court system needs reform, protects the guilty	3
Basic laws poorly designed	3
Lack of public confidence, trust in government	2
Any other answer	7

Source: *Confidence and Concern: Citizens View American Government, A Survey of Public Attitudes,* Committee Print, Subcommittee on Intergovernmental Relations of the Senate Committee on Government Operations, 93 Cong. 1 sess. (GPO, 1973), pt. 1, pp. 296–97. The questions were: "In your own job, do you feel you are impeded substantially, only some, or hardly at all by the following things?" (CLOSED-ENDED ITEMS); "Are there any other things which you feel impede your own job substantially?" (VOLUNTEERED RESPONSES).

TABLE 5. *What People Feel Would Have to Be Done to Make the Government a More Exciting Place to Work, 1973*

Volunteered response	Percent[a]
Eliminate corruption	12
Think it's exciting enough now with Watergate	10
Eliminate red tape	9
Have more involvement with the public	8
Emphasize hard work	7
Make duties more interesting	6
Salaries based on merit, not favoritism	5
Raise morale by making work more progressive	5
Do away with tenure	5
Pay higher salaries	5
It's dull—can't do much	3
Have younger people	3
Government work no different than other work	2
Take politics out of government	2
More job security	1
Decentralize government	1
Reeducate public on way government is run	1
Reorganize and start over	1
Limit campaign spending	1
Employ more minority groups	1
Stop making unnecessary laws	*
Other answers	6
Don't know	39

Source: *Confidence and Concern*, pt. 1, p. 312. The question was: "What two or three things do you think would have to be done to make the government a more exciting place to work? Anything else?"
* Less than 1 percent.
a. Percentages add to more than 100 because some respondents mentioned more than one item.

make the government a more exciting place to work." The wording of this question explicitly invited respondents to mention factors that might increase the attractiveness of public service; yet the results were inconclusive (see table 5).

The leading suggestion, mentioned by 12 percent of the respondents, was simply to "eliminate corruption." Ten percent thought government service was already sufficiently exciting. Other respondents mentioned factors that paralleled those mentioned by government officials themselves: elimination of red tape, more public involvement, more interesting work. Only 5 percent felt that higher salaries would be an inducement. (These were, of course, volunteered answers rather than answers suggested by interviewers, so that relatively few citizens mentioned any one item.) The overall impression conveyed by these figures is that the American people, in 1973 at least, had not yet focused on the question of attracting people to government service; that many people thought sufficient incentives for government service already existed; and that when asked to propose further incentives, large numbers of people mentioned more restrictions or higher standards (for example, eliminate corruption, emphasize hard work) rather than additional rewards. Whatever the accuracy of the public's view, it is certainly consistent with the widespread distrust of government and its officials.

For at least one interest group dedicated to procedural and structural reform of government, the story is not much different: the issue of attracting leadership personnel was apparently not perceived as urgent. In its 1978 membership (mail) poll of issues, the "public interest" lobby Common Cause asked its members to rank a series of proposals intended to improve government performance. "Recruit and appoint high quality people" ranked fifth out of six items offered in the questionnaire. Only about 8 percent of Common Cause's 38,724 respondents put this item first.[9] Somewhat higher in the respondents' priorities was a suggestion resembling President Carter's civil service reform proposal ("make it easier to reward productive employees and replace incompetent employees"), which was ranked first by 18 percent of the respondents (and third overall). Other proposals, in order of their ranking, were regular evaluation of government agencies, programs, and tax expenditures; reorganization and streamlining of the federal bureaucracy; reorganization of congressional committees and procedures; and establishment of a long-range planning body divorced from day-to-day issues.

The Common Cause respondents, it should be emphasized, are by no means representative of the general public. They constitute an elite group of sorts, being undoubtedly far better informed than the average citizen, and they would be expected to hold favorable views about the importance of government activity and the need for reform.

What is suggestive about this is that the Common Cause respondents

9. "Results of 1978 CC Issues Poll," *In Common*, vol. 9 (Spring 1978), pp. 18–24. The question was: "Making Government Work has been a major theme of Common Cause activities. Dissatisfaction with the performance of government, quite apart from its policies, is prevalent among the public and within government itself. In your opinion, what are the most important steps—beyond CC's accountability proposals—that the federal government could take to improve its performance?" Respondents were asked to mark the top three proposals in order. Findings are based on the proportion of respondents marking the issue as 1, 2, or 3 in priority.

are a potential constituency for reformist proposals, the type of constituency that would have to be mobilized to support greater incentives for federal service. The poll revealed, however, that Common Cause members echo the general public's disenchantment with government performance and seeming preference for more restrictive rather than more permissive treatment of government employees. Conceivably the Common Cause members could be persuaded to support additional incentives for government service; but when the poll was taken they were not ready.

Attitudes toward Salaries and Perquisites

Discussion of public attitudes toward the specific issue of federal compensation is necessarily more speculative. Recent studies by major survey organizations include few items directly aimed at this question and no efforts to probe it in depth. A systematic study of public attitudes toward federal compensation ought to be high on the agenda of policymakers concerned with the issue. Such a study would place in perspective the existing incentive structure, nonmonetary as well as monetary, and would identify which alternatives fall within the boundaries of public tolerance and which do not.

Despite the paucity of data, there can be little doubt about citizens' reactions to federal compensation. Every fragment of evidence suggests that large government salaries are a red flag to the average American. At every level of government—city, county, and state, as well as federal—top officials' salaries have repeatedly drawn heated political controversy. Legislators are not exhibiting cowardice when they exercise caution in raising their own salaries or those of other high-level officials; they are representing their constituents.

High government salaries are a sensitive public issue for several reasons. A salary figure is simple; everybody can relate to it. No matter how ill informed citizens may be about other issues in government, they know their own income and can readily make comparisons with the published salary figures of government officials. Nothing is more natural than making such comparisons, for people spend most of their lives matching their resources and life-styles with those of others around them. And when government managers' salaries are pegged far above the incomes of all but a tiny minority of Americans, it is not surprising that a vast majority of citizens react negatively. I am not talking here of fairness or economic propriety but of predictable attitudes in American society, with its emphasis on materialism and egalitarianism.

Top-echelon government salaries are visible to the average citizen and are prime targets for investigative journalists. Salary disputes in Congress are given wide exposure by the press. The same goes for debates in state legislatures, county boards, and city councils. In 1977 the press gave extensive coverage to the salaries (in the $40,000 to $50,000 range) being paid President Carter's White House staff aides, many of whom were young and inexperienced. Later, there were articles about the Carter administration's "$100,000 families"—husband-and-wife teams with huge combined incomes because both partners held top-level managerial jobs. The intricacies of government pension systems receive less coverage; but articles have exposed the "double dippers"—military retirees drawing pensions while holding down civilian government posts, sometimes resulting in annual incomes of $75,000 or more (a practice curtailed by the 1978 civil service reforms).

One may object that publicizing such figures out of context is misleading and even irresponsible. Yet these figures have meaning for the people who read the news stories—the general public. Gross figures are more easily reported and understood than are the intricacies of the compensation question. And government officials' salaries are all the more conspicuous because comparable private sector pay levels—while undoubtedly higher—are usually not known or reported by the media.

Would the American people endorse higher compensation for government managers? Only a foolhardy analyst would predict a positive response. For example, higher salaries were given low priority by respondents who were asked what could be done to make government service more rewarding (see table 5). The public's dissatisfaction with and cynicism about government performance and officialdom do not augur well for public support of higher compensation levels. American citizens currently stress greater sacrifices by and restrictions on, rather than greater rewards for, public leaders. The recent taxpayer "revolt," needless to say, was a direct result of the public's cynical mood.

Even though public opinion studies have not probed attitudes toward high-level federal salaries, a 1978 *Washington Post* survey casts further light on the matter.[10] The survey confirmed earlier findings of public cynicism and desire for more efficient government. It also emphasized the low esteem in which public workers are held. By a two-to-one margin among those expressing an opinion, private sector salespeople and office

10. Barry Sussman, " 'Tax Revolt' Targeted at Poor Services," *Washington Post,* October 1, 1978. Findings were drawn from a September 7–17, 1978, telephone survey of 1,756 people.

clerks were viewed as more courteous and honest than public employees; by a three-to-one edge, they were seen as working harder and faster to get a job done. In only one category, intelligence, were private and public workers rated comparably. Government workers themselves seem to share these views. Eighteen percent of the *Post*'s respondents said they or someone in their household were employed by local, state, or federal government. These same respondents gave only slightly better ratings to public employees in every comparison than did the rest of the population. Although the question applied mostly to lower- and middle-level workers, the responses clearly reflected general criticism of public sector employees.[11]

Citizens appear to believe that the federal government employs too many people and pays them too much. Four out of five respondents in the *Post*'s survey claimed that there were more people in the federal government than necessary "to do the work that must be done"—63 percent saying "far too many" and 17 percent saying "somewhat too many." More than half of the interviewees believed that federal employees were paid more than people in comparable jobs outside the government. Only 8 percent believed federal workers were paid less. Asked what areas of spending ought to be reduced, 23 percent of the respondents said they would cut the number of government employees, government pay and pensions, and other items they regarded as outright waste. This figure was almost twice as high as cuts proposed for other areas of spending.

At the same time, fragmentary survey findings indicate areas of public tolerance for more generous compensation of public officials. In the 1973 Senate survey, citizens who were themselves on higher rungs of the socioeconomic ladder were more apt to mention "higher salaries" as a means of making government service more attractive. This suggests that the prime supporters of higher compensation are people who are college educated, hold professional or managerial jobs, or have high incomes. Though constituting a minority of the populace, these people wield disproportionate power in politics because they tend to be better informed and more active than those of lower socioeconomic status. In short, America's upper class is the most promising constituency for the issue of higher

11. The question was: "Think about your dealings with public employees you have come in contact with compared to your dealings with salespeople and office clerks not in the government. Who do you think are more (courteous, honest, hardworking, speedy in getting a job done, intelligent), public employees or salespeople and office clerks?"

compensation, assuming that its members could be mobilized on the issue. The constituency might embrace top-echelon public-sector workers in the few states and localities that pay at the same levels as the federal government.

Americans seem willing, moreover, to underwrite government expenses they regard as legitimate. A 1977 survey sponsored by the House Commission on Administrative Review included a number of questions concerning various perquisites enjoyed by members of the House (though compensation per se was not covered by the study). Majorities of respondents endorsed government reimbursement for congressmen's moving expenses, official travel between Washington and their home districts, and official travel within their districts.[12] And a majority of citizens seemed to support President Carter's civil service reorganization, although it is likely that they saw it more as a means of ensuring efficiency than of raising compensation levels.

These fragmentary data hint that nonsalary benefits designed to increase the attractiveness of top federal jobs might meet with public approval. Benefits might include relocation allowances, educational expenses, and perhaps cost-of-living differences for different parts of the country. Needless to say, benefits would have to be closely linked to job performance, strictly policed to prevent abuses, and immune from being interpreted as "frivolous." Here again, a systematic public opinion survey would clarify the types of compensation that might meet with public approval.

To make major changes in federal compensation levels, a public sense of urgency would have to exist. Only then would there be public pressure for reform, or at least recognition of the problem's seriousness that would pave the way for steps that would otherwise seem drastic or unpleasant. That sense of urgency is not now discernible. Informational and mobilizational efforts to sensitize the general public or attentive groups would no doubt have to be mounted to stimulate such a sense of urgency. One impetus would be public anger at major government scandals. The past decade has witnessed no dearth of scandals, some of which have involved inept or corrupt federal leaders. Yet citizens see these incidents as arguing for tighter controls on federal managers rather than greater rewards.

The mobilizing effect of a scandal, moreover, is diffuse and short-lived. To exploit public anger over a scandal, reformers must ride the wave of

12. *Final Report of the Commission on Administrative Review,* vol. 2, p. 853.

dissatisfaction before it has dissipated into general cynicism, and must link the proposed reform to the causes of the scandal. Heclo describes the Civil Service Commission's valiant efforts to prevent politicization of the "career-status" assistant secretaries for administration in the late 1960s. For a period the commission resisted White House attempts to fill these posts with political appointees, warning of a possible public outcry. Little or no public outrage materialized, however, and the commission was obliged to abandon its efforts.[13] The public's attention span is apt to be equally short in the matter of incentives for federal service.

Summary

Understanding the politics of federal managerial compensation begins with the study of public attitudes. This is necessary not because public opinion determines each and every public policy choice—it assuredly does not—but because resolution of the compensation issue hinges on public attitudes that severely limit decisionmakers' choices. Decisionmakers who are directly responsible to voters through the electoral process are particularly sensitive to these boundaries of public tolerance, a fact of political life that underlies the failure to achieve consensus on the compensation issue during the past decade or so.

In summary, several findings of public opinion surveys are pertinent to federal managerial compensation.

1. The public expresses marked cynicism about leaders of government and other major social institutions. While faith in the institutions themselves seems unshaken, the public believes that leaders have betrayed their trust.

2. In expressing their views about the ideal attributes of public officials, today's citizens tend to place honesty above substantive ability. They endorse more stringent codes of ethics for government leaders, placing greater faith in such formal checks than in leaders' inherent qualities.

3. Holding such views, the general public has not focused on the problem of attracting people to government service—and may not realize that it is a problem. The subject is rarely cited by respondents in surveys and stands relatively low in the expressed priorities of state and local leaders or civic-lobby activists.

4. Citizens would unquestionably resist the notion of higher salaries for

---

13. Hugh Heclo, *A Government of Strangers: Executive Politics in Washington* (Brookings Institution, 1977), pp. 77–78.

public leaders. Publicized salaries of government officials at all levels are flashpoints of controversy.

5. Receptivity to more generous compensation for government managers would undoubtedly be greatest among people of high socioeconomic status—those who are college educated, who draw high incomes themselves, and who are professionals or managers. Receptivity to certain carefully defined forms of compensation other than salary might be greater than to salary increases.

An understanding of public attitudes goes a long way toward explaining the seemingly erratic workings of political marketplaces on the issue of federal managerial compensation. When they seek to avoid pay hikes or to freeze high-level officials' pay, members of Congress are responding to genuine popular feelings on the matter. On this issue, they act as delegates of popular opinion rather than as trustees of the public good. With the current antipathy toward bureaucrats, red tape, and high taxes, it is hard to fault the accuracy of these legislators' readings of their constituents' sentiments. Whether the public's viewpoint is justified is quite a different issue.

This survey of the public's view of compensation makes it easier to comprehend the activities of decisionmakers, especially those in Congress, in determining pay levels for government managers.

Congressional Politics and the Compensation Issue

Few issues place senators and representatives in a more precarious position than salary adjustment for top federal employees, including themselves. Conflicting pressures—from budget-conscious administrations, pay-conscious employee organizations, and tax-conscious citizens—strain democratic decisionmaking processes to their limits. Legislators' worry about reelection not infrequently causes posturing or grandstanding, which lends the issue of compensation a notoriety it does not deserve.

The issue's persistent constituency flavor has prevented the emergence of a consensus on either policy objectives or procedures. The history of pay legislation has therefore been one of piecemeal adjustments, punctuated occasionally by broad revisions designed to "solve" the problem once and for all. None of these "solutions" have proved durable, however, and after a decade and a half of congressional deliberations, some conscientious and some frivolous, the matter is as far from being settled as ever.

From all accounts, voters react bitterly to each federal pay raise, making their views known through letters and personal visits. It is doubtful that their revulsion is intense enough to induce them to vote against incumbent legislators. Yet criticism of pay hikes is real, as is the threat that potential opponents will make use of the issue in the next election. Legislators from competitive or marginal constituencies (as well as those philosophically opposed to higher salaries) are most likely to produce statements and press releases demonstrating their fealty to the principle of parsimony. In explaining their votes or actions, legislators strive to set themselves apart in voters' minds from their colleagues and from Congress as an institution. As Fenno points out in his study of legislators' "home style," this is a common strategy for explaining Washington life to the folks back home. "Members of Congress run *for* Congress by running *against* Congress," he writes. "The strategy is ubiquitous, addictive, cost-free, and foolproof."[14]

The Committee Setting

Constituency politics exert a powerful pull upon the committees that deal with the compensation issue in both houses of Congress. Traditionally, members have gravitated to these panels to fulfill reelection and constituency needs. Large numbers of civil service or postal employees, or the needs of constituencies for postal facilities, are cited as reasons for seeking membership on the committees. The making of public policy per se is not paramount in the minds of members, at least of the House committee. (Because Senate constituencies are broader and more heterogeneous, the influence of federal or postal employees on senators is diluted.) Fenno describes his interviews with House Post Office and Civil Service Committee members in the 1965–68 period: "It is conceivable that a House member might have an interest in government-employee problems or in the postal service, such that he would seek membership because of the subject matter. But no such instances were discovered in the interviewing."[15] Not surprisingly, then, public employees' needs receive little attention from most members of Congress.

The House Post Office and Civil Service Committee attracts a dispro-

---

14. Richard F. Fenno, Jr., *Home Style: House Members in Their Districts* (Little, Brown, 1978), p. 168.
15. Richard F. Fenno, Jr., *Congressmen in Committees* (Little, Brown, 1973), p. 7.

portionate number of members with low seniority, many of whom move to other assignments when the opportunity arises. Turnover is relatively high, and according to Fenno's study of the Eighty-fourth through the Eighty-ninth Congresses, 53 percent of those assigned to the committee did not request the assignment. It is usually considered a "second committee" for its members. Of the six committees Fenno compared—Appropriations, Ways and Means, Foreign Affairs, Education and Labor, Interior, and Post Office—Post Office had the largest proportion of members holding more than one assignment—77 percent.[16]

The House Post Office and Civil Service Committee is thus a clientele-oriented committee whose members seek membership on it (to the extent that they do) for constituency reasons. The premises for its decisions could be summarized as "support maximum pay increases and improvements in benefits for employee groups and . . . oppose all rate increases for mail users."[17] Most members do not remain interested in the committee's constricted domain; many of them eventually transfer to more prestigious committees. Those who remain on the committee quickly climb the seniority ladder, which gives them a stake in perpetuating the body.

In 1970 a blow was dealt the House and Senate postal committees by the passage of the Postal Reorganization Act, which shifted authority over postal rates and employees' salaries to a newly created government corporation, the U.S. Postal Service. The postal reforms, stimulated by public unrest about the postal system, removed the committees' most valuable resource, control of postal salaries and rates. Their legislative workload was concomitantly reduced—in the House, from 1,182 bills introduced in the Ninetieth Congress (1967–68) to 729 bills in the Ninety-second (1971–72).

In the Ninety-third Congress, the House contemplated abolishing its postal committee and folding its functions into another body. That, at least, was recommended by the Select Committee on Committees, which was chaired by Democrat Richard Bolling from Missouri and charged with submitting a comprehensive committee reform plan. At first, few came forward to defend the panel. In the Bolling Committee, there was less argument over abolishing the panel than over the disposition of its jurisdiction.[18] However, anticipating opposition from postal and govern-

16. Ibid., pp. 16, 20.
17. Ibid., p. 64.
18. The story is detailed in Roger H. Davidson and Walter J. Oleszek, *Congress Against Itself* (Indiana University Press, 1977), pp. 164–68.

ment employee unions, Bolling and his colleagues proposed shifting the jurisdiction to the liberal-oriented Labor Committee rather than to the Government Operations Committee. Even so, the unions labored frantically to preserve the panel, fearing their useful access to legislators would be impaired. Although relatively few House members came to the committee's defense, the unions were backed by committee staff members (whose jobs were jeopardized) and a few senior committee members who, as Fenno puts it, had "made a big investment in their clientele group relations."[19] Union resistance to abolishing the Post Office panel was only one segment of the opposition to the Bolling Committee report. This report was eventually voted down in favor of a watered-down reorganization drafted by a Democratic caucus group; in deference to union demands, the substitute plan left the Post Office and Civil Service Committee intact.

In the Senate the story was much the same, except that in 1977 the Post Office and Civil Service Committee was actually abolished. The Senate panel was even less attractive than its House counterpart, no doubt because the interest groups served by the committee are less important to senators. The starting point for understanding the committee, according to Fenno, was this typical comment by one member: "I didn't ask for Post Office. It was the only vacancy when I came and that was it. I said, 'Don't I get any choice?' They said, 'That's all there is left.' "[20] Thus, when in 1976 the temporary Select Committee to Study the Senate Committee System recommended transferring postal and civil service matters to the Governmental Affairs Committee, little outcry was heard. Few senators were eager to see it retained. Indeed, membership on the panel had turned from an unrewarding burden into a liability. Chairmanship of the committee was widely cited as a factor in the 1976 defeat of veteran Senator Gale W. McGee of Wyoming, whose opponent used a series of innovative television commercials attacking bureaucracy and postal inefficiency.

A floor bid to revive the Post Office and Civil Service Committee was turned back. The sponsor of the move, Senator Quentin N. Burdick of North Dakota, acting chairman of the committee, argued that the problems faced by the Postal Service and the government's civilian workers warranted attention by a full Senate committee. These arguments were backed by a lobbying effort by organized labor. Senator Adlai E. Stevenson of Illinois, author of the committee reform plan, countered that, while the

19. Fenno, *Congressmen in Committees*, p. 255.
20. Ibid., p. 170.

committee had nine members and a fiscal 1977 budget of $564,000, it had reported only 1.6 percent of all bills reported by Senate committees during that year. By a 55–42 vote, the Senate on February 2, 1977, tabled Burdick's amendment and sustained the Stevenson reform plan. Supporting the postal panel was a curious coalition of liberals susceptible to union pressure and conservatives opposed to committee reorganization.[21]

In the two houses, therefore, different committees currently deal with civil service and compensation matters. In the Senate civil service legislation is handled by a five-person subcommittee of Governmental Affairs. The parent committee, however, is a force to be reckoned with. Although historically Governmental Affairs has had more investigative duties than legislative ones, this is proving an asset in an era when liberals as well as conservatives are stressing oversight and review. Not only did the panel acquire new legislative jurisdiction in the 1977 reorganization, but it deals with such timely issues as reorganization, civil service reform, and "sunset" procedures.

In the House the twenty-five-member Post Office and Civil Service Committee remains intact, although its leadership and jurisdiction have fluctuated in the past few years. Normally, public employee matters are referred to one of two subcommittees: Civil Service or Compensation and Employee Benefits. To consider the President's 1977 pay recommendation, the chairman at the time, Robert N. C. Nix of Pennsylvania, created an Ad Hoc Subcommittee on Presidential Pay Recommendations, whose chairman was Stephen J. Solarz of New York. The subcommittee assumed jurisdiction over procedures for fixing top-level federal pay as well as over the 1977 pay recommendations. In 1978 President Carter's civil service reform package was split between two committees: the reorganization of the Civil Service Commission went to the House Government Operations Committee, procedural changes to the Post Office and Civil Service Committee.

Interest in public employee matters in the parent houses is typically minimal. When interest does appear, it is of limited duration and scope. Debate on the Federal Salary Act of 1967, for example, was primarily on the quadrennial mechanism for executive, legislative, and judicial salary adjustments—not, as might be expected, on the act's pay hikes. In recent years, in contrast, controversy has focused on the pay hikes, especially those affecting members of Congress.

21. *Congressional Quarterly* (February 5, 1977), pp. 197, 240.

The First "Solution": The Federal Salary Act of 1967

The first major enactment on the question of managerial compensation, the Postal Revenue and Federal Salary Act of 1967 (Public Law
90-206), established an objective, automatic decisionmaking process.
Under the act a nine-member Commission on Executive, Legislative, and
Judicial Salaries—the quadrennial commission—is created every four
years. The President appoints three members to the commission; the
president of the Senate, the Speaker of the House, and the chief justice
of the United States each appoint two members. Operating during the
fiscal year in which the appointments are made, the commission reviews
the salaries of members of Congress, members of the federal judiciary, and
executive schedule employees. The commission submits its findings to
the President, who in turn embodies his own recommendations in his next
budget message. He may accept or modify the commission's recommendations. Under the 1967 provisions the President's proposals would take effect thirty days after transmittal to Congress, unless in the meantime either
house had formally voted disapproval or Congress had enacted a statute
establishing alternative pay rates. Congress substantially changed this
procedure in 1977.

The 1967 act was explicitly designed to avoid the annual struggle over
pay, with its political embarrassments and costs. As Congressman Morris
K. Udall argued on the House floor:

We need a more rational system of fixing pay . . . if we are ever to get out of
the annual struggle on the pay that we are fighting today, with people and
clerks lobbying in our offices.

We have raised [congressional] pay seven times since 1787, since the time
of George Washington. They went for 78 years before they raised it from $6
to $8 a day, because they were afraid of what some demagog opponent might
say about it.[22]

This tendency not to raise executive, congressional, and judicial salaries
has caused compression of salaries at the higher general schedule (GS)
ranges. The problem arises because legislators' salaries are linked to those
of high-level managers in the other two branches, and because by law
employees in the general schedule can be paid no more than those in the
lowest level of the executive schedule (level V). A semiautomatic procedure—with its blue-ribbon commission, presidential recommendation,

---

22. *Congressional Record* (October 11, 1967), p. 28642.

and a legislative veto feature—would, it was hoped, deliver Congress from its quandary over the issue.

This hope proved to be ill founded, however. Actually, close inspection of the history of the 1967 act shows that its congressional base of support was quite slender. The notion of the quadrennial commission (as it is usually called) was not new, having surfaced in the House version of the 1965 federal salary bill. Two years later, the scheme was incorporated in the House version of the 1967 act (House bill 8261, later House bill 7977) because of the strong backing of Udall, Committee Chairman Thaddeus J. Dulski, and the full Post Office and Civil Service Committee. On the House floor it encountered stiff opposition from legislators who argued that it violated separation of powers and gave undue power to the President. The attack was led by Republican Congressman H. R. Gross of Iowa, the famed conservative "watchdog." Gross's amendment deleting the plan from the bill was defeated on a voice vote; but his motion to recommit with instructions to delete both the quadrennial commission provision and much of the pay hike was defeated by only a narrow margin, 211–199.

The Senate Post Office and Civil Service Committee dropped the quadrennial commission from its version of the measure, stating in its report:

> The committee is unanimously opposed to any legislative proposal which would vest in the executive branch the authority to establish, affirmatively or negatively, the salaries of the Members of Congress. What we pay ourselves is a constitutional responsibility vested in us and to be exercised by us. To shirk that positive duty by handing the responsibility to the President, a salary commission, or any other person or group, and then to allow his or their recommendations to take effect is an abdication of constitutional responsibility.[23]

There was no move on the Senate floor to reinstate the proposal. However, in the House-Senate conference the Senate managers backed down and the House provision was restored, albeit with a stipulation that the quadrennial commission be denied jurisdiction over the amount and kinds of expenses for legislators, judges, and executive schedule officers. The conference report was accepted overwhelmingly, by a 327–63 roll-call vote in the House and a 72–0 roll-call vote in the Senate. Yet its history indicated a shaky base of support on Capitol Hill for the new pay-setting procedure.

---

23. *Postal Rates and Federal Salaries,* S. Rept. 90-801, 90 Cong. 1 sess. (GPO, 1967), p. 25.

Ever since 1969, when Congress considered the first salary recommendation under the 1967 act, compensation bills have been greeted by a chorus of objections from individual legislators. Opposition to pay adjustments offers an inexpensive and seemingly irresistible opportunity to demonstrate commitment to governmental economy and self-denial. The lightning rod for controversy is the fact that congressional pay is a part of the President's recommendations. As Senate Majority Leader Robert C. Byrd explained:

> Having Members vote on their own pay increases has always invited political grandstanding, posturing and demagoguery—both by Members and potential opponents—thus feeding public opposition to congressional pay increases. As a result, congressional salaries have always lagged far behind comparable positions of responsibility in the private sector.[24]

This periodic grandstanding on the congressional pay issue has defeated the purpose of the Federal Salary Act of 1967 and the Federal Pay Comparability Act of 1970, which was to remove these very decisions from political controversy and relieve legislators of the risky business of voting on them.

From the very first, it was obvious that the "automatic" pay adjustments would be nothing of the sort. When the first quadrennial commission submitted its recommendations in December 1968, a number of legislators urged President Johnson to lower the dollar amounts, especially of congressional salaries. In his State of the Union address of January 14, 1969, Johnson indicated he would accede to these requests, and in his budget message of January 17 he made good his promise.[25] Even so, a number of resolutions of disapproval were introduced in both houses. On February 4, 1969, the Senate rejected, by a 47–34 vote, a disapproval resolution drafted by Senator John J. Williams of Delaware. The next day, the House Rules Committee prevented resolutions of disapproval from reaching the House floor. Thus a scaled-down version of the first quadrennial commission's recommendations went into effect.

The second quadrennial commission's recommendations encountered more intense opposition, even though by this time there had been no pay raises in five years. As submitted to Congress by President Nixon on

24. *Congressional Record,* daily edition (April 29, 1977), p. S6801.
25. "Annual Message to the Congress on the State of the Union, January 14, 1969," *Public Papers of the Presidents: Lyndon B. Johnson, 1968–69* (GPO, 1970), vol. 2, p. 1267; "Special Message to the Congress Recommending Salary Reforms for Top Officials in the Executive, Legislative, and Judicial Branches, January 17, 1969," ibid., pp. 1345–46.

February 4, 1974, the recommended amounts were slightly reduced, especially at the very top levels.[26] No less than sixty-three resolutions of disapproval were introduced in the House and eight in the Senate. Some proposals would have excepted members of Congress from the pay raise; others would have scaled down or delayed the increases. House sponsors came disproportionately from the ranks of conservatives of both parties; sponsorship in the Senate was more diffuse. All resolutions were referred to the respective Post Office and Civil Service committees, whose members struggled to find acceptable compromises that would minimize political costs.

The Senate acted first. Under consideration was Senate Resolution 293, a committee-sponsored compromise written by Chairman McGee, which would have barred the proposed salary increase for members of Congress but authorized them for executive and judicial officers. During two days of debate (March 4 and 6, 1974), two compromises offered by committee members were turned down decisively: one, sponsored by Senator Hiram L. Fong of Hawaii, would have postponed the effective date of the increases; another, by Chairman McGee, would have reduced them and forbidden further increases for the next two years. Finally, by a 69–28 vote, the Senate adopted a substitute amendment introduced by Senators Frank Church of Idaho and Peter H. Dominick of Colorado barring any pay raises for officials covered by the 1967 act. Final passage of Senate Resolution 293, as amended, came on a similar vote of 71–26.

Because the 1967 act stipulated that a disapproval vote by either house would nullify the President's recommendations, the Senate's action killed the 1974 pay increase. Before the Senate's action, however, the House Post Office and Civil Service Committee had been wrestling with several alternatives to the President's recommendations. The committee went so far as to introduce a resolution of total disapproval (House Resolution 807), just in case the Senate voted to nullify the pay increase for legislators while approving it for other officials. Committee members contended that pay increases should be approved for everyone or for no one.

The second quadrennial commission's procedural recommendations, which were designed to alleviate the political liability of pay adjustments by making them more frequent and hence more modest, fared no better than its salary recommendations. The commission proposed that Congress alter the 1967 act to create a biennial commission that would recommend

26. See *Congressional Quarterly* (March 9, 1974), pp. 637–39, 641, 645.

pay adjustments for top-level officials. Replacing the four-year cycle with a two-year cycle, it was alleged, would minimize the growing problem of compression and would reduce the size of the increases:

A system involving salary changes every 4 years is simply incompatible with one that is adjusted each year during an inflationary period, particularly when the 4-year system "puts a lid on" the 1-year system. A 2-year cycle of adjustment for the Executive Schedule reduces the distortion resulting from inflation by half. . . . The 2-year period also sharply reduces the size of the necessary salary increase, hence would lessen the misunderstanding among the electorate that seems to follow any boost in government salaries. Being accustomed to annual pay raises himself, the average voter overlooks the fact that 4 years normally elapse between increases in the Executive Schedule.[27]

Thus biennial adjustments were intended to remedy both political and economic flaws inherent in the longer cycle.

Senate bill 1989, which embodied the notion of biennial adjustments, was reported by the Senate committee and passed the Senate by voice vote on July 9, 1973. According to the timetable set up by this bill, presidential commissions would be established in each odd-numbered year beginning in 1975. Reports to be made by the President by June 30 of the fiscal year in which the review was conducted would go into effect in thirty days if neither house disapproved. (It is hard to see how this plan solved the political problem, inasmuch as its pay adjustments would occur only a month before biennial congressional elections.) The measure was killed in the House later that month, when members, by a 237–156 vote, turned down a "rule" for considering the measure.

Other bills introduced in the Ninety-third Congress failed to make their way out of committee. Of thirty-six House bills, eight would have abolished the quadrennial commission and increased legislators' salaries. Others would have altered the timing of the pay adjustment process, made congressional pay raises effective in the Congress following the vote, or changed House procedures for handling pay measures. Of four bills introduced in the Senate, two would have put the commission on an annual basis, one would have abolished the commission, and one would have tied pay adjustments to government cost-of-living statistics.

The Second "Solution": The Comparability Mechanism

In the Ninety-fourth Congress, another method of setting managers' salaries was adopted: the Executive Salary Cost-of-Living Adjustment

27. *Report of the Commission on Executive, Legislative, and Judicial Salaries, June 1973* (GPO, 1973), p. 15.

Act. This move, supplementing the 1967 act, brought managerial posts under the comparability system used for other federal workers, as established by the Federal Pay Comparability Act of 1970. Under the 1975 law, members of Congress, executive schedule officers, and certain members of the judiciary gain pay adjustments whenever a comparability adjustment is made in the statutory pay systems covered by the 1970 act. The adjustment is to equal the average general schedule worker's pay increase. The President designates a committee, called the pay agent (currently the chairman of the Civil Service Commission, the secretary of labor, and the director of the Office of Management and Budget), to prepare comparability figures and report to him; the President's recommendations are submitted to Congress by September 1 of each year, taking effect in thirty days unless vetoed by either house.

Although this annual procedure seemed a logical solution to the pay problem, the congressional consensus behind it was, to say the least, unclear. The Senate approved the new plan (presented as an amendment to House bill 2559, the Postal Service's compliance with the Occupational Safety and Health Act) by a 58–29 roll-call vote after defeating several crippling amendments. In the House, however, the Senate's plan was approved by the narrowest of margins: 214–213, with one member voting only "present."

The first adjustment under the new annual procedure was successful, as had been the initial adjustment under the quadrennial system. Following the procedures of the 1970 comparability act, President Gerald Ford for the first time recommended a salary increase (5 percent) for managerial officers, identical to the increase slated for general schedule employees. Although his advisers had urged a larger increase for general schedule workers, the President limited his recommendation to 5 percent because "pay comparability must be viewed in light of the country's current economic situation."[28] The Senate committee voted 7–2 to report Senate Resolution 239 disapproving the President's downward modification of his advisers' adjustment figures.[29] This resolution was rejected by the full Senate by a vote of 53–39, upholding the President's position. The procedural maneuvers in the House were more complicated, but again the result was to uphold the President's position. The House Post Office and Civil Service Committee voted to take no action, and a motion to dis-

28. *Federal Pay Comparability Alternative Plan, Message from the President of the United States,* H. Doc. 94-233, 94 Cong. 1 sess. (GPO, 1975), p. 1.

29. *Disapproval of the Federal Statutory Pay Reduction,* S. Rept. 94-371, 94 Cong. 1 sess. (GPO, 1975).

charge the committee from considering the matter was tabled, 278–123. The 5 percent pay increase, which took effect on October 1, 1975, was the first increase since 1969 for the government's top managers.

The following year, election-year jitters proved too much for the second annual comparability adjustment for federal managers, which was slated to become effective on October 1. In May, a House Republican—Larry Pressler, who was contemplating a Senate race—filed suit in a federal district court challenging the constitutionality of automatic pay raises for Congress without a vote and seeking an injunction against the disbursal of scheduled salary increases for top managerial employees. At the end of August, House Minority Leader John J. Rhodes of Arizona disclosed that Republicans would try to block automatic pay increases for legislators by bringing the issue to a vote. Rhodes accused the Democratic leadership of planning to prevent a vote on a disapproval motion.[30] As it turned out, the motion was allowed and passed by the election-minded House. At the urging of the House Post Office Committee, the measure as passed (House bill 14238) applied not only to members of Congress but to executive and judicial officers. The Senate's version, approved on September 8, applied only to members of Congress. In conference the House position prevailed, and President Ford signed the measure into law (Public Law 94-440). Although he considered vetoing the measure, the President noted that Congress would have a chance to reconsider the compensation question early the following year.[31]

The third quadrennial commission, whose report was presented in December 1976, proposed a formula designed to make its recommended pay increases politically palatable: a trade-off between pay hikes and the adoption of a code of ethics. While recommending substantial salary increases (for example, from $44,600 to $57,500 for members of Congress), the commission argued that it would be "an exercise in political futility (a judgment Congress has confirmed more than once) to propose any significant increase in executive, legislative, and judicial salaries unless you [the President] are satisfied that the leaders of the other branches of government will join you in a commitment to major reform."[32]

30. *New York Times,* August 28, 1976.

31. "Statement by the President on Signing H.R. 14238 Into Law, October 1, 1976," *Weekly Compilation of Presidential Documents,* vol. 12 (October 4, 1976), p. 1428.

32. *Report of the Commission on Executive, Legislative, and Judicial Salaries, December 1976* (GPO, 1977), p. 26.

The package addressed the post-Watergate crisis of confidence and had the advantage of reaching Congress early in 1977, just after congressional elections. With the concurrence of President-elect Jimmy Carter, President Ford transmitted his pay recommendations, modified downward from the commission's salary levels, to Capitol Hill in his budget message of January 17, 1977.

Democratic leaders in both houses succeeded in blocking attempts to disapprove the pay raise, but not without protracted maneuvering and protests from many individual senators and representatives. In the House thirty-three resolutions, many of them applying exclusively to members of Congress, were sponsored or cosponsored by no fewer than 176 representatives. Speaker Thomas P. O'Neill, a firm advocate of the salary increase, referred these measures to the Post Office and Civil Service Committee. To stall for time, it was decided to create an Ad Hoc Subcommittee on Presidential Pay Recommendations to take testimony and report. In three days of hearings (February 7–9, 1977), 33 witnesses were heard and 103 members submitted written statements. Of the 131 members who testified or submitted statements, 44 flatly opposed the pay raise, 30 recommended that the increase be deferred until the next Congress, and 100 demanded that the House be permitted to vote on the issue. Only 9 members publicly supported the raise.[33] (Some members were found to be in more than one category.)

In the ad hoc subcommittee all motions to disapprove the pay boosts were defeated. The subcommittee and the full committee thus declined to report resolutions disapproving the pay adjustment, although changes in adjustment procedures were proposed and later reported to the full House. Helped by the intervention of the Lincoln's Birthday recess, the House leadership succeeded in preventing a House vote on the salary adjustment.[34]

In the Senate a different tactic was employed to prevent a vote on the President's recommendations. A resolution can be considered in the Senate only after one legislative day has ended. Instead of adjourning each day from January 19 through February 1, the Senate merely recessed, thereby maintaining the same legislative day. This and other delaying tactics prevented Senator James B. Allen of Alabama from bring-

33. *Presidential Pay Recommendations*, Hearings before the Ad Hoc Subcommittee on Presidential Pay Recommendations of the House Committee on Post Office and Civil Service, 95 Cong. 1 sess. (GPO, 1977).

34. *Congressional Quarterly* (February 5, 1977), p. 196.

ing the pay issue to the Senate floor until February 2. It arrived in the form of a proposed amendment to Senate Resolution 4, a Senate committee reorganization plan. Allen's amendment provided senators with a forum for airing their views on the pay raise. Majority Leader Byrd argued that the amendment would delay action on the reorganization plan, thus preventing early seating of new senators on standing committees.[35] Eventually the Senate voted, 56–42, to table the Allen amendment. Pressing for a Senate vote on the matter was a heterogeneous coalition of southerners, conservatives, those who were newly elected or up for reelection in 1978, and a few liberal reformers.

Because neither house voted disapproval during the allotted thirty-day period, the recommended pay adjustments went into effect on February 20, 1977.

Repercussions continued to be felt throughout the Ninety-fifth Congress, however. In allowing the President's recommendations to go into effect, House and Senate leaders repeatedly promised strict ethics codes as the "price" of the pay raises. Less than a month after the pay raise took effect, the House completed work on its new code of ethics (House Resolution 287). The code embraced a variety of provisions: broadened financial disclosure requirements, prohibition of unofficial office accounts, prohibition of travel by "lame-duck" members, and restrictions on gifts from lobbyists. But the chief feature of the code was that it limited members' annual outside income to 15 percent of their official salary ($8,625 of the current salary of $57,500). However, the limit did not apply to unearned income, and many members, especially those of modest means, argued passionately that it discriminated in favor of the wealthy. Responding that the limit on outside income was "the heart and soul of the entire package," Speaker O'Neill whipped his troops into line and won passage of the measure.[36] The critical vote, on the "modified closed rule" for debating the measure, was 267–153—a party-line vote, with only three Republicans favoring the rule and fifteen Democrats opposing it.[37]

Within a month the Senate approved its new ethics code (Senate Resolution 110) by an overwhelming vote of 86–9. While it differed in particulars from the House code, its outside income limitation was the same —15 percent of a senator's annual salary. The House and Senate codes reinforced the concept of the full-time legislator. By curtailing outside

---

35. *Congressional Record,* daily edition (February 2, 1977), pp. S2008–09.
36. Ibid. (March 2, 1977), p. H1630.
37. See *Congressional Quarterly Almanac, 1977,* p. 767.

income and shutting off methods of "cashing out" office accounts for personal use, the codes also make it more difficult for legislators to raise their allowances in lieu of pay. More than ever, legislators will depend on the pay adjustment process for their livelihood.[38]

The impetus for the House and Senate ethics codes came from a variety of sources, most of them independent of the third quadrennial commission. One factor was certainly public reaction to the $12,900 pay raise of February 1977. But while this reaction hastened passage of the codes, longer-range factors gave them impetus. The most important was public reaction to a series of scandals in 1976 involving House members, including the case of Democrat Wayne L. Hays of Ohio. The Hays case led to creation of the House Commission on Administrative Review (the Obey Commission), which prepared the ethics recommendations. In the Senate a special ethics committee was created in January 1977 to draft a code of conduct.

There were numerous efforts in the Ninety-fifth Congress to undo the February 1977 pay raise. Attempts to nullify the pay raise itself were beaten back. But maneuvering during the congressional budget and appropriations debates was aimed at denying funds for the raise. Finally, the scheduled comparability pay adjustment (for October 1977) was prohibited by the passage of Senate bill 964, signed into law on July 11, 1977. The act (Public Law 95-66), applying to all officials who had been awarded pay increases in February 1977, passed the two houses by commanding margins: 93–1 in the Senate and 397–20 in the House.

The most significant fallout of the 1977 adjustment was passage of an amendment to the Postal Revenue and Federal Salary Act of 1967, requiring roll-call votes in both the House and the Senate on future pay adjustments for officials within the purview of the quadrennial commission. Separate votes would be permitted for each pay category. Sponsored by Senator Dewey F. Bartlett of Oklahoma, it was an amendment to the Emergency Unemployment Compensation Extension Act of 1977. Although House and Senate leaders were not enthusiastic about the Bartlett amendment and although its inclusion in the unemployment compensation bill violated the House's rule against nongermane conference amendments, the measure had an irresistible appeal: it passed the Senate by a

---

38. See testimony of Congressman David R. Obey, in *Staff Report to the Commission on Executive, Legislative, and Judicial Salaries* (GPO, 1977), pp. 219–21. However, in March 1979, the Senate voted to postpone the effective date of the rule on outside earned income until January 1, 1983.

vote of 82–13 (after a motion to table failed, 64–30); later the House adopted the conference report by 406–2. At the beginning of the Ninety-sixth Congress, House Democrats strengthened the Bartlett amendment by gaining their leaders' promise to give due notice before bringing up members' salary and benefit measures.

What types of legislators vote for managerial pay raises? What legislators vote against them? Generalizations are hazardous, inasmuch as the issue's context shifts from vote to vote. Procedural considerations often mask the substance. Selected for analysis here is one of the crucial recent votes: the amendment, proposed by Charles E. Grassley of Iowa, to the legislative branch appropriations bill for fiscal year 1978, which would have prohibited using funds for the March 1977 managerial pay raise. The amendment was rejected on June 29, 1977, 241–181.[39] The vote put the managerial pay issue quite vividly, and it epitomizes current Capitol Hill viewpoints on the subject.

Several factors clearly influence voting on compensation. One is political party: Democrats are more inclined than Republicans to support higher managerial pay. In this case Democrats rejected the Grassley amendment by a two-to-one margin, whereas Republicans voted for it by almost as great a margin. By the same token, liberals of both parties support pay raises (at least when there is a Democratic president) more readily than conservatives do.[40] Voting on the Grassley amendment, the few liberal Republicans were as likely to back the 1977 pay hike as were liberal Democrats. Conservatives of both parties voted against the pay raise (that is, in favor of the amendment), though the margin of opposition was much narrower among Democrats than among Republicans.

Seniority and electoral vulnerability also influence votes. Senior members and those from safe districts are freer to support federal pay raises than are junior legislators and those from marginal districts. In the Grassley amendment vote, one- and two-term members and those who won election in 1976 by less than 55 percent of the vote were far less supportive of the pay raise than were other categories of legislators. These

39. The vote is tabulated in *Congressional Quarterly* (July 2, 1977), pp. 1388–89.

40. To tap members' ideological positions, a "liberalism" score was constructed from *Congressional Quarterly*'s "opposition to conservative coalition" score, with figures recomputed to eliminate the effect of absences from the House floor. "Conservative coalition" scores for 1977 can be found in *Congressional Quarterly* (January 7, 1978), pp. 6–8. The vote on the Grassley amendment was not a "conservative coalition" vote, which means that there was no contamination between the independent and dependent variables.

two factors—seniority and marginality—are related (that is, senior members are more likely to win by large margins), but they seem to operate independently to influence voting on this question.

There are numerous exceptions to these generalizations, for today's legislators cultivate unique viewpoints and develop unique strategies for explaining their viewpoints to constituents. In general, however, the supporters of managerial pay raises are currently most likely to be drawn from the ranks of Democrats, liberals, senior members, and those who are electorally safe. Opposition most frequently emanates from Republicans, conservatives, junior members, and those from marginal districts.

Summary

Within a decade Congress came nearly full circle on the issue of making salary adjustments for top-level federal officers. In 1967 Congress seemed to have accepted the principle of automatic adjustments on a four-year cycle, made pursuant to presidential recommendations and study by a prestigious independent body. The system worked reasonably smoothly the first time around but soon ran afoul of constituency politics. In 1975 a second "automatic" procedure was added, simply by including top-level workers in the federal government's annual adjustment process. Before long, this too broke down. Finally, in 1977 the 1967 act's principle that the President's salary proposals should take effect unless vetoed by Congress was severely compromised by the requirement for roll-call votes on the President's recommendations. In this respect, the legislative branch was virtually back to the pre-1967 situation in which it could not escape frequent votes on pay adjustments.

The foregoing account of the pay problem during that decade is not intended as a comprehensive legislative history; rather, it is designed to highlight some of the procedural and political aspects of the question. Public sector pay issues are politically awkward by their very nature. This inherent awkwardness is overlaid, however, by Congress's procedural and political anomalies, which complicate decisionmaking. It might be well to review these anomalies, as they emerge from this brief account of legislative events between 1967 and 1977.

The legislative veto. Under the Postal Revenue and Federal Salary Act of 1967, the President's pay recommendations take effect thirty days after he submits them to Congress, unless one or both houses vote to disapprove them. This provision was modified by the 1977 Bartlett amendment, which makes congressional votes on pay adjustments mandatory rather than optional. Both provisions are forms of legislative veto, but they differ in where they place the burden of political effort. When a congressional vote is optional, opponents of the President's course of action assume the burden of nullifying it. Supporters of the President's proposed action can maneuver to prevent a vote—no easy task, but one accomplished by congressional leaders in 1969 and again in 1977. Under the Bartlett procedure, such a vote presumably cannot be avoided. This places opponents of the President's actions in a far stronger position, for they do not have to fight the legislative time clock to force a vote.

The legislative veto, as a general proposition, has aroused controversy. Some criticize Congress for abdicating its legislative duties to the President; others argue that Congress is only facing reality by giving leeway to the President and limiting its own attention to broad policy matters. The congressional pay issue presents legislators with the added problem of conflict of interest. Some commentators raise constitutional objections to the legislative veto. Allowing only one house of Congress to negate a presidential initiative, they argue, violates the notion that Congress should legislate as an entity, with both houses taking action. Actually, Congress routinely delegates responsibilities to its committees and subcommittees in the day-to-day processing of legislation; and the action of a single house (often, in practice, a single committee) can kill legislation.

Conflict of interest. Resolution of the pay issue foundered on the issue of congressional compensation, the political conflict of interest involved when members' votes result in raising their own pay. One widely proposed solution for the potential conflict of interest—deferring pay increases until the Congress after the one that votes—would work well for the House of Representatives with its two-year terms, less well for the Senate with its six-year terms.

The conflict of interest is not a legal one, inasmuch as members of Congress (and the other branches, for that matter) have constitutional duties for determining the federal government's structure and conduct, even when applied to themselves. But in a political sense, with its inevitable effect on the public image of Congress, the conflict of interest cannot be ignored.

Problems of timing. Any system that requires election-year legislative votes on pay adjustments invites trouble. As the House's Ad Hoc Subcommittee on Presidential Pay Recommendations stated pointedly in 1977, "The subcommittee firmly believes that the politics of any pay adjustment are such that it *must* be considered by the Congress in a nonelection year. The political pressure experienced by the subcommittee members in this nonelection year was awesome."[41] It is not surprising, then, that election-year attempts to adjust the pay of top-level employees have failed, even with two supposedly "automatic" mechanisms for making such adjustments. The three most recent pay adjustments (1969, 1975, and 1977) all occurred in nonelection years.

On the other hand, it is virtually impossible to avoid election-year deliberations on such an explosive issue. Even if the President's quadrennial recommendations were meshed with the political timetable, the annual comparability adjustments would naturally fall in election years. Moreover, multiple opportunities for committee and floor votes—especially on congressional budget resolutions and legislative appropriations bills—ensure that the pay issue will be aired virtually every year, quite apart from any "automatic" adjustment mechanisms. It offers so many temptations for members to gain political mileage that Congress is almost certain to devote inordinate amounts of time to it. "While the pay issue is important," the House committee observed, "much of the time spent debating that issue could better be spent on the more significant issues facing the country and the Congress."[42]

Another problem of timing arises from the quadrennial pay adjustment formula. While the four-year cycle was designed to reduce the frequency of congressional votes on pay, in an inflationary era this results in inordinately large proposed increases.

The complexity of congressional procedures. Congress is a complicated, decentralized institution. Not only are its two houses separated by constitutional mandate and historical traditions, but in each house more than one set of committees can be involved in the matter of managerial pay adjustments. The primary committees are, to be sure, Post Office and Civil Service in the House and Governmental Affairs in the Senate. Yet although these committees process authorizing legislation, appropriations subcommittees handle the actual funding bills. Budget resolutions, reported by the House and Senate Budget committees, also produce votes on funding relevant to the compensation issue. Finally, votes on compensation can be forced by attaching amendments to other pieces of legis-

41. *Report of the Subcommittee on Presidential Pay Recommendations, Together with Additional Views,* Committee Print, House Committee on Post Office and Civil Service, 95 Cong. 1 sess. (GPO, 1977), p. 10.
42. *Congressional Salary Deferral,* H. Rept. 95-717, 95 Cong. 1 sess. (GPO, 1977), pt. 1, p. 5.

lation. No matter how automatic or orderly the procedures for processing pay adjustments may appear on paper, their actual implementation on Capitol Hill is bound to be open-ended and complex. That is the nature of the legislative process.

Other Actors in the Compensation Process

Since 1967 compensation for high-echelon federal officers has been shaped by the interplay of public attitudes on the subject and legislators' penchant for taking positions that accord with those attitudes. Only three times in the past twelve years has this pattern been breached and pay adjustments actually awarded to executive, legislative, and judicial managers. The rest of the time the pattern has been one of inaction. However, other actors are involved; and the role of each must be considered to complete the picture of the politics of compensation.

The President

Presidential leadership is a strategy frequently advanced to resolve issues that have been mired down by particularist forces. Only the President, it is argued, can transcend narrow interests, attract public attention, and mobilize public support for causes that are otherwise unglamorous or invisible. Speculating on the prospects for recasting the federal civil service, Heclo maintains that a prerequisite would be a president "willing to give strong priority to personnel matters."[43] President Jimmy Carter, for example, declared that civil service reform was the centerpiece of his government reorganization effort and successfully pressed for legislation in 1978; without his personal commitment, there would assuredly have been no action at all.

Yet evidence indicates that federal structural and personnel issues are relatively low in presidential priorities and that initiatives like President Carter's civil service reforms are rare. In Cronin's job description for the presidency, personnel issues fall near the bottom of the list of priorities.[44] In general, presidents have little to do with staffing the federal establishment and even less to do with incentives for federal service. The excep-

43. Heclo, *Government of Strangers,* p. 263.
44. Thomas E. Cronin, *The State of the Presidency* (Little, Brown, 1975), pp. 250–56.

tions are selecting staff associates and appointing cabinet members (who, as often as not, choose *their* staff aides) and coping with public and press criticism of appointees enmeshed in scandal or controversy. For the most part, however, presidents are happiest when they hear nothing about personnel matters. They have scant incentive, moreover, to delve into such matters. It is unglamorous work, and its benefits are scattered and all but invisible.

The political volatility of the compensation issue reinforces presidents' disposition to maintain a low profile. A natural tactic is to call on special blue-ribbon panels to help dispel potential opposition to pay adjustments. In 1967 President Johnson appointed an advisory group headed by retired AT&T chairman Frederick R. Kappel; eight years later President Ford gave a panel headed by Vice-President Nelson A. Rockefeller the assignment of making recommendations on the federal pay problem. The use of blue-ribbon advisory panels, of course, gained statutory basis with the 1967 Federal Salary Act's quadrennial commissions.

Although they appoint independent commissions, presidents hesitate to follow their advice concerning compensation adjustments. President Johnson delayed and scaled down recommendations based on the confidential Kappel Commission report of 1967; two years later, following the advice of advisers and members of Congress, he trimmed the recommendations of the first quadrennial commission, also headed by Kappel. President Nixon modified the second quadrennial commission's proposals in his January 30, 1974, budget message. President Ford tempered both the 1975 recommendations of the Advisory Committee on Federal Pay (from 8.66 percent to 5 percent) and the 1976 proposals of the third quadrennial commission. It is an accident of timing, but thus far the three quadrennial commissions' reports have been presented near the end of the chief executive's term of office.

Presidents historically exhibit restraint in endorsing salary adjustments —in the Postal Service, the Civil Service, and the managerial posts covered by the 1967 act. Although declaring allegiance to management principles of compensation (for example, linkage and comparability), presidents have rejected excessive employee demands and, in inflationary times, tried to minimize the inflationary impact of generous pay hikes. Presidents and employee unions have maneuvered for advantage, a pattern that began during the Eisenhower administration, before the 1967 act. Presidents Nixon and Ford repeatedly tried to delay comparability adjustments or hold them below the recommended levels. In 1972 Nixon refused to submit an alternative comparability plan, but his action was held by an appellate court to violate the law.[45] Inflationary fears led President Carter to trim three percentage points from 1978 comparability adjustments.

The federal pay question was injected into the 1976 presidential campaign. The 1975 pay raise (the first under the annual comparability system) drew strong criticism from at least four leading presidential contenders—Republican Ronald Reagan and Democrats Jimmy Carter, Senator Henry M. Jackson, and Senator Frank Church. Carter, who commented on the issue on several occasions, said he favored "going back to the old system" under which Congress had to vote on each pay raise it received. He also said that members of Congress should be prohibited from raising their salaries during their current terms. Questioned about the issue at several campaign stops, President Ford criticized efforts to repeal the raise. "I think that a member of the House and Senate ought to have fair treatment," he said, "and I think it is demagoguery to isolate them from all other people who work for the federal government."[46]

In short, while presidents might be expected to take the "large view" of compensation for federal managers, they are under a variety of pressures, political and economic, to exercise restraint. And presidential candidates, no less than congressional candidates, must heed public attitudes in tempering compensation adjustments.

The Advisory Commissions

The notion of independent, blue-ribbon advisers was incorporated into the managerial salary-setting process by the 1967 Federal Salary Act. The salary commission's powers, it must be stressed, are only advisory. It does not set salary levels; it can only study and recommend. Were it to exercise formal powers over compensation levels, it is doubtful that its constitutionality would be sustained. In dealing with an analogous and equally delicate political problem, federal campaign finance regulation, Congress passed and President Ford signed the Federal Election Campaign Act Amendments of 1974. To implement campaign rules, the law created a Federal Election Commission with mixed membership similar to that of the quadrennial commissions. Ruling on the law's constitutionality, the

45. *National Treasury Employees Union* v. *Nixon,* 492 F.2d 587 (D.C. Cir. 1974).

46. *Congressional Quarterly* (April 17, 1976), p. 883.

Supreme Court in January 1976 held that the Federal Election Commission violated the separation of powers doctrine.[47] Congress subsequently passed a revised version of the law, providing for a six-member commission appointed by the President and confirmed by the Senate. Interestingly, early congressional opponents of the quadrennial commission employed the separation of powers doctrine during debates on the 1967 act.

Members of the quadrennial commissions have been drawn from an elite group of lawyers, labor leaders, business managers, management specialists, and educational managers. Perhaps even more than the federal managers whose compensation they consider, these persons represent a relatively narrow segment of the nation's managerial and professional class. Nor do they represent public sector managers at the state or local levels. The nature of commission membership has not escaped comment from Capitol Hill critics. Representative Patricia Shroeder of Colorado, a member of the ad hoc subcommittee that considered the President's 1977 recommendations, complained that the commission was a "stacked deck": it was composed of people who were entering federal service, who had left it, or who were lobbying federal officials.[48] Because of close ties with the federal government, she asserted, they would be reluctant to support anything but a substantial pay raise. Ralph Nader, appearing before the ad hoc subcommittee, also questioned a commission composed of members in the "upper one percentile of wealth" to recommend pay levels for federal managers, many of whom are drawn from the same elite groups. If the commission were staffed and run by people whose average income was $11,000 a year, he remarked, the recommendations might have had "a greater level of credibility."[49]

Actually, the third quadrennial commission, recognizing the political sensitivity of the compensation issue, followed a moderate course and proposed a number of palliatives. Most important, the commission proposed a code of conduct for federal managers that would help restore public confidence and render the proposed pay boosts more defensible. Also suggested were changes in the quadrennial timetable and creation of a permanent quadrennial commission of private citizens supported by an Office of Personnel Management. The advisory panel soft-pedaled the need for comparability, acknowledging that a variety of benefits, including

47. *Buckley* v. *Valeo*, 424 U.S. 1 (1976).
48. *Presidential Pay Recommendations*, Hearings, p. 327.
49. Ibid., p. 445.

"psychic income," should be weighed in assessing the true compensation levels of federal managers.

An impartial blue-ribbon commission, introduced to make salary adjustments more acceptable to members of Congress and the general public, has not achieved this objective. As the legislative history of the 1967–77 decade reveals, legislators' pronouncements gain far more publicity than the studies made by the commissions even when, as in the case of the third commission, these studies are thorough and politically astute.

Lobbying for the Managers

In federal personnel politics a primary influence is that of employee unions. By all accounts the most powerful are the postal workers' unions, which represent a large majority of the half million Postal Service employees. Before 1970 they dominated the environment of the House Post Office and Civil Service Committee, and to a lesser extent its counterpart in the Senate.[50] Today they bargain directly with the Postal Service for salaries and benefits. Trailing the postal workers in influence are the other federal employees' unions, which have successfully lobbied for generous salaries and benefits. These unions deal most effectively with bread-and-butter issues—salaries, benefits, and retirement plans. But they also fight for proposals designed to better their bargaining position: most notably, organizing rights, the right to strike, and modifications in the Hatch Act's restrictions on political activity. Bargaining on such issues forced significant modifications in President Carter's civil service reorganization plan.[51]

Compared to lower-level workers, the federal managerial class is virtually impotent. In fact, compression has occurred because compensation for the majority of federal workers has moved upward far more rapidly than that of top-level managers, producing a squeeze. In large part this is the result of the managers' small numbers and lack of political organization. Congressman Udall said as early as 1967:

I think the professional people in the Federal Government should learn that there is nothing improper or dirty about political contributions or raising money. The postal unions and the others know how campaigns are fought. . . .

[Of the] 2.8 million Federal employees, about 200,000 or 300,000 of them —really a relatively small portion—in many instances have had the political

---

50. Fenno, *Congressmen in Committees*, pp. 37, 39, 247, 253.
51. *Congressional Quarterly* (July 15, 1978), pp. 1777–84.

muscle, the expertise, and the know-how to shape Federal salary legislation year in and year out, and in numbers. . . . But there has been no organization and no interest shown by the middle and upper grades and this is why they have lost out year after year in these across-the-board salary raises.[52]

The situation is no different today. Of course, employee unions generally support at least nominally higher management salaries—for the simple reason that they set the ceiling for the general schedule—but give little attention to the question.

Federal managers have few incentives to speak up for their own interests. The managerial group is varied; it is constituted of leaders from the three branches whose motives, jobs, and career patterns are hardly comparable. Even political executives in the executive branch are not a coherent group. They follow varied paths into federal service, and they remain for only a brief time. They have few opportunities to work with their counterparts in other agencies. In Heclo's suggestive phrase, they are a "government of strangers."[53] The lack of coherent politics in the United States has led to the lack of a coherent class of political managers.

If federal service is for most a way station in their careers, managers typically show their dissatisfaction with compensation by deciding to leave—a quiet but eloquent form of protest. A few years ago 140 federal district and circuit court judges filed suit for a salary hike, arguing that the loss of buying power from inflation (34 percent between 1969 and 1975) violated the Constitution's guarantee that judges' compensation "shall not be diminished during their Continuance in Office" (Article III, section 1). Hardly an argument worthy of the nation's judicial leaders, it was rejected by the U.S. court of claims, and late in 1976 the Supreme Court declined to review the case.[54] More eloquent testimony to the judges' plight is found in the flow of judicial talent into private legal practice. The same phenomenon occurs in the other two branches. Many legislators who protest against congressional pay raises have been equally vociferous in denouncing the ethics codes' disclosure provisions and limits on outside income. From all accounts, members' frustration is genuine.

---

52. *Federal Salary Act of 1967,* Hearings before the Subcommittee on Compensation of the Committee on Post Office and Civil Service on H.R. 8261 and related bills, 90 Cong. 1 sess. (GPO, 1967), p. 360.

53. Heclo, *Government of Strangers,* pp. 66–73, 87–88, 103 ff.

54. *C. Clyde Atkins, et al.* v. *United States; Louis C. Bechtle, et al.* v. *United States; Ruggero J. Aldisert* v. *United States,* 214 Ct. Cl. 186 (1977); *Atkins, U.S. District Judge, et al.* v. *United States,* 426 U.S. 944 (1976).

Congressional retirements are at their highest level in years, and financial considerations probably contribute to this.[55]

What is the federal managers' constituency? If they cannot or will not speak for themselves, who can speak for them? Who worries about their competence and well-being? No one, it would seem.

One effort to lobby for higher managerial pay was launched by the third quadrennial commission late in 1976. Even before the commission's report was released, several newspapers across the country came out in favor of raises for top-level officials in the three branches. The *New York Times,* for example, faulted Congress for a lack of political nerve: though reluctant to pay other employees more than themselves, Congress does not have the courage to vote itself a pay increase for fear of voter response.[56] The *Times'* editors also cited as reasons for failure to approve pay adjustments a "covert" hostility toward liberal federal judges and a widespread belief that federal executives do not deserve salaries comparable with their counterparts in private industry.

Following the commission's report, chairman Peter G. Peterson organized the Citizens' Committee for Restoring Public Trust in Government. The group sponsored full-page advertisements in major newspapers across the nation, calling attention to "The Hidden Crisis in the Federal Government." According to the ads, the "profound crisis" was made up of four parts:

> The government has a desperate need for outstanding executives; it will not get and keep them unless the salary freeze is unfrozen; Congress does not dare to take such action until the public is in a more receptive mood, and this will not happen until the people's trust in government is restored.[57]

The ads' purpose was to sell the idea of a pay raise to the public and to stimulate the writing of letters to senators and representatives who were wary of voting for it. Peterson's efforts represent the only campaign to influence public opinion on managerial compensation.

To shift public opinion, a sustained effort would unquestionably have to be undertaken. Since underlying public attitudes are hostile to the notion that federal officials require further incentives to serve their country, the challenge of educating the public is a formidable one.

---

55. Roger H. Davidson, "Congress: The Blahs Take Their Toll," *Los Angeles Times,* February 14, 1978.

56. *New York Times,* editorial, November 19, 1976.

57. *New York Times,* January 13, 1977.

Proposals for Change

In view of the breakdown of existing procedures for adjusting federal managers' salaries, it is not surprising that numerous proposals for change have been introduced in Congress. Some proposals contemplate alterations in the quadrennial mechanism, others in the annual adjustment procedures, and still others in congressional procedures for handling the issue. Among the major proposals are the following four.

1. Revise statutory procedures for adjusting federal compensation. Bills have been introduced to abolish the quadrennial commissions and to remove high-level officers from the annual comparability system. These two "solutions" to the compensation problem were designed to remove it from annual congressional debate and give the entire process an objective, nonpolitical character. However, support for these mechanisms is slight at best.

2. Separate members of Congress from other categories of federal managers for the purpose of pay adjustments—from either the quadrennial commission's jurisdiction or the annual comparability process, or both. Such a move would help executives and judges but would be a disadvantage for legislators. Taking as an article of faith the parity of the three branches, more than a few members feel that *they* are the government's true managers and should receive compensation comparable to that of all but a few government officials. Many legislators sense, moreover, that separating the congressional pay issue would intensify the political risks of adjusting their own compensation. This problem is even more acute with the passage of House and Senate ethics codes requiring income disclosure and limiting outside income sources. Setting executive and judicial salaries would thus be made easier, but the political quagmire surrounding congressional pay would become deeper. Required votes on recommended pay adjustments (based on the so-called Bartlett amendment) have the potential effect of isolating the congressional pay issue, at least insofar as the quadrennial commissions' reports are concerned. The same direction was followed in the Civil Service Reform Act of 1978, which ignored the linkage principle, notably for the Senior Executive Service.

3. Delay any pay raises for members of Congress until the beginning of the Congress following the one that makes the adjustment. This provi-

sion is intended to blunt the political repercussions of pay raises and to moderate the conflict of interest members encounter in voting their own pay. This revision would work reasonably well for the House of Representatives but less well for the Senate with its longer terms.

4. Change congressional procedures for considering or voting on compensation recommendations. After the 1977 procedural maneuvers by the Democratic leadership, Minority Leader Rhodes proposed that it be made easier to take disapproval resolutions out of committees' hands and force floor votes. Members' desires for a chance to vote on the House or Senate floor should be satisfied by the Bartlett amendment (requiring separate votes on the President's recommendations) and subsequent pledges by House leaders to give adequate notice of such votes.

The multiplicity of proposals accentuates the lack of consensus on the process of making salary adjustments for federal managers. It reflects the wide range of options, even after more than a decade of experience under so-called automatic salary adjustment procedures. The fact that many of the proposals move in the direction of greater congressional involvement and away from automatic procedures suggests further that debate over the issue has advanced little in the years since the passage of the 1967 Federal Salary Act. The issue is as perilous as ever, and no obvious resolution is in sight.

Part Two

Alternative Approaches

Edward Lazear and Sherwin Rosen

The Economics of Compensation of Government Officials

THIS ESSAY examines the compensation of government officials in the framework of the economic theory of occupational choice. Particular emphasis is placed on relative supply conditions and how various policy instruments might affect the kind and number of people attracted into the political arena. Many of these issues have been publicly discussed for years. However, the most recent point of discussion is the "principle of comparability"—that public officials, elected or otherwise, should have salaries comparable to those of similar positions elsewhere in the economy.

The Principle of Comparability

Public service has always been viewed as a social obligation, somehow different from other careers, and the responsibilities, duties, and personal conduct of public officials have been regarded somewhat differently from those of people holding positions in the private economy. Furthermore, increasing government involvement at all levels of economic and social activity has been accompanied by increased specialization of those concerned in public choices. Making these collective decisions, which often have wide repercussions, requires superior knowledge of complex social institutions and the likely economic reactions of the affected parties, as well as detailed technical knowledge. Not only are extensive support services needed for these purposes, but officials must acquire decisionmaking skills. If executive or legislative responsibility was ever regarded as a part-time job or a moonlighting activity of an otherwise occupied citizen, that is not the case now or in the foreseeable future, particularly at the federal level.

Legislative bodies are in the peculiar position of approving appropriations for their own salaries and expense schedules; and apparently have frequently felt constrained by the prospect of adverse reactions from their constituents (an occupational hazard). In this century, at least, congressional pay, exclusive of fringe benefits, has not kept pace with the compensation of workers in the private economy. For example, the pay of congressmen at the turn of the century was $5,000 a year. The $42,500 level reached in 1969 represents a compound annual rate of increase of only 3.1 percent over the sixty-nine-year period, whereas the annual rate of money wage growth for workers in manufacturing over the same period was roughly 5 percent. To put it another way, a job in manufacturing paying $5,000 a year at the turn of the century would, if it enjoyed the average rate of increase of money wages in the economy, have paid about $140,000 in 1969 rather than $40,000. The freeze on congressional pay from 1969 to 1975 accentuates these differences. Although it is undoubtedly true that the monetary value of the fringe benefits and perquisites of office has risen over that period, the same is true for workers in the private sector. There is no need to extrapolate these simple figures to all government workers, and they do not apply to most of them. Nevertheless, a declining relative wage is one of the usual correlates of a declining industry, serving as an economic signal to repel the entry of resources into that activity. Americans expect more from their elected representatives than ever before but seem to want to pay them less.

Though the principle of comparability is one way of addressing the question of designing compensation systems for government workers, it does not offer a sufficiently systematic approach to resolve the problem with much precision. The primary appeal of the concept must be its simplicity and equity. It is a generally accepted precept in American society that those who contribute more to the economy are entitled to a greater share of its proceeds. Yet comparability may also be useful in ensuring an adequate supply of public servants. At its simplest level, then, the principle of comparability may be regarded as a primitive application of the theory of supply, independent of its appeal on equity grounds. To induce people to enter government service government employees must be paid salaries commensurate with what similar kinds of people in similar kinds of positions earn outside the government. Without such treatment, few would be surprised to find a systematic exit of qualified people from government service.

It is probably true that the principle of comparability is an adequate basis for compensation of the simplest and most well-defined jobs in government service for which there are well-defined private alternatives. Clerical positions readily come to mind as such a case. But these need not be confined to a particularly narrow range in the skill distribution. Nurses, medical practitioners, carpenters, lawyers, printers, and economists have salaries in government service geared to readily found alternatives in the private sector.

The problem becomes much more difficult with activities that are more specific to government, for which few counterparts outside that sector can be found. What is the counterpart in the private sector of a superior court judge, of a state legislator, of a governor, indeed of the President? But this problem is not peculiar to the government sector; it applies to all sectors of the economy. Thus a large firm operating in a major metropolitan area must pay its clerical and professional staff about what they could earn elsewhere, since their skills are used by many firms in the same general market. However, every enterprise has a cadre of personnel engaged in activities that are peculiar to itself; for instance, the second-level administrative staff that has detailed knowledge of the inner workings of the organization and that makes the operation work smoothly. Knowledge of the formal rules and channels of communication and exchange is so strongly linked to the organization itself and has so little relevance to other enterprises that the principle of comparability can be given no operational meaning and cannot be applied effectively.

These difficulties make a much broader approach necessary. A more general conceptual model, however, has both benefits and costs. Its chief benefit is to serve as an aid for thought and for organizing all the factors that bear on the question. Its chief cost is to add more unknowns to the analysis, many of which must be investigated empirically before specific recommendations can be made. For example, if a class B secretary earns $9,000 in the private market, it takes little expertise to conclude that the government sector should pay about that amount. How can a parallel role be defined for, say, the mayor of Chicago? Asking the question immediately raises enormous conceptual difficulties. Evidently one needs to know quite a bit about the supply conditions of candidates and how the structure and size of compensation affects both the number and the quality of candidates who might consider entering the race.

The quality issue is of paramount importance. It is desirable to guarantee as far as possible that those in positions of public decisionmaking authority will, in some sense, make the "best" decisions from the alternatives available (including, of course, the alternative that no public intervention is warranted). Part of the difficulty in dealing with the market for political agents is that there is no inherent, well-defined way to measure results. In the private sector the quality of a decision is ultimately reflected in the profitability of the enterprise. The analogue for the government sector is a measure of social welfare. For activities involving the outright provision of public services, government services should be efficiently provided, both in getting the most out of the resources devoted to projects and in achieving the appropriate scale of operations. But also, a great deal of government activity involves transfers of resources among different groups in the population. Surely there are differences of opinion among the people about the extent and nature of these transfers and the appropriate level of government services that are not easily measured, though presumably representative government somehow mediates these differences through the political process.

The Attributes of Public Jobs

The design of incentive and compensation systems obviously plays a role in whether a career attracts or repels people. The fundamental principle was eloquently elucidated by Adam Smith more than two hundred years ago in *An Inquiry into the Nature and Causes of the Wealth of Nations:* people consider all the advantages and disadvantages when choosing among alternative careers and occupations. A modern economist would say that a person tends to choose the occupation that maximizes (expected) utility—or the difference between expected benefits and costs, subject to information limitations and wealth constraints at the time the choice is made.

It should be stressed that the level and structure of compensation is only one of a myriad of factors affecting the net attractiveness of an occupation. In this respect job choices are not conceptually different from other economic choices. In choosing a product such as an automobile, considerations of performance, comfort, and safety as well as price are likely to be important. A manufacturer might make his product more marketable either by lowering its price or by changing some design component to make it more attractive to a greater number of potential buyers. Choice among jobs involves the same principles. All jobs have varying amounts of what are essentially consumption items that increase or detract from their net advantage. Some jobs entail more concentrated effort or greater decisionmaking responsibility than others; some provide greater potential for public service, public esteem, and assistance to people, or are subject to greater public scrutiny and place those who hold them in the limelight. This complex of factors produces a "psychic" income in addition to monetary remuneration. Many of these attributes, or working conditions, are merely by-products of the tasks to be performed, which themselves are determined by a complicated network of specialization and division of labor in the economic system. Though the list of consumption attributes embodied in any given career may change, both in the number of items and in their intensity, these changes usually occur so slowly that they are rather clumsy instruments for changing the attractiveness of any given career. The level of remuneration in one activity relative to others is a much more flexible instrument and much more adaptable to changing circumstances, since most people consider general purchasing power to be an attraction.

In a normal labor market, variations in the level of compensation in a given activity (relative to other activities) are servomechanisms for adjusting differences between the number of jobs available and the number of people seeking to fill them. Increases in the relative wage for a given occupation obviously raise its net advantage and tend to induce more people to enter it. Conversely, decreases in remuneration make the position less attractive, discouraging new entry and encouraging those who chose it to look for alternatives. If academic economists were ever skeptical of this mechanism, declining enrollments in graduate history departments should be convincing. There is a substantial body of research that supports this proposition in several of the professions.[1]

While it is clear that changing levels of remuneration change the net attractiveness of an occupation, it is still crucial to determine empirically the responsiveness of entry to salary and other monetary inducements. In general, it can be said that the magnitude of the response (the elasticity of supply) is determined by differences of opinion about the relative merits and disadvantages of the occupation among people who are in a position to choose it. If there are few differences of opinion among these people, the entry response to an increase in salary can be expected to be great, whereas if there are wide differences the response will be much smaller.

1. See, for example, Richard B. Freeman, *The Market for College-Trained Manpower: A Study in the Economics of Career Choice* (Harvard University Press, 1971).

The logic of this proposition is straightforward. If tastes are highly concentrated, people who are not currently in a given occupation will have only a slight preference for the occupation they are in. A small increase in the salary of one occupation will induce all those in other occupations to switch jobs. On the other hand, if preferences are disparate, it may take a significant increase in the salary of one occupation to induce those in another occupation to switch.

The equilibrium level of remuneration in a given occupation compared with relevant alternatives also depends on how potential entrants evaluate its psychic components. If the population is fairly homogeneous in its valuations and the occupation has attributes that are better than average, the wage necessary to attract applicants will be lower than average. Conversely, occupations with attributes that are considered to be below average require higher than average remuneration to attract personnel. When valuations are markedly different, the situation becomes more complex, and it is not possible to make a general statement without more information. The necessary monetary inducement is then determined by both the number of positions to be filled and the number of people who place a positive value on the job's psychic components. Those who value the psychic components most highly will choose the job at a relatively low wage. As the wage rises, net attractiveness grows and induces additional people, who value these components less highly, to enter. If the number of jobholders required is large enough to exhaust the group of people who value the psychic attributes positively, the wage has to be above average to attract people who place a negative value on the psychic components of the activity.

While there is no systematic evidence in the public sphere, it is widely believed that the number of public positions is small enough relative to the supply of persons with "noble motives" to require lower than comparable compensation levels to attract them, at least at higher levels of government. This belief is supported by the Weber and Burman study done in 1976 for the Commission on Executive, Legislative, and Judicial Salaries (the Peterson Commission),[2] in which 528 persons who occu-

2. See summary of the study by Arnold R. Weber and George R. Burman in *Report of the Commission on Executive, Legislative, and Judicial Salaries, December 1976* (Government Printing Office, 1977), pp. 36–43. The study, "Compensation and Federal Executive Service, Survey and Analysis," is contained in *Staff Report to the Commission on Executive, Legislative, and Judicial Salaries, February 1977* (GPO, 1977), pp. 1–69.

pied or had left senior positions in the executive, legislative, and judicial branches of the federal government were questioned about the role of compensation in their choice of a career. The crucial statistic is that the average person in the sample had accepted an actual decrease in salary of more than 20 percent at the time of entry into government service. However, there were marked differences between the branches. Those in executive and judicial positions (who were appointed, not elected) suffered monetary losses of 23 to 33 percent, whereas the average among legislators was not a loss at all, but a modest 2 percent gain (notice here that the average pregovernment salary for legislators was more than 25 percent lower than that of the other groups in the sample). The following table, taken from the report, illustrates the point:[3]

	Executive schedule I–V	Judicial	Legislative
Average adjusted salary immediately before government employment (dollars)	39,800	44,500	28,300
Average adjusted salary at entry to government service (dollars)	30,800	30,000	29,000
Average change in salary (dollars)	−9,000	−14,500	700
Average change as percent of original salary	−23	−33	2

It is not surprising, given these data, that almost none of the respondents indicated that compensation was a major influence on their decision to enter government service. In fact, the desire to perform public service and the challenge of the job were stated as being the most important influences. It is impossible to apply these results to all elected officials (since the sample was not random and the bulk of it referred to nonelective office). However, it is what would be expected of a sample of incumbents in any job in the presence of rising supply price, for in that case the average incumbent would be a considerable distance away from the range where salary and pecuniary considerations would be dominant. Since those with the greatest taste for public service would be the most probable applicants and the first to enter, the average respondent would be willing

3. *Report of the Commission on Executive, Legislative, and Judicial Salaries, December 1976*, p. 41. All dollars in the Weber and Burman study are constant 1967 dollars.

to hold the position at an even lower salary than was actually paid. To put this another way, the responses might well have been different if nonincumbents had been sampled, precisely because their perception of the virtues of public office could be expected to be different from that of incumbents. Thus though this kind of evidence is interesting, it is not very useful for ascertaining general supply conditions because it primarily indicates the preferences of the average person who has already chosen the position, whereas supply conditions are determined primarily by people at the edge of the range, not at the average.

Yet the Weber and Burman study does provide some information relevant to those near the margin because it paid special attention to people who had departed from government service. More than 75 percent of those who had left executive and judicial positions stated that income was a factor in their decision. In fact, the average salary in the private sector was an astonishing 87 percent higher than the last government salary for executives and 84 percent higher for judges. The following table presents these results from the Weber and Burman study:[4]

	Last salary before leaving government (dollars)	Salary in first job after leaving government (dollars)	Percentage change
Executive schedule I–V	26,200	48,900	87
Judicial	24,700	45,500	84
Legislative	30,800	41,400	34

Evidently, while these people were willing to accept a 23 to 33 percent income loss to enter government service, by the time of their departure to take a job in the private sector, they valued the nonmonetary aspects of their public jobs no less. The situation for the legislators surveyed was quite different. Here only 26 percent indicated that income influenced their decision to leave the federal government, and in fact their postgovernment salaries were "only" 34 percent higher than their congressional salaries. Here such things as health and the adverse outcome of an election might have played a larger role—involuntary departures—than for appointed officeholders. If so, the survey does not provide much evidence on legislators close to the margin, and in any case does not reveal anything about disappointed office seekers or about those who did not

4. *Report of the Commission on Executive, Legislative, and Judicial Salaries, December 1976*, p. 42.

seek office at the existing salary and other conditions of work. Nevertheless, the overall evidence does seem to support the proposition that remuneration is more than a trivial factor in the behavior of those seeking and leaving government office.

Lifetime Income and Career Considerations

One of the obvious difficulties in interpreting the data discussed above relates to differences in the nature of compensation and in work activity among the three branches. An important development in modern labor economics in the past two decades is the recognition that one needs a lifetime income or wealth concept to investigate career choices adequately. When it comes to the details of developing a salary schedule for a wide variety of positions, something needs to be known about the interrelationships of these positions in the government sector and about their relationship to alternatives in the private sector. That is to say, a career invariably involves a sequence of different jobs or work activities over the life cycle (a "track"), and while it is easy to think about occupational choices in general—for example, in the medical and legal professions and in politics—the task becomes increasingly difficult in practice as it is narrowed down to particular positions within these broad fields. The problem is that career tracks are rarely well defined and involve considerable uncertainty. Progression along the track is not wholly determined by the career, but also depends on the match between the job and the person holding it and the effort spent in attempting to advance to a better position. Luck, other random events, and unforeseen contingencies play major roles as well.

However difficult these complicated factors render any detailed analysis, the fundamental point remains that the nature of career advancement affects the net attractiveness to applicants at given points on the track. Thus if holding one office increases the probability of advancing to another that is even more attractive, the net advantage of the first is greater. These factors are not qualitatively different from the purely psychic components of income discussed above, except that they may be subject to more uncertainty. Future possibilities have to be added to the general list of "working conditions" offered by any job or office. The point is illustrated by Weber and Burman's data. Expected job tenure of those in high executive branch positions undoubtedly was shorter than that of those in the legislative or the judicial branch. The future financial payoff in the private sector from holding such positions reduces the supply price of potential entrants to them just as much as, if not more than, the opportunity for public service, and is a major factor accounting for the relatively low remuneration that the government needs to pay people in these jobs.

This issue may be put a little differently. A career is characterized by the accumulation of knowledge, or "human capital." The accumulation of knowledge at any given point on the track is partially a by-product of the work activities to be performed (as in learning by experience), but the amount accumulated is also substantially controlled by the jobholder. The amount of "capital" accumulated determines prospects at a later point in the career. Hence it is important to examine lifetime prospects or lifetime income opportunities. As a rule, the greater the potential for advancement offered by a given job, the lower the salary necessary to attract applicants. Moreover, the applicants most eager to accept will be those who believe they can make the most capital out of it. This parallels the point made above that those valuing the psychic components of income most highly will be the most eager applicants. The price an applicant must pay for an opportunity for career advancement is the difference between the salary paid on the job in question and that paid on a different job that does not offer the same chances for future development. The willingness to pay for such an opportunity, however, cannot exceed the expected increment of wealth it offers an applicant. For this reason "dead-end" jobs require higher pay to attract applicants of given quality than jobs offering greater possibilities for a bigger future prize.

Compensation and Turnover

Two kinds of knowledge produced in conjunction with holding a particular job have been recognized in the literature.[5] One type is specific to the job itself; the other is more generally applicable to a variety of jobs as well as to the one in question. The first is usually related to factors that make turnover—through separation and accession—costly. For some purposes it is useful to think of this as related to the costs associated with initially holding the job, including learning its specific details and work

5. See, for instance, Gary S. Becker, *Human Capital: A Theoretical and Empirical Analysis, with Special Reference to Education,* 2d ed. (Columbia University Press for National Bureau of Economic Research, 1975).

routines. A significant component of these costs for elected officials may be associated with building up a constituency in a particular political district, with learning the coalition structure in the legislative body, and so forth. Insofar as this kind of knowledge is specific to the office in question and has little or no value in other work activities, it acts as a wedge that insulates incumbents from the outside market and establishes a range of indeterminacy in the wage structure: there is little competition from other activities if the capital accumulated is job specific. Moreover, job turnover among those who have accumulated specific skills represents a cost to society, since the skills are valueless when the person is separated from the job.

On the other hand, the accumulation of more general knowledge that has significant value for other activities automatically forges a link between the remuneration of a particular office and that available for other positions inside or outside government. Building a constituency in one district may be of benefit in an election campaign for a higher office in a broader jurisdiction. Favorable publicity that an incumbent receives in a "visible" office has a similar kind of value. In such cases any prospective officeholder would be willing to pay something, in the form of a salary reduction, to get access to these qualities of a job. Such jobs would be attractive to qualified office seekers at lower salaries, and again, those who believed they could make the most capital out of these opportunities would be the most attracted to them.

Knowledge accumulated during tenure in elective office that has value in other positions takes a wide variety of forms, and detailed analysis requires case-by-case examination. In general, it includes all kinds of special knowledge about particular industries and ethnic groups arising from economic regulation, budgetary items (such as the military), and transfer or incentive programs instituted by the government. It also includes details of tax legislation and complexities affecting special interest groups and the probable legal interpretation of particular acts. Such mundane things as honoraria and "free lunches" offered for speaking engagements and junkets abroad associated with "site visits" on particular bills must be tallied in the accounting. Publicity acquired in politics may not only help one gain higher office, but can also be of value for, say, paid testimonials for credit card companies or the writing of one's memoirs. In a world in which the existence of many private firms hangs on their ability to obtain government contracts, the value of government connections may be incalculable. A reputation in the government and knowledge of the inner workings of the bureaucracy may swing government-related business to one's present or former law firm and associates. And if one does lose an election, the knowledge gained while in office has much value in the private sector.[6] Many state legislators and city council members do not hold full-time jobs because they meet for a sufficiently large portion of the year to effectively preclude their engaging in full-time activities outside the government sector. Is it any wonder that a large fraction of incumbents are members of group practice law firms or otherwise engage in outside activities for which connections in government may be complementary?

The possibility of accumulating knowledge on the job forces certain kinds of conformity between the income available from holding public office and alternatives available in the private sector. If income available from officeholding is too small but holding the job creates the kind of capital discussed above, plenty of people may still seek to fill public posts. But office seekers will be of a different character when monetary compensation is low than when it is high. In particular, the value of capital-creating opportunities is larger for the young than for others because the young will have a longer time to collect returns on the income they forgo in taking a low-paying public job. Also, if public salaries are too low, less capital is likely to be acquired. In the first effect lies the rationale for the assertion that less than adequate compensation in the public sector tends to produce a government of the young and inexperienced. In the second effect lies the possibility that low pay will provoke high turnover and short tenure in office. Of course, the opposite tendencies are manifested if income available in the public sector is more than adequate.

Many of the factors under discussion underlie some of the main recommendations of the Peterson Commission's report of 1976. One of the important problems addressed by the commission was increased turnover of personnel in high-level executive positions. The freezing of congressional pay from 1969 to 1975 had the unfortunate by-product of also freezing the upper portion of the federal pay structure, even though the earnings of comparable positions in the private sector were rising fairly rapidly. In other words, the price a jobholder had to pay to gain access to the opportunities offered in the federal government markedly increased over the period.

There are two natural responses to such a situation. First, since the executive level pay *schedule* was frozen, a possible circumvention was to

6. See George J. Stigler, "The Theory of Economic Regulation," *Bell Journal of Economics and Management Science,* vol. 2 (Spring 1971), pp. 3–21.

elevate the classification of a job. The simple expedient of reclassifying a position to a higher grade level, with superficial or cosmetic changes in responsibility, is an effective way of granting a pay increase that could not be obtained any other way. The 1976 commission contracted with private wage and salary specialists to examine a sample of jobs of executive levels II–V and general schedule grades 16–18. Sixty-three out of the 5,512 jobs were examined in two surveys (whether this was random sample is not known). Of the 63 jobs, 28 were found to be incorrectly classified in grade level, and of these 28, 4 were found to be classified too low and 24 to be classified too high.[7] Similarly, it is reputed that outside consultants working for the government were allowed to bill for a larger number of days to get around unrealistic restrictions on daily consultation rates. The result of imperfect approaches to circumventing pay restrictions is lower quality workers and performance in government jobs.

The defects of this first response are evident. If the original executive and general service salary schedules were based on logic and market conditions, any inflation-induced reclassification would quickly destroy their rationale and create marked inequities among agencies. This would not be a defect at all had it been possible to maintain relative uniformity in the classification structure (say, by uniform escalation of all grades). However, the lid on the schedule resulted in a marked compression of the salary structure at the top, with those closest to the top bearing the greatest financial costs of the freeze. For example, it is unrealistic to rely on noble motives when hiring a chief actuary for the social security system at an annual pay, exclusive of the value of pensions, in the neighborhood of $40,000 when a person of the required capability might be able to earn three or four times that amount in the private insurance industry. Thus, the second natural response consisted of a reported difficulty in filling these high positions and, though the turnover in these positions is never very high, a notable increase in departures. This is precisely what could be expected to happen.

Differences in the potential for personal development and investment probably go some distance toward explaining some of the differences in the responses of officeholders in the executive, judicial, and legislative branches to Weber and Burman's survey questions. As noted, tenure is expected to be markedly shorter in the first than in the other two branches. Also, the types of people in these different jobs are at different points in

7. *Staff Report to the Commission on Executive, Legislative, and Judicial Salaries, February 1977*, pp. 173–87.

their careers. This is especially the case for the judicial branch, where the term of appointment is quite long and usually follows a record of distinguished performance in the private sector. Most judges, when first appointed, do not anticipate returning to their private legal careers. This is not to say that many high-level executive appointments do not represent a prize following a distinguished career in the private sector or in other sectors of government, but rather that there are relatively more of those kinds of appointments in the judiciary. Nevertheless, the pull of monetary incentives in the private sector (or the push of monetary incentives on the bench) was clearly an important factor for those who left judicial positions.

Perhaps similar considerations apply to those in the legislative branch who are close to the top of the political hierarchy. Moreover, their expected and actual tenure may be quite long. An incumbent's advantage in an election campaign is due in no small part to the specific capital he has built up with his constituency through publicity and performance, capital that an opponent does not have to draw upon. If a large component of the capital accumulated in legislative positions is specific to a position at the top, the push-pull forces of relative remuneration will not be as strong as in the other branches. These considerations undoubtedly have far less force for legislative officeholders outside the federal government—those in state and local government. Even if the failure of members of Congress to alter their remuneration on the basis of supply factors in the 1969–75 period did not affect the supply response at first, continuing such a policy would have adverse consequences for those preparing themselves for entry into the federal government. Thus concentrating on federal legislators may be similar to examining the tip of an iceberg. In any case it is clear that declining relative wages caused by the freeze had adverse spillover effects on the institutional linkages in pay structure among the branches. If there was ever an economic rationale for maintaining these rigid linkages, surely there is none under present-day circumstances.

Variations in retention rates are the natural response to wage conditions at a given position that are out of sync with other positions on the track or with outside opportunities. The important point is that decisions are controlled by the jobholder and are not inherent in the job. Thus if capital accumulation is geared to job tenure, a decision not to stay in the job is also a decision to derive less capital from it. This is an extreme case, perhaps, but there are other aspects of working conditions and performance that do not necessarily involve all-or-nothing behavior. Everyone is familiar with the consequences of a group of workers "working to the rules." Imperfect monitoring of any job situation allows a worker some flexibility to choose among activities to suit his own interests, as when an officeholder accepts an honorarium to help finance two residences. Similarly, if the pay for a particular position is too low, shorter job tenure and reduced effort to acquire skills might be expected. This may also be correlated with the intensity of effort devoted to performance and satisfactory outcomes.

Salary and a Code of Conduct

Consistent with the discussion of the nonpecuniary value of a job, the adoption of a new code of public conduct for elected officials is bound to change the overall attractiveness of officeholding at existing levels of remuneration. It will therefore require changes in the structure of monetary compensation and may also change the type of people seeking to fill these positions. For example, the requirement for "full financial disclosure" might make public jobs more attractive to those with nothing to hide, depending on the technique of disclosure. As far as investment in personal development and career opportunities is concerned, codes that restrict transition from one type of activity to another can have particularly important side effects on supply conditions. For example, consider the effects of barring holders of government employment from ever subsequently holding a position in the private sector with a firm that had business dealings with the government.

We are not experts in the legalities and fine points of what constitutes conflict of interest and are not willing to say when such restrictions are warranted and when they are not. However, it seems useful to point out that codes and other restrictions (along with an enforcement mechanism) cannot be elaborated entirely on the basis of abstract principles of how elected and other officials "should" behave; the implications of how these restrictions affect the supply of office seekers by changing the net monetary and nonpecuniary attractiveness of certain career choices must be taken into account. It is worth stressing that large alterations in working conditions through conduct and other behavioral restrictions must be examined jointly with commensurate alterations in the structure of compensation.

Salary and the Quality of the Labor Force

A compensation system affects more than the tastes of people choosing a position and how they behave on the job. It affects the skill mix of the people who choose it as well. There are no reticent lawyers and politicians, short basketball players, tone-deaf musicians, or clumsy structural steel workers. Since the productive capacities of members of the labor force vary markedly in different work activities in the economy, an important task of an allocation mechanism of labor resources, if not its most important task, is to place the correct type of worker in the correct type of job.

A freely competitive labor market with informed choice duplicates an ideal allocation in assigning the proper type of worker (a worker with the appropriate innate talent) to the productive requirements of the job. The allocation is ideal in the sense that any other set of job assignments could not increase the value of income produced in the economy. This proposition is true for two reasons. First, competitive bidding among demanders of labor guarantees that a person's potential earnings in each job will equal the value of his production in it. Second, each person will choose the activity that offers the largest net advantage—in the case where psychic components are ignored this is equivalent to choosing the job that offers the largest possible wage (subject to informational limitations at the time choices are made). The conclusion that the allocation is ideal in the sense stated follows almost immediately.

A conceptual experiment might begin with an allocation of workers of various talents to a large number of different occupations (broadly defined). Consider the reallocation that would result from an increase in the relative wage in one occupation. Define the "quality" of a person observed in any occupation by some measure of his output. As explained before, as the relative wage in one occupation rises, more people will choose to enter it because its net advantages increase. Can more be said? In particular, will the average quality of workers observed in the occupation increase as well?

Consideration of two extreme cases is instructive. First, suppose that talents are hierarchical, along the lines of a single ability dimension (such as IQ). Evidently, if the occupation whose relative wage has increased is at the top of the heap (in a sense, having already selected those at the top of the IQ distribution), there is only one way to go and that is down: new entrants will be of lower quality than those who initially chose the occupation. But if the occupation is not at the top of the distribution, an increased wage will make it somewhat more attractive to those in the higher occupations, who will be higher quality people than those who chose it in the first instance. The job will also become more attractive to those slightly further down in the hierarchy, who will be of lower quality than the incumbents. Hence, the average quality of applicants may increase or decrease.[8]

This is an extreme case of positive correlation in earnings prospects of people across occupations, in which the most able person would earn the most in all occupations, the second most able person would earn the second largest amount in all of them, and so forth. A more realistic story would involve multidimensional talents, but the correlation among them could be so high (and positive) that the hierarchical simplification might not be a serious distortion. The second extreme depends crucially on multidimensional attributes, but these are negatively correlated. Then the persons observed in any given occupation would tend to be no better than average and possibly worse than average in occupations they did not choose, and among the best in occupations they did choose.[9]

There are several qualifications to this line of argument. First, differences in the value placed on nonpecuniary factors will affect the distribution of quality in occupations. Casual observation suggests, though, that those who are talented at something like doing it (there is a positive correlation between productivity and psychic income). If this is so, the observed quality distribution will not be much different than it would be if there were no nonpecuniary considerations.

Second, how skills are distributed across occupations depends on the level of aggregation implicit in the definitions of the occupations. As the definition of occupation becomes finer, positive correlations in quality across occupations might be expected to be more important, if only because "neighboring" occupations are now more similar. For example, many people in political (legislative) life are drawn from the legal profession, for obvious reasons. Considering a finer classification would therefore increase the likelihood that the first case would be more applicable than the second.

8. This does not take account of changes in investment incentives through schooling, but these may be expected to go in the same direction.
9. For elaboration of this kind of argument, see Sherwin Rosen, "Substitution and Division of Labor," *Economica*, vol. 45 (August 1978), pp. 235–50.

Third, the effects of monetary remuneration on the quality of applicants depend crucially on the possibility that people will be paid in proportion to their productivity in each occupation (again, apart from psychic income). While many economists consider this to be a straightforward outcome of competitive markets, the conclusion rests on the assumption that there is a mechanism for determining and monitoring productivity. It is easy to ascertain a baseball player's productivity by a variety of statistics on hits, errors, and so forth, but there are no generally accepted counterparts for elected officials. Of course, there are many productive activities outside government (namely, activities where one cannot "see" the work) for which it is difficult to establish simple productivity measures.

The public sector differs from the private sector in that a median voting system, as applicable to the public sector, makes it less economical for a person to be well informed about political decisions than about other types of decisions. The absence of median voting rules in the private sector tends to create better-informed actors.

Fourth, the ability to attain elective office depends on skill in running a political campaign. Is this skill positively correlated with productivity in office? It is a fact that much campaign activity is subcontracted to a political party and to outside agents such as public relations experts.

Fifth, the ability of the electorate to select the highest quality candidate from a pool of applicants who vary in quality is a force in the direction of a positive association between pay and the quality of the officeholder. Although the quality of the applicant pool may change in either direction with an increase in salary for a given occupation, the ability of the electorate to select the best applicants reduces the probability of an actual decrease in performance as the result of an increase in pay.

All things considered, there is some reason to expect that higher monetary remuneration will lead to a higher quality of elective office seekers, but it is by no means a certainty.

Compensation and Performance Incentives

One of the chief difficulties in making a definitive study of the effects of compensation on the conduct and performance of public officials is the actual measurement of compensation. For example, our empirical results, discussed below, were based on measured annual salary without any imputations for other perquisites of office, the value of deferred pay, pension rights, and so forth. In a more extensive study it would be possible, at least in principle, to measure many of these items and incorporate them into the analysis. However, there is another aspect of "compensation" and behavior that by its very nature almost defies measurement. Some have termed this "political income," or less easily observed compensation, which is in addition to the status and explicit monetary aspects of compensation associated with the office. The explicit terms are tied to the office, take it or leave it, whereas political income is subject to control by the officeholder. In fact, political income is important only insofar as it changes the incentive structure and behavioral patterns of public officials in ways that make them take actions in their private interests that diverge from the public interest. For example, it has been suggested that access to political income is geared to the scale of government activity through employment of favored groups, award of lucrative contracts to favored suppliers, and overpayment to factors engaged in government business more generally.[10] If so, then, without incentives to the contrary, there is a tendency for the government sector to expand beyond its optimal limits. There are, of course, other, more obvious manifestations of conflict of interest as well.

The major issue, which applies to virtually all exchanges of labor services and employment contracts, is one that economists call "the agency problem."[11] One party to a labor contract agrees to perform work for another party. The former (employee) is called the agent and the latter (employer) is called the principal. (Thus the common use of the term "agent," as in "an elected official is an agent of the electorate," fits these definitions.) The agency problem arises when the interests of the principal and the agent are not identical. To deal with this problem, it may be possible to devise contract terms that harmonize the interests of the agent and the principal.

In a world with perfect information the principal would know precisely what was in his best interests and could specify the nature of the tasks to be performed as well as the probable outcome. Then the contract could

10. See Robert J. Barro, "The Control of Politicians: An Economic Model," *Public Choice,* vol. 14 (Spring 1973), pp. 19–42.

11. See, for example, Stephen A. Ross, "The Economic Theory of Agency: The Principal's Problem," *American Economic Review,* vol. 63 (May 1973, *Papers and Proceedings, 1972*), pp. 134–39; Gary S. Becker and George J. Stigler, "Law Enforcement, Malfeasance and Compensation of Enforcers," *Journal of Legal Studies,* vol. 3 (January 1974), pp. 1–18.

contain a clause terminating the arrangement (possibly with penalty) if the outcome was not satisfactory. This would require monitoring to ascertain performance and determine when the contract terms had been fulfilled that was acceptable to both parties.

But information is hardly perfect. In some types of exchange the principal is not well informed about the detailed procedures that might have to be used in any given contingency, and also may find it difficult even to specify a satisfactory outcome. In effect, part of the contractual exchange involves the buyer's purchasing the detailed technical knowledge and expertise of the seller. Everyday examples are doctor-patient and lawyer-client relationships. Here the principal would be concerned that the agent was making the proper effort and using his knowledge wisely on the principal's behalf, because so much discretion is turned over to the agent in these circumstances.

Since the agent is interested in allocating his resources in his own best interest and the same information is not available to both parties, conflict of interest is possible. In some circumstances the difficulties of monitoring may be so great as to preclude contractual arrangements. However, there are mutually acceptable contracts that give the agent the proper incentives. A contingent fee for real estate brokers and lawyers is a simple example. A lump-sum payment for house remodeling rather than payment by the hour is another example. Here any differences of interest between the parties are partially resolved by gearing payment to some measure of outcome or productivity rather than to measures of input. Sometimes insurance arrangements, with the insurance company serving as a monitoring agent (as in some medical insurance plans), can lessen some of the risks in these kinds of exchanges. The key to all of these examples is the amount of discretion allowed the agent, which seems to be inherent in the production of certain services. Thus bonuses and promotions are a control mechanism in a business world with wide separation of ownership and management, and—more to the point here—the role of the election process and public monitoring is a control in the case of public decisions.

The relation between compensation and trust was recognized two hundred years ago by Adam Smith:

The wages of labour vary according to the small or great trust which must be reposed in the workmen.

The wages of goldsmiths and jewellers are every-where superior to those of many other workmen, not only of equal, but of much superior ingenuity; on account of the precious materials with which they are intrusted.

We trust our health to the physician; our fortune and sometimes our life and reputation to the lawyer and attorney. Such confidence could not safely be reposed in people of a very mean or low condition. Their reward must be such, therefore, as may give them that rank in the society which so important a trust requires.[12]

David Hume made a similar observation:

It is a familiar rule in all business, that every man should be paid, in proportion to the trust reposed in him, and to the power, which he enjoys.[13]

Both statements are terse and cryptic. Does high pay affect the supply of honest people for activities requiring honesty? It is simply not clear how high wages in and of themselves can filter those with a greater propensity for honesty into a profession. Probably, providing an incentive to act in a socially desirable way once the occupation has been chosen is more effective. For if a high wage is paid, a person, if detected, has a great deal to lose by engaging in dishonest acts.

A compensation system can decrease malfeasance only to the extent that it renders socially undesirable actions more costly for the officeholder or, to turn the issue around, only to the extent that it rewards socially desirable activities. In a long employment relationship, an obvious way of doing this is to increase the wage in such positions to a level higher than the opportunity wage available in alternative jobs. However, in all agency problems there is an "end play" difficulty: at the point at which the employment is to be terminated, all incentive control is lost because salary will cease. Here the solution is to effectively extend the salary beyond the formal end of the employment period with a terminal prize, such as a pension to be collected for some period after the conclusion of the contract. The size of both the pension and the increase in salary would be geared to the officeholder's potential gain from malfeasant acts. This gain consists of two components: one, the probability of being detected and the penalty; the other, the value of malfeasance to the agent if undetected. Thus there is a trade-off in the government budget: using resources for detection and penalties versus using them to increase salaries and pensions.

12. *An Inquiry into the Nature and Causes of the Wealth of Nations* (London: Oxford University Press, 1976), vol. 1, p. 122.

13. *The History of England from the Invasion of Julius Caesar to the Abdication of James the Second, 1688* (1773 ed.), vol. 8, p. 325.

The Optimal Pension Structure

To elaborate, suppose the government chooses the strategy of paying a very high pension to those who are deemed "worthy."[14] Elected officials will then have an incentive to behave in a manner consistent with the public's preferences. That is, if malfeasant behavior increases the probability that an official will lose his pension benefits, the larger the pension is, the greater the incentive to refrain from dishonest activity will be. However, consider what the payment of a large pension to elected officials would do to the supply of people for that occupation.

The initial effect would be to produce an oversupply of people for government service. If wages early in life met some notion of comparability, the pension would increase the value of being an elected official over that of other occupations. This would be mitigated to some extent by the fact that the probability of winning the election is less than one, but the point is still valid. If compensation is increased at the end of life in the form of pensions, it can be reduced earlier in life to offset this. There are two ways to make this reduction.

The first would be to lower the salaries of elected officials so that the total value of this lower salary and a larger pension equaled the higher salary and smaller pension given similar workers in private industry (other forms of payment are ignored for the moment). This might include varying the salary over the working lifetime as well: a less extreme form of the same model shows that senior workers are paid a great deal and junior workers very little, giving the young an incentive to grow old in the job.

An even more extreme method of varying the payment over the lifetime to ensure honest behavior would be to require individuals to in effect post a "bond" before entering office, which would be returned to them as a large pension. This bond would not have to be an actual transfer of money from the officeholder to the government, but could take the form of campaign expenditures or time and resources devoted to the acquisition of skills that are useful primarily in elective office. If these costs were high, a large pension at the end of the career would be needed to adjust the supply of candidates to the correct level. But is this good from society's point of view? Consider campaign expenditures. If the salary of elected

---

14. Some of this argument parallels those of Becker and Stigler, "Law Enforcement," and Edward Lazear, "Why Is There Mandatory Retirement?" *Journal of Political Economy,* vol. 88 (December 1979).

officials was held constant, raising the pensions available to them would increase the amount they spent on campaigning to acquire that job. An increase in salary has the same effect on campaign expenditures as an increase in pensions. This suggests that the sum of the official salary and pension value should be set so as to determine the optimal amount of campaign expenditures. Altering the ratio of pension to salary while keeping the total amount constant could affect the probability of a person's remaining honest throughout his term. A low initial salary but extremely high pension based on satisfactory performance over the lifetime will induce behavior on the part of government officials quite different from that induced by a high initial salary and very low pension. The point is that the current value of salary plus pension should be selected so as to elicit the optimal amount of campaigning, and after that, the salary-to-pension ratio should be altered so as to achieve the optimal amount of honesty.

Some caveats are in order. First, placing a large part of the compensation for government service in a person's pension, which is contingent on successful performance, tends to increase the risk associated with his compensation. If, as is often argued, government workers are averse to taking risks, they will have to be compensated for bearing this risk by higher salaries or pensions, or both. Second, increasing the amount of compensation in the form of a pension reduces the amount of mobility into and out of this particular occupation, although the costs of this loss of mobility could be lessened by selecting appropriate severance pay arrangements. For example, if a defeated incumbent were eligible to receive a portion of his pension benefits upon his departure from office, the costs of his lack of mobility would be mitigated.

Is the optimal amount of dishonesty zero? Not necessarily. The above scheme makes it seem as though complete honesty could be achieved merely by making the pension large enough for retired officials. In a world where mistakes were never made, this would be valid. However, we said above that only the "worthy" officeholders would receive large pensions or high wages as they acquired seniority. But the determination of worthiness is not a trivial task. Suppose a commission was set up to ascertain the worthiness of retiring officeholders. If, at one extreme, the commission was capricious and uninfluenced by the actual behavior of officeholders, the officeholders would have no incentive to behave honestly no matter how large the pension. Since the probability of their receiving it is independent of their own malfeasance, they might as well enjoy the returns from dishonesty and hope for the best when review time rolls around. A less extreme view yields similar problems. If the commission was wise but not omniscient, it might occasionally err by awarding a dishonest official a pension or depriving an honest one of his. If the actual behavior of the official has some effect on the outcome of this decision but cannot guarantee its justice, the officeholder will have an incentive to invest resources in other ways to convince the public of his worthiness. But too large a pension will elicit an overuse of these resources. That is, some dishonesty will be optimal because the extra resources devoted to convincing the public of the official's honesty as the result of the higher pension incentive exceed the value of the additional honesty to society. The conclusion is that even with varying wage rates and pensions the optimal amount of dishonesty is likely to be greater than zero. However, adjusting the total value of salary and pension to bring campaign expenditures into equilibrium is still a valid concept.

The current system of pensions to government officials is generous by private standards. In 1979, for those retiring at sixty-five after thirty-five years of service the pension consisted of 66.25 percent of the high three-year average salary for the executive branch and 80 percent of final pay for members of Congress; and those retiring at the age of seventy after ten years of service in the federal judiciary received 100 percent of final salary. If it seems more important to provide incentives for honesty in the judiciary than in the executive branch, the hierarchy of pension benefits is appropriate. On the other hand, pensions are not explicitly contingent on performance. This is a necessary, though operationally difficult, requirement of an optimal pension scheme.

The Social Costs of Malfeasance

Certain kinds of malfeasance do not have socially harmful effects. For example, a law enforcer accepting a side payment imposes the same cost and deterrence effect on an offender as if a fine were paid directly to the state. Moreover, the availability of such income to the law enforcer would tend to reduce the price of labor in such activities because it would add to the net "advantage" of the job (from the worker's point of view). Hence the bribe would in effect be transferred to the state anyway.

There would be a national reluctance to rely on such a mechanism even if it had no immoral connotations, because it is unlikely to create the optimal amount of deterrence if agents compete for side payments and this competition makes the payments lower than the expected value of punishment in the penal system. The million or two sometimes found in the vault of a deceased politician may represent a far greater cost to the public in tax payments, perhaps by orders of magnitude, through excessive payments to factors on government contracts and influence peddling. There is no reason to expect that those in positions of power and authority would be capable of expropriating all the economic rent. Hence additional incentives to discourage malfeasance are socially desirable.

Clearly, incentives for malfeasance are related to the term of the contract and the intervals between periodic reviews of performance. The well-known tendency of professors to fall asleep after achieving tenure must be weighed against the protection tenure gives the free exchange of unpopular, if not heretical, ideas, and many believe it is not too high a price to pay. A similar case for long terms of appointment for members of the judiciary could be made, on the grounds of protecting minority interests, though we are not convinced that lifetime appointments are optimal. Certainly the same case could not be made for legislative officials. Here logic would suggest shorter rather than longer review periods (it is indeed difficult to understand on these grounds the different elective terms of the President, members of the Senate, and members of the House, even though the number of presidential terms is restricted). If production in public office is inherently variable, determining the optimal length of the review period would face a "signal-noise extraction" problem. Not only would very short terms increase monitoring costs because of the costs of campaigning and the costs to voters in time, but it would be difficult to detect malfeasance or incompetence against a background of noisy events. Surely if monitoring costs were sufficiently small, however, a shorter period of review would be better.

How to monitor public officials is the most difficult problem of all. In the business world, when conflicts of interest arise as the result of separation of ownership and control, the possibility of takeover provides a mechanism for restoring efficiency to management. This mechanism, although an imperfect one, has an analogue in politics—the periodic election. The fundamental difficulty here, however, is that the institution of majority voting reduces the value of acquiring information to any individual in society. That is, no one voter has an incentive to acquire a great deal of information about a particular elected official since his influence on the outcome of the election is trivial. It is true that the ability of a free press to capitalize on information-gathering activities encourages their provision, but it is by no means obvious that the amount of information provided by the press is in any sense optimal.

It is clear that a wage system cannot bring about efficient government without some form of monitoring. To the extent that a code of conduct or ethics makes deviations from appropriate behavior clearer either to the electorate or to its servants, the wage system will become a more effective tool for affecting the quality of performance in office. The less costly information can be made to the electorate, the better the information available to the group will be. This implies that elected officials will be more likely to take into account the effect of deviations from appropriate behavior on their reelection possibilities. Although this will reduce the benefit of officeholding to the officials, it will simultaneously provide an incentive to perform in a manner that society finds more desirable.

Evidence of the Relationship between Compensation and Quality of Performance

The discussion to this point has raised a number of issues about the compensation of elected officials. We have repeatedly said that the resolution of a question is empirical in nature, but at the same time it is difficult to present sensible empirical evidence. A major question in this analysis relates to the connection between the compensation of elected officials and the quality of their output. Does the public receive more when it pays more? This issue is so central that, despite the pitfalls, we have attempted to provide some evidence. The complete analysis is contained in an appendix; however, in this section the methodology and results of that analysis are briefly summarized.

To obtain information on the relationship between the salary and the performance of an elected official, we conducted a cross-sectional analysis of the relationship between mayors' salaries and the level of certain amenities in their cities. The basic notion is that people in different cities prefer different amenities. As they exercise their preference they reveal a relationship between the level of amenities produced and the level of compensation of their elected officials. For example, residents in city A may give higher priority to a low crime rate than those in city B do. If so, city A may choose to pay the mayor a higher salary in the hope of inducing a more qualified person to fill the job. A better mayor will in turn produce a lower crime rate in the city than would be expected of one paid a lower salary. If, on the other hand, compensation has no effect on mayoral quality, the crime rate of cities should vary independently of mayoral compensation. In the first part of the empirical section we examine the relationship between mayoral salary and seven amenities or "disamenities" that, it is hoped, approximate mayoral output. These seven are the unemployment rate, the proportion of housing that is dilapidated, a per capita measure of parks, a measure of water pollution, the infant mortality rate, the total crime rate, and the per capita level of library books.

Data for the analysis were obtained from two sources. The first was a file from the International City Management Association 1970 tape on the salaries of municipal officials in the United States. The second was the Environmental Protection Agency's data on quality of life indicators in U.S. metropolitan areas for 1970. With these two sources we were able to look at the relationship between the characteristics of a given city and the mayor's salary.

The initial results were somewhat puzzling. In general, the relationships estimated were of the wrong sign. For example, the partial relationship between the mayor's salary and the unemployment rate was positive; that is, cities that paid their mayors more also had higher unemployment rates. This perverse relationship was found throughout.

We believe that the reason for the inconsistent findings, at least in part, lies in the correlation between these measured characteristics and the difficulty of the mayor's job. For example, other things being equal, the job of the mayor in a city with high unemployment is likely to be more difficult than that of the mayor in a city with low unemployment. To induce a person with the same qualifications to work in this more difficult setting a higher salary must be paid. Therefore, there is a positive correlation between the mayor's salary and the unemployment rate, not because paying the mayor a higher salary provokes a higher unemployment rate, but because the higher unemployment rate is viewed negatively by the mayoral candidate and his compensation is a partial offset to this. To deal with this problem we used a two-stage approach. We first inferred the amount by which a mayor would have to be compensated to make a city with a lower level of amenities paying a higher salary as attractive to him as one with a higher level of amenities paying a lower salary. We then netted out this effect from the coefficients obtained in the initial regressions and thereby estimated a cleaned effect of mayors' salaries on the amenities.

The results were generally consistent with the theory. First, mayors in less attractive environments had to be compensated with higher salaries. Second, with this effect held constant, mayors who were paid higher salaries in general produced improved characteristics. This suggests at least some positive relation between the compensation of an elected official and the output that one can expect from him. Since much of our discussion in the first part of the paper hinges on salary having a positive effect on performance, these results are reassuring. On the other hand, they should be cautiously interpreted. The standard errors of the coefficients were quite high so that our effects were rarely estimated with precision. The relationship between a mayor's salary and his performance is at best a subtle one, and only glimpses of that relationship were given in these data.

Concluding Comment

In closing, we acknowledge that this paper has given no easy prescription or rules for adjusting salaries of elected officials. Rather, what we hope we have accomplished is to set out a systematic way of thinking about these matters. Our own empirical investigation appears to lend support to the main ideas of this paper, but the estimates must be regarded as highly tentative, to be supplemented by further, more detailed studies.

Appendix[15]

The relationship between salary and productivity is fundamental to this paper. Identification of this connection, which is difficult enough for the private sector, becomes even more difficult for the public sector. The most obvious problems are that the product is hard to define and observe and that the actual salary may be a very poor measure of true compensation. Despite these obstacles, we have attempted to provide a preliminary empirical investigation of the connection between the compensation of elected officials and resulting productivity.

The basic approach is to relate mayors' salaries in 1970 to the output of city services, holding constant other factors of production and city

15. Computations were financed by a grant from the National Science Foundation.

characteristics. We attempt to identify city service production functions by postulating a simple theoretical framework and then estimating it.

A Framework

Consider a world in which people sort themselves among communities so that in any one community all have the same tastes, though the tastes of the communities may differ. Denote the utility function of the representative individual in community i as

(1) $$U_i = U_i(I, X),$$

where X is a vector of public goods or ills that constitute "local amenities" and I is income spent on all other goods. The budget constraint is

(2) $$I = W(X, P) - T,$$

where T is per capita tax, P is a vector of local population characteristics, and W is the pecuniary earnings of the individual. Note that W depends on X since, if the individual works in a community with different X, his job may be easier or more difficult and his pecuniary wage will be driven down or up to compensate. Furthermore,

(3) $$N \times T = M + T_0,$$

where N is the population size, M is the salary of the mayor, and T_0 is other local expenditure. The technical relationship to be estimated is

(4) $$X = X(\tilde{M}, T_0, P),$$

where $\tilde{M}$ is the total compensation received by the mayor, defined as

(5) $$\tilde{M} \equiv M + f(X) - T,$$

where $f(X)$ is the psychic income received from amenities denominated in dollars. The hypothesis to be tested is that $\partial X / \partial \tilde{M} > 0$.

In this model, equation 4 is assumed to be the same across communities. Since utility functions differ across cities, however, maximization of equation 1, subject to equations 2–5, will yield combinations of M and X that lie along equation 4. That is, communities with tastes for amenities will raise taxes and the mayor's salary for the additional amenities produced as the result. Thus $X(\tilde{M}, T_0, P)$ will be traced out.[16]

16. For a complete discussion of this issue, see Sherwin Rosen, "Hedonic Prices and Implicit Markets: Product Differentiation in Pure Competition," *Journal of Political Economy*, vol. 82 (January–February 1974), pp. 34–55.

Some Empirical Problems

This simple model allows us to speak more concretely about some of the difficulties encountered in the empirical analysis.

First, and most obvious, is that $\tilde{M}$ is relevant for estimation but difficult to observe. One needs to know $f(X)$ in order to know $\tilde{M}$, so the shadow value of amenities to the mayor must be ascertained. This by itself is no small task. But probably more important is that the mayor's current salary, M, may be a very poor measure of total compensation, $\tilde{M}$.

Another empirical difficulty is that P is difficult to measure. It reflects the population characteristics of the city, and many relevant characteristics may be unobservable. If the functional form of equation 4 is such that $\partial^2 X / \partial M \partial P_i^* \neq 0$, where P_i^* is the unobservable characteristic, estimates of equation 4 will be biased. For example, suppose one unobservable population characteristic is worker quality (IQ) and that low IQ cities can produce fewer amenities, other things being constant (that is, $\partial X / \partial IQ > 0$), but allow that a high-quality mayor makes more difference to low IQ cities than to high IQ cities (that is, $\partial^2 X / \partial M \partial (IQ) < 0$). The best mayors will then be in the toughest cities.[17] If we estimated equation 4 and left out IQ, we might find a negative relationship between $\tilde{M}$ and X because $\tilde{M}$ captures the effect of IQ on X through this negative sorting mechanism. This problem is pervasive in economics and is in no way confined to politics. However, it does appear to be quite serious in this context.

Even if all population variables were measured correctly, however, a third difficulty would arise. Consider regressing X on $\tilde{M}$, T, and P. One must consider the nature of the error term. Suppose a community has experienced random, unanticipated good fortune which allows greater amenities for given $\tilde{M}$, P, and T. Some of this good fortune may be used to employ a mayor with a lower $\tilde{M}$ so that X rises, but not by the maximum amount obtainable holding $\tilde{M}$, P, and T constant. This introduces systematic correlation between M and the error, and estimates of the relevant parameters will be inconsistent.

In the next section but one we present estimates relating to equation 4. Some of the difficulties mentioned in this section will be taken into account, but most remain unsolved problems.

---

17. Unless, of course, the best mayors find "tough" cities much more distasteful than the worst mayors.

Data

The data were created by merging the International City Management Association's 1970 tape on salaries of elected officials with the EPA's 1970 data on quality of life indicators.[18] The former set of data is a survey of the salaries of a selected group of municipal officials (including mayor). The sample includes all larger cities and contains data on 2,055 cities in all. The latter data set provides detailed information on 125 city characteristics for the 243 largest U.S. cities in 1970. Information was missing for four cities, so the total merged sample size for analysis is 239 cities.

The Estimating Equations

Two approaches may be adopted here. The partial approach allows a separate look at each amenity. In effect, it specifies an equation 4 for each amenity. If that approach is adopted, the estimating equation is

$$(6) \qquad X^j = \alpha_0^j + \alpha_1^j \tilde{M} + \alpha_2^j P_2 + \ldots + \alpha_K^j P_K + \alpha_T^j T$$

for each X^j. Then α_1^j is positive if X^j is a good characteristic and negative if X^j is a bad one. That is, when other inputs and population characteristics are held constant, paying a mayor more produces more goods and fewer ills. Although we will look at these simple relationships below, their interpretation is not straightforward. This is because X is really multidimensional so that optimization becomes multidimensional and interaction effects can be important. For example, X^1 may be a good and the simple relationship between X^1 and $\tilde{M}$ may well be negative (for the population parameters as well as the estimates). Communities that use higher $\tilde{M}$ might find it advantageous to produce a significantly higher level of, say, X^2, so much higher in fact that X^1 may fall. (This requires at least that $U_{x^1x^2} < 0$ or that $X_{x^1x^2} < 0$.) With normal assumptions this is unlikely, but the possibility suggests that, instead of equation 6, a function such as the following should be estimated.

$$(7) \qquad G(X^1, X^2, \ldots, X^N, \tilde{M}, T, P) = 0.$$

18. This data set is a transcription of Ben-Chieh Liu, *Quality of Life Indicators in U.S. Metropolitan Areas, 1970: A Comprehensive Assessment,* U.S. Environmental Protection Agency, Washington Environmental Research Center (GPO, 1975), appendix tables A-1 to C-5, pp. 232–83.

The problem with equation 7 is that the notion of dependent variable becomes meaningless; since $X^1, \ldots, X^N, \tilde{M}$ are all determined simultaneously, the choice of dependent variable is arbitrary. Econometrically, this implies that a simultaneous estimation technique is appropriate. Unfortunately, that is currently unworkable, so we arbitrarily chose a dependent variable and hoped for some reasonable information. The obvious choice for a dependent variable was $\tilde{M}$, and below are presented estimates of equation 7 obtained this way.

Results

Table 1 contains definitions and means of the variables used in the analysis. Table 2 presents ordinary least squares (OLS) regressions of equations 6 and 7.

Columns 1–7 of table 2 contain results of the estimation when the question is framed in terms of equation 6. That is, each amenity is treated as a dependent variable, and the relationship between it and the mayor's salary is determined as the coefficient on M. Column 8 contains the more appropriately specified version (relating to equation 7). Both versions tell a similar story, but that story is a fuzzy one at best.

In columns 1–7, we find that the coefficients on M in each equation are estimated imprecisely. Standard errors are large in all cases, and with the exception of water pollution, coefficients are statistically indistinguishable from zero at conventional levels. In the one case where the coefficient is relatively precise (water pollution), it has the wrong sign. If water pollution is an ill, the effect of paying a mayor a higher salary should be to reduce it. The reverse is true. Thus, if increasing the mayor's salary has a positive effect on the production of amenities, it is too subtle to show up here.

The same story is told by the coefficients in column 8. In this more general equilibrium version, the sign of the coefficient on any given amenity always has the same sign as M in the corresponding regression in columns 1–7. That is, M carries a positive but insignificant coefficient in column 1 and *UNEMPRT* carries a positive but insignificant coefficient in column 8. Again, water pollution is the only relationship that is estimated precisely at conventional levels, and its sign is incorrect.

Some of the other variables lend themselves to cleaner interpretation. Population variables generally have the expected signs when their coefficients are sharply estimated. For example, a city with high birth and

TABLE 1. *Definitions and Means of Variables*

Variable	Mean	Definition
INCPC	3,039	Personal income per capita (dollars)
POP70	251,034	1970 city population
POP65	246,133	1965 city population
M	13,111	Mayor's 1970 nominal salary in dollars divided by a cost-of-living index = 1 for the U.S. as a whole (mean is based only on cities with a paid mayor)
INCGTPV	90.1	Percent of families with income above poverty level
UNEMPRT	4.36	Unemployment rate
NEWSPPR	770	Local Sunday newspaper circulation per 1,000 population
DILAPHSG	2.61	Percent of housing units dilapidated
PARKS	44.8	Park acres per 1,000 population
POPDENS	4,362	Population density in central city
WATPOLLU	3.17	Water pollution index
INFMORT	20.63	Infant mortality per 1,000 live births
EDMEAN	11.94	Mean level of schooling completed
INSCHPOP	54.5	Percent of population 3–34 years old enrolled in school
LFPR	65.7	Labor force participation rate
SEGREG	0.73	Housing segregation index
TOTCRIM	2,851	Total crimes per 100,000 population
LIBBOOK	942	Books in main public library per 1,000 population
DEATH	8.85	Deaths per 1,000 population
BIRTH	18.20	Births per 1,000 population
POPCHNG	0.052	Population change: $(POP70 - POP65)/POP65$
NOMAYOR	0.098	Dummy = 1 if no mayor
FEDREV	13.1	Federal revenue to local government
LOCTAX	290.7	Local expenditures minus federal revenue
INCDIST	−0.007	Index of income distribution
BWINCM	0.79	Ratio of median black to median white family income adjusted for education
BWUNM	2.28	Ratio of black to white male unemployment rate adjusted for education
BWUNF	1.80	Ratio of black to white female unemployment rate adjusted for education
MGR	14,384	City manager's salary (corrected as in *M*)
CLERK	12,516	City clerk's salary (corrected as in *M*)
FINDIR	17,672	City financial director's salary (corrected as in *M*)
ENGNR	16,406	City engineer's salary (corrected as in *M*)
PWRKS	18,372	City public works superintendent's salary (corrected as in *M*)
STSUPT	12,712	City street superintendent's salary (corrected as in *M*)
TEACHSAL	663	Teacher's monthly salary (corrected as in *M*)
FIRESAL	6,827	Fireman's annual salary (corrected as in *M*)
POLICSAL	6,971	Policeman's annual salary (corrected as in *M*)
OTHSAL	441	Other municipal employees' monthly salary

TABLE 2. *Coefficients and Summary Statistics of Equations 6 and 7 Estimating Relation between Mayor's Salary and Quality of Life*[a]

Independent variable	Dependent variable							
	UNEMPRT (1)	DILAPHSG (2)	PARKS (3)	WATPOLLU (4)	INFMORT (5)	TOTCRIM (6)	LIBBOOKS (7)	M (8)
Constant	−0.755	17.8	103.0	17.4	44.6	5,758.0	−4,207.0	−56,502.0
	(3.08)	(2.91)	(566.0)	(13.2)	(9.28)	(2,366.0)	(1,381.0)	(26,445.0)
M	0.00000673	0.00000136	−0.000799	0.000137	−0.0000213	0.00608	0.00692	...
	(0.00000956)	(0.00000901)	(0.00175)	(0.0000411)	(0.0000287)	(0.00732)	(0.00427)	
POP70	−0.00000021	−0.00000012	−0.0000225	0.00000156	0.00000024	0.000126	−0.000116	0.00388
	(0.00000017)	(0.00000016)	(0.0000308)	(0.00000072)	(0.00000051)	(0.000128)	(0.0000752)	(0.00125)
POPCHNG	−0.724	0.559	−8.95	−1.90	0.0563	520.0	−84.8	4,721.0
	(0.405)	(0.382)	(74.3)	(1.74)	(1.21)	(310.0)	(181.0)	(3,074.0)
NEWSPPR	−0.000565	0.000298	0.0300	0.00104	0.000815	0.212	−0.0825	−1.43
	(0.000233)	(0.000220)	(0.0429)	(0.00100)	(0.000703)	(0.179)	(0.104)	(1.79)
POPDENS	−0.00000930	0.0000335	−0.000135	0.0000660	0.0000226	0.0184	−0.00729	0.751
	(0.0000376)	(0.0000355)	(0.00691)	(0.000162)	(0.000113)	(0.0288)	(0.0168)	(0.276)
EDMEAN	−0.173	−0.642	13.6	−0.108	0.0795	124.0	102.0	2,474.0
	(0.176)	(0.166)	(32.3)	(0.759)	(0.530)	(135.0)	(78.8)	(1,365.0)
INSCHPOP	0.0480	0.00331	−6.45	0.0713	−0.353	−10.9	8.47	−105.0
	(0.0197)	(0.0186)	(3.62)	(0.0851)	(0.0594)	(15.1)	(8.83)	(162.0)
LFPR	−0.0795	0.00609	0.683	−0.173	−0.0279	−7.85	9.18	223.0
	(0.0146)	(0.0138)	(2.69)	(0.0632)	(0.0441)	(11.2)	(6.56)	(118.0)
SEGREG	0.284	−0.0932	−15.0	0.344	−0.324	−276.0	−203.0	1,796.0
	(0.156)	(0.147)	(28.7)	(0.673)	(0.470)	(119.0)	(69.9)	(1,216.0)
DEATH	0.174	−0.0169	1.63	0.0741	0.451	−66.0	30.9	1,138.0
	(0.0640)	(0.0603)	(11.7)	(0.275)	(0.192)	(49.0)	(28.6)	(489.0)
BIRTH	0.142	−0.116	2.26	−0.346	−0.0973	−12.4	23.1	811.0
	(0.0427)	(0.0402)	(7.84)	(0.184)	(0.128)	(32.7)	(19.1)	(333.0)
NOMAYOR	0.261	0.0787	−25.2	2.75	−1.47	480.0	28.1	−12.8
	(0.288)	(0.272)	(52.9)	(1.24)	(0.868)	(221.0)	(129.0)	(8.25)

Variable	(1)	(2)	(3)	(4)	(5)	(6)	(7)	(8)
LOCTAX	0.00665	−0.000751	0.376	−0.00261	−0.00324	3.86	0.361	...
	(0.000973)	(0.000917)	(0.178)	(0.00419)	(0.000493)	(0.745)	(0.435)	
UNEMPRT	...	...	...	...	...	...	...	354.0
								(524.0)
DILAPHSG	...	...	...	...	...	...	...	42.0
								(538.0)
PARKS	...	...	...	...	...	...	...	−0.862
								(2.79)
WATPOLLU	...	...	...	...	...	...	...	313.0
								(114.0)
INFMORT	...	...	...	...	...	...	...	−17.7
								(173.0)
TOTCRIM	...	...	...	...	...	...	...	0.00522
								(0.700)
LIBBOOK	...	...	...	...	...	...	...	1.85
								(1.12)
INCPC	−0.00015	−0.000400	−0.0092	0.00100	0.00074	0.215	0.0261	−0.876
	(0.00016)	(0.000150)	(0.0300)	(0.0007)	(0.00049)	(0.125)	(0.0733)	(1.26)
INCGTPOV	0.0609	−0.0296	1.0	−0.0961	−0.00744	−27.4	18.3	9,933.0
	(0.0276)	(0.0260)	(5.06)	(0.118)	(0.0830)	(21.1)	(12.3)	(10,487.0)
INCDIST	−4.10	3.23	−18.3	5.65	3.37	4,147.0	239.0	−2,955.0
	(1.29)	(1.22)	(237.0)	(5.58)	(3.89)	(993.0)	(579.0)	(5,636.0)
BWINCM	−0.676	−1.95	−96.1	3.52	−0.196	−1,875.0	397.0	−378.0
	(0.718)	(0.676)	(131.0)	(3.09)	(2.16)	(550.0)	(321.0)	(567.0)
BWUNM	−0.126	−0.00590	−9.11	−0.225	−0.138	−102.0	31.9	700.0
	(0.0749)	(0.0706)	(13.7)	(0.322)	(0.225)	(57.0)	(33.5)	(774.0)
BWUNF	−0.140	−0.0199	−21.7	0.446	0.178	−127.0	70.0	53.9
	(0.102)	(0.0962)	(18.7)	(0.439)	(0.307)	(78.0)	(45.6)	(211.0)
R^2	0.409	0.286	0.0545	0.251	0.277	0.409	0.194	0.384
SEE[b]	1.07	1.01	197.0	4.63	3.23	824.0	481.0	8,044.0
Number	239	239	239	239	239	239	239	239

a. Variables are defined in table 1. Numbers in parentheses are standard errors. Columns 1–7 contain results of equation 6. Column 8 contains results of corrected equation 7.
b. Standard error of estimate.

death rates has old and young populations larger than its middle-aged population. Since the first two groups have relatively high rates of unemployment, we expect the coefficients on *BIRTH* and *DEATH* to be positive in column 1. *INSCHPOP* has the same effect. In column 7, cities with higher mean levels of education are found to also have more library books per capita, as one would expect. Column 3 shows that cities with higher local taxes also have more parks and recreational areas per capita.

Furthermore, the *NOMAYOR* variable in general carries the correct sign and its effect is sometimes estimated sharply. For example, cities without mayors have higher unemployment, more dilapidated housing, fewer parks, more water pollution, and more crime. This suggests that mayors may have a positive effect on city services, but that there is something wrong with the estimation of the salary relationship. A number of possibilities have been mentioned above: M is a poor measure of actual pecuniary compensation; $\tilde{M}$ is correlated with omitted variables, which confound the relationship; M does not take into account the amenities that the mayor receives by living in the city and so brings in systematic biases in estimation. Although we can do very little about the first two problems, the third one is dealt with in the next section.

A More Sophisticated Approach

In this section we recognize explicitly that the mayor resides in the city of which he is mayor. If people in the city care about X, as we have assumed, it is inconsistent to claim that the mayor does not, especially if X affects the difficulty of his job. If so, part of his compensation is utility or psychic income derived from the working conditions of the office. Equation 5 says that the mayor's salary is the sum of pecuniary earnings and psychic income net of taxes. As an approximation, let

$$(8) \qquad f(X) \equiv \sum_{j=1}^{N} P_{X^j} X^j,$$

where P_{x^j} is the shadow value of attribute X^j. Since the X's are observable, all that is required is the estimation of P_{x^j}. The standard way to obtain these[19] is to regress the pecuniary salary on the attributes. The

19. See Richard Thaler and Sherwin Rosen, "The Value of Saving a Life: Evidence from the Labor Market," in Nestor E. Terleckyj, ed., *Household Production and Consumption,* Studies in Income and Wealth 40 (Columbia University Press for National Bureau of Economic Research, 1976), pp. 265–98; and Charles Brown, "Equalizing Differences in the Labor Market," Bureau of Labor Statistics Working Paper 72 (BLS, 1977); forthcoming in *Quarterly Journal of Economics.*

coefficients are then minus the shadow value of the attribute: the coefficient on X^j tells how much salary the worker will forgo to obtain one more unit of X^j so that minus that coefficient is the value of X^j. Suppose we specify

$$(9) \qquad M = \beta_0 + \beta_1 X^1 + \beta_2 X^2 + \ldots + \beta_N X^N.$$

Then if the β's were estimated properly, $f(X)$ would be

$$(10) \qquad f(X) = - \sum_{j=1}^{N} X^i \beta_j.$$

Two problems arise immediately. First, equation 9 does not take into account the fact that mayors have different abilities. Second, if equation 9 holds, equation 7 is no longer identified. The solution to both problems is the same. Equation 9 must include an ability shifter. Since no information on the particular mayor's characteristics is available, the obvious choice for ability shifter will be some measure of the community's average ability. We have chosen to use a vector of community salary characteristics. Equation 9 is therefore rewritten as

$$(11) \quad M = \beta_0 + \beta_1 X_1 + \ldots + \beta_N X_N + \beta_{N+1} \, OTHSAL + \beta_{N+2} \, FIRESAL$$
$$+ \beta_{N+3} \, TEACHSAL + \beta_{N+4} \, POLICSAL + \beta_{N+5} \, CLERK$$
$$+ \beta_{N+6} \, FINDIR + \beta_{N+7} \, MGR + \beta_{N+8} \, ENGNR$$
$$+ \beta_{N+9} \, PWRKS + \beta_{N+10} \, STSUPT.$$

The variables are defined in table 1. Equation 10 remains the same and equations 7 and 11 are both identified.[20]

Now equation 7 can be rewritten as

$$(12) \quad \tilde{M} = \gamma_0 + \gamma_1 X_1 + \ldots + \gamma_N X_N + \gamma_{N+1} P_1 + \ldots + \gamma_{N+K} P_K.$$

20. Equation 11 would be a simple regression except for two difficulties. First, simultaneity with equation 7 suggests caution in the use of OLS for estimation. Second, the error in equation 11 is likely to be correlated with X. This is because additional income (as the result, say, of unobserved ability differences) will be taken partly in higher salary and partly in increased amenities. This suggests the need for an instrumental variable or two-stage-least-squares approach, where P and the salary variables (other than the mayor's) are exogenous. (This may not be completely valid.) These results were compared with the OLS results. They did not differ substantially. In addition, Zellner and Park have argued that OLS may be a better choice for small samples in a simultaneous equations model; see Arnold Zellner and Soo-Bin Park, "Minimum Expected Loss (MELO) Estimates for Functions of Parameters and Structural Coefficients of Econometric Models," *Journal of the American Statistical Association,* vol. 74 (March 1979), pp. 185–93. As the result, we have chosen to present the OLS results in table 3.

But substituting equation 11 into 10 and 10 into 5, we get

(13) $\tilde{M} = M - \beta_1 X_1 - \beta_2 X_2 - \ldots - \beta_N X_N - T.$

Substitution of equation 13 into 12 yields

$$(14) \quad M = \gamma_0 + (\gamma_1 + \beta_1)X_1 + \ldots + (\gamma_N + \beta_N)X_N + \gamma_{N+1}P_1 + \ldots$$
$$+ \gamma_{N+(K-1)}P_{K-1} + (\gamma_{N+K} + 1)P_K,$$

where $P_K \equiv T.$

This says that in order to rid estimates of equation 7 of the bias that results because unattractive cities must pay higher wages, we need only subtract estimates of the β_i obtained by estimating equation 11 from the relevant coefficients in column 7 of table 2. Column 1 of table 3 contains the estimates of equation 11 and column 2 contains corrected estimates of $\gamma_1, \ldots, \gamma_N$. (Standard errors are computed on the assumption that errors in the two equations are uncorrelated.)

Table 3 is informative and the results are much more reasonable than those in table 2. First note that the estimates of equation 11 in column 1 are sensible. Dilapidated housing, water pollution, infant mortality, and crime are ills. As these rise, the mayor's salary must increase to compensate for what are likely to be tougher working conditions. Parks are good and so carry a negative coefficient. *UNEMPRT* and *LIBBOOK* carry unanticipated signs, but standard errors are large. The salary variables used as instruments seem to work as one would expect if they truly reflect quality. Most are positive and sharply estimated. One that is not is *MGR*. This, too, makes sense. In cities with a highly paid city manager, the mayor is likely to be of low quality or even work part time. Mayors in these cities therefore receive lower salaries.

Column 2 reveals more. The corrected estimates of γ carry the anticipated sign in four of the seven cases, whereas only two of the seven are expected when uncorrected. Further, in none of the cases where the signs are incorrect is the coefficient ever significantly positive, in either an economic or a statistical sense. On the other hand, the results that go in the right direction are noisy, also. These numbers, which appear to be consistent with the hypothesis that higher pay produces elected officials of higher quality, must therefore be interpreted with a great deal of caution. The results should be regarded at best as only suggesting a positive causal line. The findings are in no way definitive.[21]

21. Ronald G. Ehrenberg and Gerald S. Goldstein obtain similar results in their analysis, "Executive Compensation in Municipalities," *Southern Economic Journal,* vol. 43 (July 1976), pp. 937–47.

TABLE 3. *Coefficients and Summary Statistics of Equations 7 and 11
Estimating Relation between Mayor's Salary and Quality of Life*[a]

Independent variable	Coefficient for equation 11	Corrected coefficient for equation 7
Constant	−9,525 (4,686)	...
UNEMPRT	−334 (353)	20.8 (500.5)
DILAPHSG	837 (392)	−795 (665)
PARKS	−0.707 (2.160)	−0.155 (3.52)
WATPOLLU	243 (84.2)	70 (141)
INFMORT	136 (117)	−153.7 (208.8)
TOTCRIM	0.465 (0.496)	−0.459 (0.857)
LIBBOOK	0.098 (0.830)	1.752 (1.394)
OTHSAL	−21.1 (9.4)	...
FIRESAL	1.81 (1.32)	...
TEACHSAL	4.56 (5.09)	...
POLICSAL	0.363 (1.36)	...
CLERK	0.597 (0.154)	...
FINDIR	0.393 (0.151)	...
MGR	−1.04 (0.07)	...
ENGNR	0.233 (0.144)	...
PWRKS	0.123 (0.139)	...
STSUPT	0.660 (0.155)	...
R^2	0.62	...
Number	239	...

a. Variables are defined in table 1. Dependent variable is M. Numbers in parentheses are standard errors.

Wesley R. Liebtag

A Private Sector Approach to Federal Executive Compensation: Illumination or Illusion?

THE SYSTEM now in use in the federal government for setting salaries for executive, legislative, and judicial positions is, as might be expected, the result of compromise and shows the influence of the political environment over the years. As such, it produces results that rarely satisfy anyone, including the positions' incumbents.

From the standpoint of sound salary administration practice, especially as carried on in the private sector, there are serious questions about a system that lumps together three such disparate groups of positions as those in the executive, legislative, and judicial branches. There are equally serious questions about the soundness of the congressional attitude, which tends to hold most executive and judicial salaries at a level equal to or below its own, an action that has produced detrimental compression in the so-called supergrade positions.

As is often the case when confronted with evidence of governmental malpractice, a strong dose of wisdom derived from practice in the private sector may be prescribed to remedy the problems of executive, legislative, and judicial compensation. Before the dose is administered, however, the applicability to government of the various approaches to executive compensation developed in private industry must be evaluated. This paper offers such an evaluation. It compares the characteristics of compensation systems in industry and government, examines the structural relationship of the salaries of the different classes of top government officials, and assesses the use of comparability concepts in making pay adjustments for these officials. Finally, recommendations are made for improving the sys-

The author thanks Dan S. Moore, retired business executive and consultant in compensation matters, for his contributions to this paper.

141

tem of executive compensation in the federal government, drawing on judgments concerning the applicability of experience in the private sector.

A Comparison of Compensation Systems in Industry and Government

The system of compensation for executive, legislative, and judicial positions has developed its own logic and principles. The special aspects of the government system may be observed by a comparison with the approach to compensation taken in the private sector.

If there is any one characteristic that typifies compensation systems found in private industry, it is that there is no set pattern. Systems differ radically from industry to industry, company to company, business unit to business unit within a company, and often between lower level employees and higher level employees in the same business unit. The many variations in industry are further emphasized by the tendency of companies to change systems reasonably frequently. In government the systems remain relatively static.

A special characteristic of the federal pay-setting system is the "linkage" mechanism, which ties together compensation at several levels of the three branches. The report of the 1976 Commission on Executive, Legislative, and Judicial Salaries offered the following observations on the concept and practice of linkage:

> The principle of fixed or automatic "linkage"—a recent historical development—seems inappropriate as a continuing way to fix salaries at these levels. Indeed . . . the most commonly referred to linkage only began in 1969 (linkage between Congress, Level II [undersecretaries], and the Judges of the Court of Appeals). There is also the "linkage" between Cabinet positions and Associate Justices in the Supreme Court.
>
> . . . There is no historic linkage among these positions, and we cannot find a persuasive rationale for its rigid application. The basis since 1969 has apparently been largely political, based on the assumption that the Circuit Judges and the Level II executives might serve as a "lifeline" to the Members of Congress, understandably unwilling to raise their own pay unilaterally. But as the public mood has intensified, the lifeline has disappeared, and it is Congress which has served as an anchor over the past eight years, dragging down the "links" and preventing any increase anywhere.
>
> There are, in fact, sound reasons for unlinking Congress, Level II (or any other level), and any of the Federal judges. Not only are these, of course,

entirely different jobs with entirely different responsibilities, but the career anticipation patterns differ sharply.[1]

The evaluation of the worth of jobs in industry is frequently based on a customized system that has been designed to suit the perceived needs of the enterprise. Sometimes the evaluation is based on a common commercial system such as that offered by a consultant. Even here customization takes place. Finally, for lower level jobs the values may be arrived at not by any measurement mechanism but by negotiation with a labor union. For example, if one looks at the hierarchy of job worth in the aluminum industry, one finds that skilled craftsmen are paid more than the rates assigned to major production machine operators. If one looks at the steel industry, one finds the same union and work of very similar content, but the pay rates of the two groups are reversed. In government, the value system is centrally controlled and is subject to few changes besides those arising from the political process. In both industry and government, measurements of job worth are based on the perceived needs of one or more parties. There is no underlying scale of intrinsic worth.

While step rates—automatic increases based on tenure—are found to some degree in industry, particularly in the lower levels, they are common in government except in the very top positions. Notwithstanding statements to the contrary, step rates in industry or government plans are rarely administered on a merit basis. In industry, single rates, after learning periods for a job or group of jobs, are typically found in the lower levels. While single rates are used in government, they are normally modified by the application of step rates.

Merit pay is usual in industry for professional, managerial, and executive positions but rare for the hourly wage group. Variations in pay between employees with common skills but different performance levels may be as much as 10–20 percent for lower level professionals and managers and as much as 20–30 percent for higher level people. Merit pay has been almost totally absent from the government compensation system. Parenthetically it may be noted that the Civil Service Reform Act of 1978 includes a commitment to the first widespread experimentation with a merit pay plan for career federal executives.

The amount of flexibility that individual managers in industry may

1. *Report of the Commission on Executive, Legislative, and Judicial Salaries, December 1976* (Government Printing Office, 1977), pp. 34–35.

and do apply in making judgments about pay increases is substantially different from that applied in government. Note that in industry they both "may" and "do." In some sectors of government they "may" but historically "do not." In at least one known instance in industry, individual managers, with the approval of the next level of management, deviate from the specific guidelines on pay, which are broad, as frequently as 30 percent of the time. While this may be an extreme case, the principle is clear: managers in industry exercise discretion in administering pay. Managers in government do not, and in fact cannot, in most cases.

While positions in the five executive levels, in the Congress, and in the judiciary are all in a one-rate system—that is, each level has one specific pay rate—step rates are used in the classified civil service. There is only limited use of the two top levels of pay in the civil service grades, according to data of March 31, 1978.[2] Most of the eighteen grades in the general schedule have a ten-step pay system; progression through most of the pay steps is more or less automatic. Despite this, in no grade level did the average pay step exceed 5.8, and the overall average pay step for the whole classified service was 4.7. The compression effect in the supergrades (16, 17, and 18) had a marked influence on the use of the top pay grades. Executive level compensation had been increased much less since 1969 than general schedule pay. In grade 18 all 407 incumbents were in the first step, since the maximum level permitted under existing law was the salary for level V in the executive classifications. In grade 17 pay step five was the maximum level in use for the same reason. In grade 16 only 7.8 percent of the 3,456 persons in positions at this level were in the ninth pay step, and none were in the tenth step.

This situation illustrates vividly the lack of flexibility in the federal system, which results from the use of a flat job rate for executive, legislative, and judicial positions, and the compression created in the upper level civil service grades and lower executive levels by the artificial ceilings on pay. Since management positions are often in grades 16, 17, and 18, the compression effect and the lack of flexibility are highly detrimental to the morale of the leaders and, in all probability, to performance.

The same lack of flexibility characterizes benefit programs. Although benefits are generally common in their basic design in both government

2. U.S. Civil Service Commission, Bureau of Personnel Management Evaluation, *Pay Structure of the Federal Civil Service,* March 31, 1978, Federal Civilian Workforce Statistics (GPO, 1978), p. 24.

and industry, different groups within vertical hierarchies have different benefits in private industry more frequently than different groups in government do.

Myths to Be Denied

In addition to recognizing the differences and similarities of compensation systems in private industry and the federal government, it is desirable to dispose of some myths that frequently have influenced compensation management.

1. *The use of position titles in the establishment of comparative compensation is useful and productive.*

There is little, if any, uniformity in the use of position titles in private industry; wide variations exist, especially from industry to industry. Because of this, titles may inhibit rather than facilitate comparisons among jobs. Titles frequently reflect the special characteristics of an industry or even the personal attributes of the incumbent. Comparisons are fruitless in these situations if they are based on title alone. (Since in the government many titles have no counterparts elsewhere, they could not be used in any case.)

If position titles are valueless in the establishment of comparative compensation, what then can be used? The obvious answer is job matching, but it is virtually impossible to match executive, legislative, and judicial positions in the government with jobs in the private sector.

2. *The general public in this country has clearly indicated its reluctance to pay executives in government significantly higher salaries than those now being paid. There is therefore little need to be concerned about the question of comparability with industry.*

Even though this statement seems to accurately describe the public attitude as perceived by some of the press and by some public officials, the reasoning is specious. Efforts must continue to be made to lift federal executive pay to levels that will help recruit the kinds of personnel needed by the nation in the positions involved.[3]

3. For details on turnover, difficulty in filling vacant positions, and early retirements, see *Report of the Commission on Executive, Legislative, and Judicial Salaries, December 1976,* pp. 19–20; and Arnold R. Weber and George R. Burman, "Compensation and Federal Executive Service, Survey and Analysis," in *Staff Report to the Commission on Executive, Legislative, and Judicial Salaries, February 1977* (GPO, 1977), pp. 1–69.

The constrictive effect of low executive pay on the rest of the federal services is a serious problem that continually undermines the morale of a large number of federal managers and supervisors. Turnover in the judicial and executive branches continues to be large enough to cause concern. A serious and continuing effort to break the logjam impeding adequate pay is a real necessity for building and maintaining an effective executive service.

3. *Federal employees, even at the executive levels, do not feel called upon to work very hard, and their pay therefore does not warrant serious consideration.*

Respect for the demands and responsibilities of a position in the federal or private sector usually depends on several factors. These include the attitude of the particular employee, the degree of discipline exerted by superiors as well as the example they set, and the rewards both inside and outside the system. Any taxpayer who has been exposed to the Washington scene knows that many executives in the government work very long hours and display a high degree of dedication. Unfortunately, there are some who behave quite differently. However, it is grossly unfair to label all government executives as lazy or inefficient because of the behavior of a limited number.

4. *The private sector is a monolith composed of many parts that are practically identical. This makes comparisons easy since all parts do the same things in the same way.*

Individual company practices in almost every area of compensation vary widely. Benefit packages are different. The number of perquisites ranges from zero in some industries to many in others. Such things as incentive bonuses are highly variable, even within one industry. Companies that are capital intensive tend to pay higher base salaries than labor-intensive enterprises. No one segment of the private sector could successfully be chosen to represent all private business.

5. *Since there are already many points of similarity between government compensation practices and those of the private sector, there is no reason why the practices of both should not be identical.*

Not only is there no one set of practices in the private sector, but the needs and therefore the practices of the many federal agencies vary widely as well, although all are subject to the limitations imposed by law. There are many differences, and probably always will be, between the two sectors. The turnover in incumbents in executive positions occasioned by a change in administration is unlike anything that occurs in the private sector. Another difference is the relatively short incumbencies that appear to be characteristic of many federal executive positions. Finally, the fact that most of these positions are in the political arena and in the public eye makes them significantly different from private sector jobs.

The Data Base Problem

The idea of developing a comparative data base of information obtained from the private sector for use in determining the compensation of top government officials is an appealing one. Superficially, it seems to offer an easy method of establishing a system of salary levels for the government service. The problem is that it is impossible to achieve with any degree of soundness. Creation of a base of this kind requires a method of position comparison that will equate work content and thus equate salaries. This is difficult to accomplish in industry at the executive levels under discussion here. Moreover, it has generally proved to be impossible across industry lines.

One difficulty lies in the fact that industry has never developed a common organizational structure, a common position-evaluation system, or a common system of position classification in the middle and high executive levels. Even among companies that use structured methods of classifying positions, there is no uniform pattern. This does not mean that classification is haphazard; on the contrary, careful procedures with emphasis on the detection of anomalies or aberrations are usual within an enterprise.

Classification levels assigned to middle level executive positions in industry are apt to reflect the particular form of organization used by the firm as well as the complexity of the company itself. Other factors that carry weight in the assignment of level and thus salary include the nature of the business and the views of senior management on the relative importance of each management position. Compensation at the higher levels thus becomes a highly personalized matter—in the sense that the special skills and accomplishments of the individuals in the positions have considerably greater influence on the determination of salary levels than is true for lower level positions.

Even within the best known point systems there are variations in how they are used by different companies. These usually reflect differences in company organization, in the degree of authority delegated from the most senior ranks, in the historic attitudes of company management toward position evaluation, and in so simple a thing as the number of pay levels management wishes to maintain for its executive ranks.

If an effort were made to assign point values to the various elements of a cabinet member's job, problems would arise immediately. How can one characterize the responsibility for dealing with congressional committees and how should points be assigned to this function? When the size of the budget for the Department of Defense or Agriculture or Health, Education, and Welfare is considered, how many points should be assigned? How many private industry jobs can accurately be compared with these? And how, using concepts of personnel administration, would one describe and evaluate the position of a senator, of the chairman of the House Ways and Means Committee, or of the majority leader in either house? Even if the three branches of the federal service were successfully separated for the purpose of fixing salaries, they could not be easily compared with private industry. It is clear that any effort to compare top federal positions with top positions in private industry would place far too much weight and importance on uncertain and ineffective measures, no matter how successful these measures might be when applied to private industry or to lower levels in the government. Using standard concepts of job evaluation for high-level federal positions would be unwise and unprofitable.

The system used in the federal government does not involve a rational comparison of the duties and responsibilities of positions. Adjustments in compensation tend to exaggerate errors in classification made in the past. If an executive position is placed on a level that is too high or too low, future adjustments in pay only confirm the incorrect classification and magnify the incorrect pay. The same circumstances could arise in private industry, except that in that environment there are two factors that are rarely encountered in government service to the same degree. One of these is the pressure of competitive positions and recruitment, and the other is the heavy emphasis on cost control that is found today in nearly every significant sector of private industry.

Another aspect of the problem for government executives is that position levels are often the result of action by political forces, specifically of the enactment of a statute that does not take into account all of the relationships. Then changes in position level are difficult to accomplish, especially if a reduction in grade is likely to result. The frequent consolidation and reorganization of agencies and bureaus also contribute to the imprecision. The maintenance of previous levels is generally a characteristic of such changes, regardless of the effect of the consolidation on the duties of the position.

The need for some interagency mechanism for periodic review of the executive levels seems imperative. Headed by a senior representative from the Office of Personnel Management, such a group could also arrange for continuing participation by competent professionals from industry to make certain that new techniques were available and used. This group could also review and endorse or question agency classification actions.

In this connection, attention is directed to the newly established Office of Personnel Management, one of the replacement agencies for the Civil Service Commission. Although the 1978 Civil Service Reform Act does not grant the OPM specific authority for overseeing classification of executive level positions, some such responsibilities might well be assumed. This is particularly relevant to the new Senior Executive Service. There appears to be a need for some nonpolitical mechanism to prevent individual department or agency abuse of its classification authority when the full gamut from GS-16 to executive level IV is opened up.

While the supergrades (GS-16, -17, and -18) have been considered in the past in proposing action on the executive levels, the relationship between the two has not been nearly as close as that which will result from the Senior Executive Service, which will encompass most positions from GS-16 to executive level IV. This change seems to say that methods of determining intragovernmental pay comparability need to be refined and improved without delay. (See the paper by Hartman, below, for further discussion of this point.) Although professionals dealing with compensation may have certain reservations about some aspects of the Senior Executive Service, on the whole it appears to be an improvement on the old system.

It should be noted that elimination of the idea of using a private industry data base for federal executive levels, as proposed here, places even greater importance on present practices as applied to the general schedule levels below the supergrades. Pay comparability for GS levels 1–15 is now established through the use of the annual national survey of professional, administrative, technical, and clerical pay made by the Bureau of Labor Statistics. (Examples are given in table 4, in the appendix to this chapter.) Over the years, reasonably good job matches in these levels have been developed. The techniques for making the wage comparisons, however, are not as satisfactory, nor are the relationships that ultimately result. Once the process for GS-1 through GS-15 has been completed, the President's pay agent extrapolates the necessary recommendations for the supergrades. This procedure should be continued, assuming the process to establish wage comparison is improved, but the necessary controls must be set up for use with the Senior Executive Service. Such extrapolation is not intended to imply that the procedure in any way represents a comparison of senior executives with industry positions. It does not and cannot provide such a comparison.

The severe limitations on using comparability do not mean that the compensation of top government officials should be insulated from external economic considerations. For purposes of determining compensation, however, these external factors are best expressed in rates of change of aggregate data. Thus adjustments in executive, legislative, and judicial compensation should be related, though not tied directly, to changes in the consumer price index, the index of average hourly earnings, and the rate of salary increase, as revealed by the annual BLS survey and studies such as those published by the Conference Board,[4] which indicate the rate of movement of executive compensation. While these data cannot be applied directly to executive salaries in the federal service, they should be considered meaningful measures that can be helpful in determining a reasonable rate of increase in these salaries.

State and Local Government Data

Although often not available quickly, historical data on salaries paid state officials such as governors, secretaries of state, and treasurers can be obtained. The *Book of the States,* published annually by the Council of State Governments, is the best source for these figures, some of which are shown in table 5 (in the appendix to this chapter).

The reason for suggesting that data of this kind be used is that there are many similarities in government positions of various kinds, even across federal and state lines, and some federal government executives, particularly presidential appointees, are recruited from and return to states and major cities and counties. While there may be no true counterpart in private industry for a major department head position in the federal government, the latter may share some characteristics with the position of a major department head in the government of a large state such as New York or California.

To a lesser degree the same is true of positions in city and county governments. Here the difference in scope, except in the larger cities, is so great as to make the comparisons considerably less significant. Also,

4. Harland Fox, *Top Executive Compensation,* Conference Board Report 753 (New York: Conference Board, 1978), and preceding editions.

city and county data are much more difficult to obtain, since the figures published in the *Municipal Year Book,* the *County Year Book,* and the *Urban Data Service Report* are aggregates and do not contain individual data points.[5] Thus their use is limited.

Despite the problems of availability and timeliness, the data from state, county, and municipal sources should be used as part of the process of determining the appropriateness of trends in federal executive pay.

The History of Federal Executive Salaries

Adjustments made in executive salary levels in the last ten years have been the product of actions by the President and the Congress and show no pattern. Actual increases in pay have ranged from less than 5 percent to as much as 71 percent. In 1977, the last year of any significant change, increases ranged from 28.9 percent at executive level II to 4.8 percent at executive level I. Table 1 gives the figures.

One serious problem shown by this pattern is the compression in the federal service that results from the artificial limits placed on pay raises by Congress and the President. Private industry in the United States and abroad has suffered to a lesser degree for a number of years from the compression in compensation that comes from a very rapid rise in the wage and salary levels (and total compensation level) of employees below the management and executive positions. In the federal service the compression is much greater than in industry primarily as a result of the arbitrary restriction on upper level salaries. Insistence by Congress, for example, that only a few federal positions may receive salaries higher than those paid congressmen and senators has been a major contributor to the problem. This means that four levels of executive positions, levels II to V, must be squeezed into the structure between the supergrades below and the cabinet member above. Congress then compounds the confusion by enacting legislation that forbids paying any general schedule position an amount in excess of the rate for executive level V. One result of this is to push the compression effect down into the GS-15 level.

The limit on pay adjustments for the executive levels since 1977 has resulted in frozen pay for large numbers of employees in the executive

5. International City Management Association, *The Municipal Year Book, 1979* (Washington: ICMA, 1979), and preceding issues; National Association of Counties and International City Management Association, *The County Year Book, 1978* (Washington: NAC and ICMA, 1978), and preceding issues; *Urban Data Service Report* (ICMA, monthly).

TABLE 1. *History of Recent Federal Executive Salary Increases, 1968–77*[a]

Dollars unless otherwise specified

Executive level	1968 salary	1969			1975			1977		
		Salary	Increase	Percentage change	Salary	Increase	Percentage change	Salary	Increase	Percentage change
I	35,000	60,000	25,000	71.43	63,000	3,000	5.00	66,000	3,000	4.76
II	30,000	42,500	12,500	41.67	44,600	2,100	4.94	57,500	12,900	28.92
III	29,500	40,000	10,500	35.59	42,000	2,000	5.00	52,500	10,500	25.00
IV	28,750	38,000	9,250	32.17	39,900	1,900	5.00	50,000	10,100	25.31
V	28,000	36,000	8,000	28.57	37,800	1,800	5.00	47,500	9,700	25.66

Sources: 1968, 1969, *Documentary History of Federal Pay Legislation, 1975*, Committee Print, Senate Committee on Post Office and Civil Service, 94 Cong. 2 sess. (GPO, 1976), p. 30; 1975, 1977, *The Budget of the United States Government—Appendix*, pt. 2: "Schedules of Permanent Positions," for the years given.

a. Since 1968, increases have been granted only in 1969, 1975, and 1977.

TABLE 2. *Annual Salaries of Federal Officials, 1977*
Dollars

Position	Salary
President	200,000
Vice-president	75,000
Speaker of the House	75,000
Chief justice of the United States	75,000
Associate justices	72,000
Cabinet members	66,000
President pro tempore—Senate	65,000
Majority leader—House and Senate	65,000
Minority leader—House and Senate	65,000
Senators and representatives	57,500
Deputy secretaries of state, defense, treasury, transportation	57,500
Deputy attorney general	57,500
Under secretaries of other executive departments	52,500
Executive level IV	50,000
Executive level V	47,500
GS-18	47,500[a]
GS-17	47,500[a]
GS-16 (step 3 and above)	47,500[a]

Source: *The Budget of the United States Government, Fiscal Year 1978—Supplement: Executive, Legislative, and Judicial Salary Recommendations,* and *Appendix,* pt. 2: "Schedules of Permanent Positions."
a. Effective rate for GS-16 to GS-18, limited by law to the rate for executive level V.

levels, the supergrades, and GS-15, as well as for government employees not in the general schedule. This also means that people employed at several different senior levels of the federal service will be receiving identical salaries, regardless of supervisory relationships, differences in position responsibility, or anything else. Table 2 illustrates the problem.

Range Increments

Table 3 shows how the intervals between federal executive pay levels have varied at different times. In 1968 the smallest increment was 1.7 percent and the largest was 16.7 percent; in 1969 the smallest was 5.3 percent and the largest was 41.2 percent; in 1977 the smallest was 5.0 percent and the largest was 14.8 percent. Study of the data suggests that no consistent rule or concept was followed in setting the intervals between levels.

Practice in industry varies somewhat, with no set figure representing

TABLE 3. *Intervals between Federal Executive Salary Levels, Selected Years, 1968–77*

Dollars unless otherwise specified

Item	1968	1969	1975	1977
Level I				
Salary	35,000	60,000	63,000	66,000
Increment from level II	5,000	17,500	18,400	8,500
Percent difference	16.67	41.18	41.26	14.78
Level II				
Salary	30,000	42,500	44,600	57,500
Increment from level III	500	2,500	2,600	5,000
Percent difference	1.69	6.25	6.19	9.52
Level III				
Salary	29,500	40,000	42,000	52,500
Increment from level IV	750	2,000	2,100	2,500
Percent difference	2.61	5.26	5.26	5.00
Level IV				
Salary	28,750	38,000	39,900	50,000
Increment from level V	750	2,000	2,100	2,500
Percent difference	2.68	5.56	5.56	5.26
Level V				
Salary	28,000	36,000	37,800	47,500

Sources: Same as table 1.

industrywide intervals; however, the intervals between executive levels in a given company have tended to remain the same. Also, there is rarely, if ever, less than 5 to 6 percent between levels. The size of the organization and its relative complexity are major factors in determining the number of ranks or levels and the intervals between them. Below the very highest executive ranks, the increment from one range (or level) to another may be as low as 8 percent or as high as over 15 percent.

The situation is different for the chief executive officer and the next highest position in a company. A private 1977 study of eleven major corporations showed that the gap between the two top positions ranged from 16.8 percent to 62.3 percent, the average being 41.2 percent. Many major companies regard the top position as being at least two levels above the next most senior position.

The interval between the salary of the second highest paid executive and the third highest paid, in that same study of eleven major companies, ranged from zero to 55.6 percent, with an average of 28.3 percent. (The zero case probably involved a recently promoted executive.) Tables 6 and 7 (in the appendix) give average changes in the compensation of executives in industry.

In the federal service the President's salary of $200,000 is nearly three times that of the vice-president, a relationship that does not exist in major private companies. On the other hand the vice-president's salary of $75,000 is only 13.6 percent above the pay of cabinet members and is the same as the salaries of the Speaker of the House and the chief justice of the United States (table 2).

Since the current interval between executive level I (cabinet members) and level II is 14.8 percent, it seems obvious that the gap between the vice-president and the cabinet members is too small at 13.6 percent. It should be increased. Similarly, the intervals between executive levels II and III, III and IV, and IV and V are too small, ranging as they do from 9.5 percent to 5.0 percent (table 3). Industry practice and the attitudes of government executives both suggest that 10 percent is about the minimum acceptable spread if real motivational differences are to exist.

It is clear that a general restructuring of the current executive salary system is imperative. There is little, if any, relation between the various levels of difficulty and responsibility and the differences in pay. Two steps might be taken to deal with this special problem.

First, a study should be made to establish the *internal* relative value of federal positions without regard to their present compensation. (Such a study should not include the positions of senators and congressmen for obvious reasons.)

Second, once this study was completed, the incremental differences between position levels should be set to reflect the perceived differences in difficulty and responsibility. For example, the position of the vice-president might be judged as representing half the value of the position of the President. Then the relative value of the cabinet positions should be established, without a requirement that all be at the same level, although this might be the result.

This kind of study would inevitably result not only in a relative rank order but also in the setting of the necessary incremental differences between levels. The size of the increments as a percentage of the next lower salary should decrease as the rank order diminishes. Thus while the difference between the job of the President and that of the vice-president should perhaps be 50 percent, the difference between the job of the vice-president and the highest ranking cabinet member might be about 30 percent, and so on.

No specific proposal is made about the size of the gaps. However, the need for a coherent, defensible system is clear and should be met.

Merit Pay in an Inflationary Economy

Merit pay for managerial and executive positions enjoys wide acceptance in private industry in this country, having developed rapidly after World War II. Experiments of various kinds have been tried in an effort to improve merit systems. These include forced appraisal distribution systems, which require comparative measurements of performance, flexible time periods between increases, and flexible amounts of increases so that truly exceptional performance may be recognized as often as necessary—sometimes more than once a year.

In general, merit systems have been successful. In some cases the system has been distorted, but they appear to be few. It may be important at this point to define the word "merit" as used herein. It simply means that the best performers get the largest increases and the poorest the smallest. It implies nothing about the average.

The major problem encountered recently by companies seeking to administer salaries on a merit basis comes from the inflationary forces at work in this country. When the portion of a salary increase that is perceived to be attributable to inflation is significantly larger than the portion that is perceived to be attributable to merit only, the merit plan suffers. If great care is not taken to preserve the importance of performance awards and to administer them correctly, merit systems may cease to have any beneficial effects.

Industry experience suggests that there may be serious problems if the two elements of the salary increase—merit and economic—are separately identified to the recipients. This is apparently the method contemplated under the merit pay plan contained in the recent civil service legislation.[6] A change might be considered to eliminate separate identification of the merit and economic portions.

Efforts to administer a merit pay system for the Senior Executive Service and for the classified civil service under the Civil Service Reform Act of 1978 should be carried out with full awareness of the problems cataloged above.

6. The Civil Service Reform Act of 1978, title V, provides for a merit pay system for supervisors and managers in GS grades 13–15.

Employee Benefits

Six types of employee benefits are significant in both the federal and the private sectors. They are life insurance, health insurance, retirement pay, sick leave, vacation or annual leave, and paid holidays. Other benefits of lesser importance include severance or termination pay, unemployment compensation, and workmen's compensation.

Private business frequently offers other benefits not usually found in the public sector, including the federal government (although the new Senior Executive Service has a bonus system). Executives in the private sector are frequently awarded bonuses, stock options, or various kinds of deferred compensation. Stock purchase plans and a variety of thrift or savings plans are sometimes made available to all employees of a company, and discounts on the purchase of company products are not uncommon. However, there is often substantial variation in the level and type of benefits offered to executives, to people in professional and managerial positions, and to those working for hourly wages.

Surveys of the costs of private industry benefits over a twenty-year period conducted by the Chamber of Commerce show that benefits as a percentage of payroll increased from 22.7 percent in 1955 to 40.3 percent in 1975. The increase from 1969 to 1975 was 26.3 percent.[7]

Efforts to compare benefits in the private sector with those in the federal sector encounter serious difficulties. Many private plans today are noncontributory with the employer paying the full cost of such things as a retirement plan. Some private plans are fully funded; others are required by law to achieve full funding. In contrast, federal retirement programs are partly contributory, but they are not fully funded. Instead, annual appropriations are made to finance a substantial share of the benefits. These differences make comparisons complicated.

Plan provisions tend to differ widely, not only between government and industry, but within industry and sometimes within a single company. Although not identified as benefits, there are attributes of federal executive service that clearly offer advantages to the jobholder. These include prestige and the demonstrable effect of such service on postgovernment careers. These advantages are much less common in private business.

7. Chamber of Commerce of the United States of America, *Employee Benefits, 1975* (Washington: Chamber of Commerce, 1976), p. 27.

All this leads to the conclusion that benefit plans must be considered by costing them through a computer-based model. Such costing can be done for most plans in both sectors, if desired, to determine whether there are significant differences and also to assist in judging the costs and value of new or modified benefit plans for the government sector.

Total Compensation Comparability

In recent years, much of private industry has used a system in which "total compensation"—base pay plus benefits—is compared with that of the competition, with other positions in the company, or with any other set of data considered desirable for comparison. Failure to make use of this sort of measurement leaves many questions unanswered and omits consideration of benefits, probably the fastest growing portion of compensation today, at least in cost.

The Office of Personnel Management is testing a method of comparing total compensation. The General Accounting Office, which suggested this procedure in 1975, had this to say about the new development:

> We believe the implementation of a total compensation system is critical in attaining the public's confidence in the Government's compensation-setting process. Therefore, we believe a need exists not only for the Commission to expedite its development and testing of a total compensation process but also for the Congress to enact appropriate legislation to insure the timely implementation of this concept.[8]

Once this technique has been tested and proved, it should be carried out.

One very difficult problem here arises from Congress' retention of the authority to modify federal benefit plans and the dispersion of that authority among various congressional committees in both houses. This system does not augur well for the orderly planning of government benefits or for flexible and rational consideration of changes. While it is assuredly difficult to be optimistic about the chances of success, a concerted effort should be made to designate one decisionmaking point for all federal government benefit plans, developments, and changes. There are many obvious advantages from the standpoint of both federal employees and taxpayers.

8. Comptroller General of the United States, *Federal Compensation Comparability: The Need for Congressional Action,* Report to the Congress, FPCD-78-60 (GAO, 1978), app. 2, pp. 5–6.

Recommendation and Proposals for Action

To assure acceptable performance in the nation's federal executive positions and to facilitate recruitment for them, it is imperative that an orderly system be used for establishing and maintaining internal compensation relationships among the executive levels. (The emphasis on internal relationships rather than external comparisons is deliberate.) The following proposals may help achieve these objectives.

1. No effort should be made to develop a data base from private industry for comparison with the level of federal executive salaries; however, private sector data should be used in the aggregate to help determine the rate of movement of executive salaries.

2. Other indicators of trends, such as the consumer price index, the index of hourly wage movement, and changes in state and local government salary levels, should be taken into account in setting compensation.

3. The intervals between federal executive level salaries should be increased and their determination should be placed on a sound and defensible basis. Compression in the Senior Executive Service and in the executive schedule should be reduced. This can only be accomplished if the salary levels for the executive levels are raised sufficiently to eliminate excessive compression.

4. Changes in the decision process used in establishing executive salary levels are clearly required if some of the problems and difficulties described above are to be overcome. This is not a new idea; it has been voiced repeatedly in the past, most recently by the Commission on Executive, Legislative, and Judicial Salaries in its 1976 report to the President. Some of the changes referred to therein are incorporated in this paper; some are not.[9]

5. A systematic method for considering changes in benefit plans, preferably with one decisionmaking point, should be developed. An effort should be made to compare individual and total benefit plans on a cost basis.

6. Care should be used in implementing the merit pay aspects of the 1978 Civil Service Reform Act in order to avoid (a) the gradual erosion of merit recognition so that the so-called merit pay is extended to all em-

9. *Report of the Commission on Executive, Legislative, and Judicial Salaries, December 1976.* The detailed proposals made by the commission appear on pp. 56–62.

ployees, and (b) the problems of merit recognition in an inflationary economy.

7. Incentive bonuses for the Senior Executive Service should be supported, provided adequate controls are established.

8. The Office of Personnel Management should continue, and expand, efforts to involve representatives of the private sector in the studies and decisionmaking processes, particularly those concerning classification and the control of levels.

9. The existing "linkage" mechanism should be disregarded. Each of the three federal services (executive, legislative, judicial) should be considered and acted upon separately for pay purposes.

It is obvious that the compensation system for executive, legislative, and judicial officials has developed its own standards and frame of reference. An attempt to rigorously apply the concepts and procedures used in private industry to the compensation of these government officials would be misguided. On the other hand, experience with executive compensation in the private sector offers models of sound practice in dealing with issues such as merit pay, optimal structural relationships, and the use of comparability data. An increased awareness of private sector practices may help to bring good sense, if not complete rationality, to the task of determining the pay of congressmen, cabinet officers, and judges.

Appendix

Tables 4–7 illustrate numerically several of the preceding discussions.

TABLE 4. *Annual Percentage Pay Increase for Private Sector Professional, Administrative, Technical, and Clerical Positions, 1969–77*

Positions comparable to general schedule levels	Average increase from previous year							
	1970	1971	1972	1973	1974	1975	1976	1977
Levels 11–15	6.4	6.2	5.6	5.7	6.2	8.8	6.5	7.7
Levels 5–10	6.3	6.3	5.2	4.4	5.7	8.6	6.4	6.3
	Index (1969 = 100)							
Levels 11–15	106.4	113.0	119.3	126.1	133.9	145.7	155.2	167.1
Levels 5–10	106.3	113.0	118.9	124.1	131.2	142.5	151.6	161.2

Source: Bureau of Labor Statistics, *National Survey of Professional, Administrative, Technical, and Clerical Pay, March 1977* (GPO, 1977), text table 2, p. 3.

TABLE 5. *Change in Salaries of the Governors of Fifteen Large States between 1969 and 1977*
Amounts in dollars

| State | Governor's salary | | Percentage increase for 8-year period | Average annual percentage increase |
	1969	1977		
California	44,100	49,100	11.3	1.3
Florida	36,000	50,000	38.9	4.2
Georgia	42,500	50,000	17.6	2.0
Illinois	45,000	50,000	11.1	1.3
Louisiana	28,374	50,000	76.2	7.3
Massachusetts	35,000	40,000	14.3	1.7
Michigan	40,000	58,000	45.0	4.8
New Jersey	35,000	65,000	85.7	8.0
New York	50,000	85,000	70.0	6.9
North Carolina	35,000	45,000	28.6	3.2
Ohio	40,000	50,000	25.0	2.8
Pennsylvania	45,000	60,000	33.3	3.7
Texas	55,000	66,800	21.5	2.5
Virginia	30,000	50,000	66.7	6.6
Washington	32,500	42,150	29.7	3.3
Average	39,565	54,070	38.3	4.0
Median	40,000	50,000	29.7	3.3

Sources: *Book of the States, 1970–71*, vol. 18 (Lexington, Ky.: Council of State Governments, 1970), p. 150; *The World Almanac and Book of Facts, 1978* (New York: Newspaper Enterprises Association, 1977), pp. 249–52.

TABLE 6. *Median Percentage Change in Salaries of Chief Executive Officers, Private Sector, 1971–77*

| Industry | Increase | | | Average annual increase, 1971–77 |
	1971–73	1973–75	1975–77	
Manufacturing	10	17	20	7.5
Utilities	9	11	18	6.1
Commercial banks	10	17	17	7.1
Insurance	12	15	16	6.9
Retail	n.a.	13	18	7.5[a]

Source: Harland Fox, *Top Executive Compensation*, Conference Board Report 753 (New York: Conference Board, 1978), p. 9. Year-to-year comparisons were made of the same firms in each period.
n.a. Not available.
a. For 1973–77.

TABLE 7. *Changes in Total Compensation of the Three Highest Paid Executives in Eight Major Companies, 1969–77*
Thousands of dollars unless otherwise specified

Rank	1969	1970	1971	1972	1973	1974	1975	1976	1977	Change, 1969–77 (percent)
Highest paid										
High	480	520	515	813	621	791	657	787	812	…
Low	330	389	394	319	339	392	371	498	534	…
Average	396	444	454	500	480	546	533	623	658	…
Change in average (percent)	…	12.1	2.3	10.1	−4.2	13.8	−2.4	16.9	5.6	66.2
Next highest paid										
High	374	390	399	395	412	526	532	604	638	…
Low	242	219	274	248	260	291	321	353	329	…
Average	313	314	320	338	327	376	410	446	472	…
Change in average (percent)	…	*	1.9	5.6	−3.4	15.0	9.0	8.8	5.8	50.8
Third highest paid										
High	329	288	322	340	396	457	366	n.a.	410	…
Low	146	143	164	186	183	235	264	n.a.	317	…
Average	227	233	253	282	267	314	318	n.a.	371	…
Change in average (percent)	…	2.6	8.6	11.5	−5.6	17.6	1.3	n.a.	16.7[a]	63.4

Sources: Proxy statements of eight companies selected from the *Fortune* list of fifty top companies. Changes in incumbents or changes in bonus awards produce sharp changes upward or downward in total compensation.
n.a. Not available.
* Less than 0.5 percent.
a. For 1975–77.

Part Three

Special Problems

James C. Kirby, Jr.

Federal Conflict of Interest Regulations and Their Relation to Official Compensation

THERE are many federal statutes, regulations, agency codes, and policies governing conflicts of interest that are indirectly related to official compensation in that they preclude specific federal officials and employees from making various types of investments or engaging in income-producing outside activity. This paper will not attempt to include matters unrelated to debatable issues of levels of compensation; it will deal principally with limits on income-producing holdings and investments and limits on compensated outside activities of upper level officials in the executive, judicial, and legislative branches. Conflict of interest regulations will be considered in depth only if they have some bearing on whether a particular class of officials should have their compensation altered because of the regulations' effect on unofficial income. It will become apparent that only in Congress are there currently any seriously debatable issues of conflict of interest that are related to issues of financial compensation.

The recent moves by both houses of Congress to limit the income members may earn for outside services added a new dimension to the concept of conflict of interest at the congressional level. In the past this concept applied only to situations in which the official action of a public official gave the appearance of being motivated by personal economic interests.

The author served as executive director of the Special Committee on Congressional Ethics of the Association of the Bar of the City of New York, which studied the subject of congressional conflict of interest in 1967–69 and issued its report as a book, *Congress and the Public Trust*. The author gratefully acknowledges the valuable and diligent research assistance of New York University law student Susan S. Baker.

There were prohibitions on specific economic interests of executive and judicial officials, but outside activities of members of Congress had not been considered by Congress itself to be a manageable matter for legal prohibitions. The Special Committee on Congressional Ethics of the Association of the Bar of the City of New York, when it studied the entire subject of congressional ethics,[1] gave little serious consideration to prohibitions on outside earned income except for that from law practice and other fiduciary relationships, such as serving as a corporate officer or director. Decisions of members of Congress to deliver speeches for honoraria or to write for royalties only involve "conflicting" interests in that the member may undergo mental conflict in determining whether to use a given period of time for official duty or for personal gain.

The 1977 codes of ethics were a major breakthrough on this front. The 1976 Commission on Executive, Legislative, and Judicial Salaries (the Peterson Commission) had linked proposed salary increases to limits on outside earned income. The new codes for ethical self-regulation that resulted were based on this condition and on consequent acceptance of the full-time nature of the job. Outside activity for income—as opposed to merely holding investments—came to be viewed as a dual evil, threatening both the time and the objectivity of members. In 1970 "moonlighting" was viewed by the Special Committee as an issue more of governmental efficiency than of morality or ethics. Such activity obviously could be at the expense of leisure or family time rather than of the performance of official duties. However, this has come to be viewed both by the public and by Congress as a conflict of interest. The possibility that time is being diverted from official duty and the possibility that the recipient member may develop a sense of obligation to the person or interest group that is the source of the income have become of great importance to the public. Also, the fact that both houses of Congress concluded, by large votes, that limitations on outside income had become necessary is highly persuasive, although many acted reluctantly. The members know best whether such things as honoraria, royalties, legal fees, and compensated corporate directorships actually or potentially endanger the objectivity and independence of judgment to which the public is entitled in congressional decisionmaking.

---

1. Association of the Bar of the City of New York, Special Committee on Congressional Ethics, *Congress and the Public Trust* (Atheneum, 1970).

Holdings and Investments

For every high-level executive official and federal judge, there are modest limits on property holdings, which raise few problems and do not merit extended discussion. For instance, from the nation's beginning, the secretary of the treasury has been prohibited by statute from investing in federal securities.[2] No member of the Interstate Commerce Commission may hold an interest in a common carrier subject to its regulation.[3] Members of the Federal Reserve Board are ineligible to hold any office or position of employment in a bank that is a member of its system.[4] No Federal Communications commissioner may invest in the communications industry or have any official relationship with persons subject to the provisions of the laws enforced by the FCC.[5]

Except for statutory restrictions on law practice, federal law contains few obstacles for the member of Congress who wishes to acquire or continue a particular property interest or business affiliation. The earliest limitation dates from 1808 and prohibits contracts between the federal government and members of Congress.[6] However, it excepts corporations of which members may be stockholders and sales of property if delivery and payment are made when the contract is executed. Thus in the present-day industrial world there is little practical limitation on members of Congress having a financial interest in commercial enterprises that are objects of their legislation. A few minor prohibitions have been added over the years, most of them related to agricultural programs. Other obscure minor prohibitions include bans on the U.S. government's acquisition of land from members for flood-control purposes and the employment of a member by a contractor or charterer who receives subsidies under the Merchant Marine Act of 1936.[7] Legal barriers to outside business involvements of members of Congress are minimal, significantly fewer than those applicable to members of the executive and judicial

2. 1 Stat. 67, as amended, 31 U.S.C. 1003.
3. 49 U.S.C. 11.
4. 12 U.S.C. 242.
5. 47 U.S.C. 154b.
6. 18 U.S.C. 431.
7. 33 U.S.C. 702m; 46 U.S.C. 1223e.

branches. Subject to political considerations and largely self-imposed ethical limitations, members of Congress may take advantage of business opportunities on about the same basis as other citizens.

Outside Earned Income

The Peterson Commission examined the outside activity of officials in all three branches of the federal government and properly concluded: "In the Executive and Judicial branches, outside activities are strictly controlled, and for practical purposes do not constitute an important source of outside income or the potential for conflict of interest."[8]

The judgment of the Peterson Commission is substantially accurate. When people are appointed to the federal bench or to a high executive position, either a specific statute or compelling institutional considerations almost invariably cause them to automatically cease pursuing their regular occupations or professions. Accordingly, for purposes of this paper, it will be assumed that continued participation in outside business or employment, including the practice of law, is not an important issue in the executive and judicial branches.

Federal judges have little problem with the matter of outside activity. They are forbidden to practice law by title 28 of the U.S. Code, section 454. Canon 5C(2) of the Code of Judicial Conduct[9] prohibits service by a judge for remuneration as officer, director, manager, adviser, or employee of any business other than a business wholly owned by members of the judge's family, all of whom are related to the judge or to his or her spouse within a particular degree. Canon 5E prohibits service as an arbitrator or mediator. Certain public service activities may be performed for compensation, particularly those related to the improvement of the legal system, such as writing, lecturing, and teaching. But permissible opportunities are few and not usually lucrative. Federal judges appear to be quite circumspect in this regard, perhaps in part because of the Fortas and Haynesworth incidents.

In Congress the most difficult and controversial provisions of the 1977 codes of ethics of both houses were the general limitations applied to

8. *Report of the Commission on Executive, Legislative, and Judicial Salaries, December 1976* (Government Printing Office, 1977), app. A, p. 86.

9. American Bar Association, *Code of Professional Responsibilities and Code of Judicial Conduct,* as amended August 1976 (ABA, 1976), pp. 61C–62C.

members and officers and employees whose compensation exceeds $35,000: their outside earned income may not exceed 15 percent of their official salary.[10] The principal reason cited is that Congress and the public have come to regard service in Congress as a full-time job. Few, if any, members publicly disagree, although some regard this as unfortunate. The special Senate committee that recommended the code stated:

Senators work long hours devoting a substantial amount of not only their own time, but also time they could be with their families, attending to Senate business on behalf of their constituents. Consistent with these duties is the notion that since service in the Senate is a full-time job, considerable skepticism is often raised in the minds of the public whenever outside income is received by a Senator because of personal services rendered outside regular Senate duties.[11]

The limit on total outside earned income, approximately $8,600 in 1979, is not unreasonable once the fixing of such limits is recognized as within the power of each house of the Congress. Although pending litigation will settle this question, the power granted each house by the Constitution to "punish members for disorderly behavior" will probably be held to include the power to establish reasonable rules defining "orderly behavior."

The distinction between investment income and earned income was frequently cited in the debates as an unfairness in the new regulations. However, members inevitably come to Congress with some form of personal property holdings. They cannot be expected to divest themselves of such holdings and bestow them on the poor. All investments present some potential conflict of interest, but they must be continued in some form. No such rule of necessity justifies allowing continued performance of personal services, which may appear to be at the expense of official duties and is undoubtedly at the expense of public confidence because of the understandable suspicion that payments for such services are used to cultivate special influence.

This does not mean that Congress cannot do more to minimize the conflicts of interest inherent in property holdings. It has ignored the 1970 recommendation of the New York Special Committee that members not be allowed to serve on legislative committees having jurisdiction over areas of their special economic interests. But members can do more by

10. But see footnote 59, below.
11. *Establishing a Code of Official Conduct for Members, Officers and Employees of the U.S. Senate,* S. Rept. 95-49, 95 Cong. 1 sess. (GPO, 1977), pp. 8–9.

diversification and by conversion of assets to investments with relatively low potential for conflicts.

Other exceptions to the limits on outside income in the 1977 codes include royalties from writing books, buy-out arrangements in professional organizations, income from family businesses, and distributive shares of partnership income. The origins and explanations for some of these exceptions are rather obscure and I will not attempt to explore them. It is safe to assume that they do not quantitatively amount to wholesale loopholes in the prohibition on outside earned income.

There are also limits on honoraria. The limit for each speaking appearance or article written is $1,000 for members of both the Senate and the House.[12] The annual aggregate of such fees is subject to the 15 percent total limit. A few members will suffer significant economic loss and bitterly oppose this provision. However, the Senate committee report is pointed and persuasive:

Honoraria for speaking engagements was a focal point of debate in the Committee. The Committee realizes that speechmaking by public figures is an old and honored American tradition. Senators are, in a very real sense, national representatives who can contribute significantly to the public dialogue by leaving Washington and speaking to audiences in states other than their own. At the same time, recent polls reveal that the public views honoraria for speaking engagements with marked concern. The Committee has attempted to balance these considerations by permitting honoraria for speeches, appearances and articles to continue while at the same time cutting back on the overall amount of honoraria a Member can collect in a year and for each appearance.[13]

Any drawing of lines by dollar amounts is necessarily somewhat arbitrary, but the figures selected appear to be reasonable. The aggregate and individual limits should combine to have a salutary effect on public confidence.

Congressional Law Practice

This source of conflict involves what is by far the largest occupational group in Congress. Lawyers consistently make up about 60 percent of its membership. A code of ethics that improves the quality of congressional

12. The original $750 limit in the House ethics code was raised in January 1979.
13. *Establishing a Code*, S. Rept. 95-49, p. 9.

service by its lawyer-members will inevitably result in considerable improvement of the group as a whole.

Discussions of the ethics of lawyers in Congress and in other public offices invariably include a critical reference to Senator Daniel Webster's professional relationship with the Second Bank of the United States. In a letter written as a "private" one in October 1833, the senator suggested to Nicholas Biddle, president of the bank, that the bank might want Webster to call congressional attention to President Jackson's contemplated withdrawal of U.S. deposits from the bank. In December, Webster again wrote to Biddle:

Sir

Since I have arrived here, I have had an application to be concerned, professionally, against the Bank, which I have declined, of course, although I believe my retainer has not been renewed, or *refreshed* as usual. If it be wished that my relation to the Bank should be continued, it may be well to send me the usual retainers.[14]

One may speculate that Webster would have championed the bank's legislative causes with the same vigor had there been no lawyer-client relationship. Neither the existence nor the success of the relationship was any secret. Webster successfully represented the bank in forty-one cases before the Supreme Court.

Webster's example was not approved by at least one other great federal legislator from New England. In 1845 John Quincy Adams was offered $5,000 to argue a constitutional issue on the separation of powers before the Supreme Court. He replied that he had long ago ceased to practice law in federal courts but as a representative would give the prospective client his opinion on the question without charge. He recorded the incident in his diary and added:

It occurs to me that this double capacity of a counsellor in courts of law and a member of a legislative body affords opportunity and temptation for contingent fees of very questionable moral purity. Of one such transaction I had knowledge last winter, which in my mind was tainted with the vilest corruption; and I have heard of others, which I shall not specify, because they are familiarly spoken of as in no wise exceptionable, but for which the only palliation of which I deemed them susceptible is that alleged by Lord Chancellor Bacon in his defence upon his trial before the English House of Peers—that

14. Letters from Daniel Webster to Nicholas Biddle, October 29 and December 21, 1833, in Reginald C. McGrane, ed., *The Correspondence of Nicholas Biddle Dealing with National Affairs* (Houghton Mifflin, 1919), pp. 216–17, 218.

there are "vitia temporum" as well as "vitia hominum." It is a sad contemplation of human nature to observe how the action of the members of legislative bodies may be bought and sold, and how some of the brightest stars in that firmament may pass in occultation without losing their lustre.[15]

However, it was not uncommon during the nineteenth century for members of Congress to represent claimants in agencies and courts against the United States. The first statutory limits on each representation grew from a public scandal created by the law practice of Senator Thomas Corwin of Ohio in the years after the Mexican War. He represented a Dr. Gardiner before the Mexican Claims Commission, claiming damages arising from the alleged destruction of a silver mine. The senator's success in recovering $500,000 for his client received little notice until 1852, when it was revealed that both Dr. Gardiner and the silver mine were frauds. The incident became one of the major public scandals of the period.[16]

A decade later congressional practitioners were representing Civil War soldiers before U.S. Army courts-martial. The utility of such representation was obvious and several members took advantage of it. Others argued publicly and logically that it was unfair because of the power of individual congressmen over the military judges before whom they appeared. Senator Lafayette S. Foster of Connecticut once complained on the Senate floor that in one court-martial a member of Congress serving as defense counsel had expressed dissatisfaction with a ruling of a member of a tribunal and had added, "You expect soon to be promoted, and I give you to understand that your confirmation will not get through the Senate without some difficulty."[17]

By the turn of the century the Populist and Progressive movements were producing widespread dissatisfaction with the power of corporate and moneyed interests in Congress. A part of this evil lay in the acceptance of legal retainers by lawyer-members. In 1906 David Graham Phillips named twenty-one senators in *The Treason of the Senate,* a polemic series that accused the body of betraying the people in favor of spe-

15. *Memoirs of John Quincy Adams, Comprising Portions of His Diary from 1795 to 1848,* Charles Francis Adams, ed. (Lippincott, 1874–77), vol. 12, pp. 224–25.

16. *Congress and the Public Trust,* p. 80.

17. Association of the Bar of the City of New York, Special Committee on the Federal Conflict of Interest Laws, *Conflict of Interest and Federal Service* (Harvard University Press, 1960), pp. 35–36.

cial interests. Sixteen of the twenty-one were lawyers and their private practices were deeply implicated.

The most noteworthy law practice discussed by Phillips was that of Senator Joseph W. Bailey of Texas, who received more than $225,000 in legal fees from a single Texas oil man for services performed over a period of months. Bailey was the only subject of Phillips's attacks to reply publicly. He challenged Phillips on several points but conceded the charges concerning his law practice with a response that probably represented the prevailing senatorial view at the time of the ethics of accepting corporate legal fees.

He says that I practice law successfully, in that I make money. If he will ask my clients, he will also find that I have practiced law successfully in the way of protecting their interests. If that is a crime, it is time the country should know it. Mr. President, I despise those public men who think they must remain poor in order to be considered honest. I am not one of them. If my constituents want a man who is willing to go to the poorhouse in his old age in order to stay in the Senate during his middle age, they will have to find another Senator. I intend to make every dollar that I can honestly make, without neglecting or interfering with my public duty; and there is no other man in this country who would not do the same, if he has sense enough to keep a churchyard.[18]

By 1916 lawyer-members who did not practice had become bolder in denouncing their colleagues who accepted retainers from special interests. In that year Senator William E. Borah openly blamed congressional law practice for the inadequacy of the legislation of the period. In a classic speech to the American Bar Association on the general subject of the responsibilities of lawyers in public office, he said:

I do not believe that a lawyer has any more right, as a matter of correct public service, to hold a retainer while writing a law in the public interest and that a law which may affect his client adversely, than has a judge to hold retainers from those who interests may be affected by the decisions which he renders. . . . Custom has inured us to a different code of ethics, but this custom has brought in its wake many inapt, inefficient statutes, timid and ineffective in their terms, shielding special interests and protecting private advantages . . . because of that timid compromising spirit born of an effort to adjust conditions which cannot be adjusted.[19]

18. *Congressional Record* (June 27, 1906), pp. 9375–76.
19. William E. Borah, "The Lawyer and the Public," *American Bar Association Journal,* vol. 2 (October 1916), pp. 776, 780.

Drew Pearson and Jack Anderson devoted an entire chapter of their 1968 book[20] to lawyers and developed several unsavory cases against individual members, some of which are of unquestionable accuracy.

Law practice has demonstrated a special potential for actual and alleged congressional improprieties and has played a disproportionate role in the history of congressional scandals. A cutting generalization in a standard reference work by a veteran political writer is relevant.

Foremost among these [political practices that raise ethical questions] is the mixed career of the lawyer-legislator. Lawyers lead all other professions in representation in the Congress and in the legislatures. It is accepted practice for a legislator to pursue his legal career and represent clients with a special interest in pending legislation—railroads, unions, manufacturing concerns, highway contractors, defense empires, vending machines, insurance companies. Such arrangements fairly shout "conflict of interest."

The legislator who accepts a $20,000 bribe for pressing a special-interest bill faces a prison term if caught, but the legislator who receives a $20,000 legal fee from a company whose interests he champions in the legislature faces no penalty. He is doing what comes naturally in American politics.[21]

However, in 1969 far fewer lawyers in Congress were found to be in active law practice than was generally assumed.[22] Seventy-one lawyers were among the 120 members interviewed, a 59 percent representation, identical to that of lawyers in the entire Ninetieth Congress. Sixteen of the senators interviewed for the report of the New York Special Committee were lawyers, as were 55 representatives. Only 26 of these 71, or 37 percent, continued any form of law practice.

One significant finding was that lawyer-representatives accounted for a disproportionate share of the members of both houses who continued to practice. A great majority of the Senate's sixty-eight lawyers had completely terminated law practice, and it was concluded that the fraction continuing any form of practice was no greater than one-fourth. In a 1967 survey of lawyer-senators the *St. Louis Post-Dispatch* located only seventeen with any involvement in law practice.[23] The committee concluded

20. *The Case Against Congress: A Compelling Indictment of Corruption on Capitol Hill* (Simon and Schuster, 1968).

21. Fletcher Knebel, "The Economics of Politics," *1968 World Book Yearbook,* pp. 62, 68–69.

22. The succeeding material concerning law practices in 1969 is based on *Congress and the Public Trust,* pp. 86–117.

23. "Congressmen and Private Law Practice," *St. Louis Post-Dispatch,* November 12, 1967.

that no more than ten or twelve senators received substantial income from such practice. Almost none actually performed legal services to any significant degree. It was notable that fourteen of the seventeen practicing senators were from states east of the Mississippi River.

The fact that in the House between 35 and 45 percent of the lawyers continued to practice called for close analysis, which was done empirically on the basis of the interviews. Two important variables were revealed, which continue to cause more representatives than senators to practice law.

The first relevant factor is length of service. Law practice by members of the House varied almost inversely according to length of service and was virtually, though not totally, nonexistent among senior members. Ten of the sixteen representatives, or 63 percent, who continued to practice had served three terms or less. At four terms the incidence of law practice dropped sharply. Of the thirty-nine who had served four terms or more, only fourteen, or 36 percent, continued to practice. Only one of the six most senior representatives interviewed, all of whom had served fifteen terms or more, continued law practice in any form.

It was concluded that abstention from law practice was the behavioral norm of a majority of all senators and of a majority of the representatives who had begun to climb the seniority ladder. These presumably were beginning to find their congressional work both more demanding and more rewarding. They also enjoyed the advantages of incumbents in election years and were gaining in the prestige and expertise that enhanced both their congressional careers and their opportunities for profitable return to private life if it became necessary.

In other words, representatives whose situation had become comparable to that of senators tended to follow the senatorial abstention from law practice. Some of the junior representatives who continued to practice were only doing so tentatively until they were reelected once or twice. Others were gradually phasing out their practices. Still, a sizable group planned to continue indefinitely.

In addition to length of service, geography emerged as an apparent explanation of continued law practice by representatives. Practicing lawyers generally account for much of the so-called Tuesday to Thursday Club, which consists largely of members from eastern states who historically have been enabled by proximity to spend long weekends in their districts.

Practicing lawyer-representatives in the interview sample were sharply divided according to whether their districts were located east or west of the Mississippi River, as shown by the following table:

	East		West		Total	
	Number	Percent	Number	Percent	Number	Percent
Practicing	21	58	3	16	24	44
Nonpracticing	15	42	16	84	31	56
Total	36	100	19	100	55	100

The salient fact to emerge was that law practice in the House is a function of geography, just as in the Senate. If continued practice is a benefit either to the profession or to the public, it is a blessing that falls unevenly across the nation. Of the twenty-four practicing representatives, only three came from states west of the Mississippi. If law practice is detrimental to efficient congressional service, eastern constituencies suffer disproportionately.

The advantage proximity gave easterners to combine professional and congressional careers may have accounted for the unusually large number of practicing lawyers among the members from such states as New York, Connecticut, and New Jersey. New York's forty-one members of the House included twenty-eight lawyers, slightly above the national average, seventeen of whom continued to practice. Connecticut's eight members were all lawyers, five of whom continued to practice. Six of the ten lawyers in the fifteen-member New Jersey delegation had practices. It is interesting, too, that four of the six senators from these states were among the minority of lawyer-senators who continued to practice.

This suggests that some members may have been attracted to congressional service in part because it permitted outside law practice, unlike most other full-time public service. The next question is whether discouraging such law practice might deter lawyers from seeking election. This is answered by comparing the number of lawyers in delegations from western states who have little potential for continuing practice. A count produced the following percentages of lawyers in delegations by East-West analysis:

	Senate	House	Total
East (327 members)	78	60	62
West (208 members)	58	51	53
Total (535 members)	68	57	59

The disparity between eastern and western delegations may be signifi-cant. Of the delegations from the twenty-five eastern states, 62 percent were lawyers; of the western delegations only 53 percent were. The con-venience of continuing to practice law may partially account for this dif-ference. Of more significance, however, is the fact that a majority of the western delegations were lawyers, despite their demonstrated low poten-tial for continued practice. This should establish that discouraging the practice of law by members of Congress will hardly cause the profession to be underrepresented though it may reduce the possibility of overrepre-sentation.

A major obstacle to actual law practice by a member is that it is severely limited by title 18 of the U.S. Code, section 203a. This statute had its ori-gin in the previously mentioned Dr. Gardiner incident and prohibits a member of Congress from receiving direct or indirect compensation for representation in "any proceeding . . . in which the United States is a party or has a direct and substantial interest, before any department, agency, court martial, officer, or any civil, military, or naval commission." More specific statutes prevent members from practicing before the U.S. Court of Claims and the Indian Claims Commission[24] and, as mentioned, bar their employment by beneficiaries of maritime subsidies. These laws should effectively insulate vast areas of typical law practice. The represen-tation of clients before such federal administrative agencies as the Securi-ties and Exchange Commission, the Interstate Commerce Commission, the National Labor Relations Board, and the Federal Trade Commission is forbidden. And representation is precluded in tax matters before the Internal Revenue Service and all matters handled by the Department of Justice and other executive departments. A major portion of the normal activity of most urban law firms is representation of the type legally for-bidden to members of Congress.

One must therefore speculate about whether the practices of a firm in which a member of Congress is a partner are actually so limited. In *Congress and the Public Trust* the committee concluded that section 203 is sometimes circumvented by the use of bookkeeping arrangements under which the firm accepts the prohibited federal practice but the partnership agreement precludes the member of Congress from receiving any part of the income so derived. It also found one instance of two firms operating under a "double door" or "dual partnership" arrangement in which the

24. 18 U.S.C. 204, originally enacted as 12 Stat. 766; 25 U.S.C. 70o.

member's name appeared only in a firm that purportedly handled the non-federal matters permitted by section 203. Such arrangements have been encouraged by a 1943 ruling of the attorney general, which indicated that, so long as the federal official does not personally share in the particular fees, section 203 is not violated if his partners render the services he is forbidden to perform. The appearance of such arrangements is of more doubtful propriety, and this has caused the obvious ones to draw deserved public criticism.[25]

Without such dual arrangements, both the member and his firm are clearly limited to nonfederal practice and should decline federal business, referring regular clients to other lawyers. Fully honoring section 203 would impose such restrictions on the firm's services that many clients might be deterred. It may be, however, that there are still sufficient non-federal areas of the law to make it worthwhile to maintain some congressional law practices.

Most interviewees who purported to be practicing law admitted that they performed no professional services. When questioned about the nature of the services they personally rendered to their firms or to clients, most were quick to disclaim any drain on their working time. They often added that their names brought business to their firms or that they referred business to the firm in exchange for a share of its income. Many of those who admitted to actually practicing claimed that estate and real-estate work accounted for most of their services. The term "consultation" was sometimes used.

Junior representatives who were phasing out practice or clinging to a foothold in their firms until reelection gave them greater security accounted for the largest incidence of practitioners in the House. Senior representatives and senators who continued to practice usually gave as a reason a need for supplemental income or the safeguard of having a firm to rejoin in case of defeat.

The second reason—the need for a cushion against defeat—is the most difficult to analyze. Some practitioners genuinely believed they would have difficulty returning to law practice if they did not maintain a law firm connection. This may be understandable in some cases, but experience is generally the opposite. A 1954 study of the American legal profession included a survey of lawyers in politics by Harry W. Jones of Columbia University, which found that lawyers' unique ease in reentering private life helps account for the large number of them in Congress. It said:

25. *Congress and the Public Trust*, pp. 111–15.

A lawyer can leave his practice for two years or six, or for an even longer time, with some assurance that he can return to his practice with professional skills unimpaired and with the prospect of newly attracted clients to replace those he might have lost during his years in Washington.[26]

The fact that most members do not find it necessary to continue law practice while in Congress is evidence that it is not essential for the small minority who do. The majority therefore deserves analysis. In general, they have more seniority and more of them are from the West, but otherwise the nonpracticing majority of lawyers in Congress have little in common. They are both liberal and conservative, Republican and Democratic, rural and urban. Some are wealthy, but many are of extremely modest means. Political considerations unquestionably influence many members. A congressman's continuing to practice law could well be a liability and seldom, if ever, a political asset. Lawyers who lose business and laymen whose interests conflict with those of the congressman's clients might understandably complain.

Apart from political considerations, many members of Congress genuinely believe they cannot practice law without raising insurmountable conflict of interest problems. A veteran lawyer-senator, who had not practiced since his election, said in an interview: "I don't think a Senator or Congressman should practice law, whatever the protective arrangements. There is a threat of conflict of interest every day. You can't even probate an estate now without some Federal involvement."[27] A letter of March 5, 1968, to the Special Committee from Democratic Congressman David Henderson of North Carolina included similar judgments:

In the second place, with the Federal government these days doing business or otherwise acting in a way that affects virtually every phase of commerce, business, and even our everyday lives, how can a member of Congress possibly be free of conflict of interest if he is practicing law? And what does he do in case of conflict of interest? Obviously, he cannot decline to vote on an issue or decline to participate in committee consideration of an issue if he represents a client who has a direct or indirect interest in the subject matter, and if he turns away every prospective client who may or might possibly some day have an interest in a matter before the Congress, I simply do not see how he can practice law.[28]

26. Albert P. Blaustein and Charles O. Porter, *The American Lawyer: A Summary of the Survey of the Legal Profession* (University of Chicago Press, 1954), p. 98.
27. *Congress and the Public Trust*, p. 97.
28. Ibid., pp. 98–99.

The reason most frequently cited by nonpracticing members was the full-time nature of congressional service. Many interviewees pointed out the increasing demands on their time and could not believe that any member of Congress could simultaneously practice law and do justice to congressional duties. Such members frequently went on to state their personal moral objections to other members' trading on congressional office by allowing a law firm to use their names although they did not actually practice. Surely, these factors are even more important now than in 1970, when *Congress and the Public Trust* was published. They were rarely mentioned but are probably felt by many nonpractitioners, who also believe it is a matter of conscience and do not want to endanger their effectiveness with their congressional colleagues. Other nonpracticing members are surprisingly suspicious and resentful of the relatively few who have law practice arrangements. They do not believe that these few are actually practicing, and many of them view congressional law practitioners as influence-peddling or improperly trading on public office for private gain, or both.

The debilitating effect of law practice on a member's effectiveness was stated eloquently by Senator Borah in 1916.

If a legislator should feel that the rights of some great corporate interests were being unjustly assailed, if he should feel that some law which seemed to favor interests then under public censure was entitled to his support, he would be perfectly powerless to be of any service to them if it was known that he held a retainer from those engaged in a similar kind of business. In other words, it is just as important that the legislator be free from entanglements and those associations which seem to direct his actions in order that he may do justice to the business and corporate interests of the country as that he may do justice to the public. If he feels called upon to make a fight for the rights of those under public censure I cannot imagine his being fitted for that fight unless he is wholly disengaged in every conceivable way from any business or personal interest in the result.[29]

The practicing lawyer is inevitably suspect when he champions the legislative interests of a client. His colleagues understandably cannot know whether he is motivated by the public interest or the client's interest. This alone should be sufficient reason for members to avoid law practice.

Most congressional law practice is believed to be what one nonpracticing senator called a "facade." When the quadrennial commission method

29. "The Lawyer and the Public," p. 782.

of setting congressional salaries was being debated in 1968, Senator John Pastore said in its defense:

Let me say that many Senators have to depend upon their Senate salary to live. They have to maintain two homes. They cannot practice law, if they are lawyers, because that would subject them to conflict of interest.

We can go around making speeches and lectures. That gives us a little money. Or we can get tied up with *a law firm where we would not do any work, but just have our names on the door, and receive some form of compensation.* Those who are lawyers but do not choose to do this have a right to stand up and say, "This is what I think we are worth." . . .

The idea seems to be prevalent that we have got to make big money in order to stay in the Senate with all its demands, unless we happen to come in here as wealthy men, unless we happen to have oil wells, or own a television station, or a radio station, or *a law practice which is only a facade.*[30]

The difficulty with facade practice is identifying the quid pro quo received by the law firm or its clients. This was pointed out in 1951 as a problem of congressional ethics by a subcommittee chaired by Senator Paul H. Douglas. After discussing the inadequacy of congressional salaries and allowances and the need for supplemental incomes, the subcommittee's report said:

The upshot is that a majority of the Members of Congress find it necessary to supplement their salary in some way. Were Congress meeting but 6 months or less a year, as it once did, there would be no serious difficulty, but membership is now practically a year-round activity, which, with the duties of campaigning, leaves little time to engage in business or professional activities. Members who are lawyers may accept fees or retainers for giving advice and counsel or for other legal services. But they have little time for very extensive service and if their duties become perfunctory, the question always arises, are they being paid for their influence and to influence their perspective? Men who pay legal retainers expect to get something for their money.[31]

When the American Bar Association canons were revised in 1969, the profession dealt expressly with the ethics of permitting law firms to display the names of full-time public officials. The public is likely to be confused about the performance of legal services by the official and about the special influence that the firm and its clients may be presumed to have with the official. The present Code of Professional Responsibility deals expressly with such facades in disciplinary rule 2-102(B), which states:

A lawyer who assumes a judicial, legislative, or public executive or administrative post or office shall not permit his name to remain in the name of a

30. *Congressional Record* (July 18, 1968), p. 22010. Emphasis added.
31. *Ethical Standards in Government,* Report of a Subcommittee of the Senate Committee on Labor and Public Welfare, 82 Cong. 1 sess. (GPO, 1951), p. 25.

law firm or to be used in professional notices of the firm during any significant period in which he is not *actively and regularly* practicing law as a member of the firm, and during such period other members of the firm shall not use his name in the firm name or in professional notices of the firm.[32]

The facade practices can be neither "active" nor "regular." Nor is the rule satisfied by professional notices that hint at the congressman's limited participation. Such terms as "of counsel," "retired," and "inactive" can no longer be used to imply the association of inactive congressional lawyers. Active and regular practice is a condition for any use of a member's name in professional notices of a firm.

The new rules of ethics were so clear on this point that facade practitioners either terminated their relationships or escalated their levels of practice activity—if they complied with the new code. Otherwise they risked disciplinary action by the bar. Those who actually engage in active practice despite its political dangers have already been shown to be few. Compliance with the new ethical code should have eliminated most law practice by members of Congress.

Based on personal congressional and professional experience, the research that produced *Congress and the Public Trust,* and the historical record, I strongly concur with the judgment of senators and representatives who refrain from all law practice because of its inherent conflicts of interest. This restraint prevents a public official from acting on matters in which he has a personal pecuniary interest. Should a lawyer in Congress be allowed to legislate on matters in which his clients are interested? Stated differently, is the relationship between lawyer and client such that the two should be treated as having a community of interests? If so, the lawyer-member should not be allowed to act on his client's interests and should avoid such relationships. It unnecessarily places his voting record in what has been called an area of "invited distrust" by former American Bar Association President Ross L. Malone. He once said of lawyer-legislators in general:

Inevitably, however, the legislature is going to consider proposed legislation affecting clients represented by the lawyer-legislator. Some of them will be regular clients of his office. He may have accepted an annual retainer from others. While accepting a retainer in no sense involves a surrender of independence of either thought or action on the part of a lawyer, it is not realistic to say that he has the same freedom of choice on matters affecting the client that would exist in the absence of such an arrangement. Regardless of the

32. ABA, *Code of Professional Responsibility,* p. 10C. Emphasis added.

subjective effect upon him and his vote as a legislator, it is certain that the public would never believe—nor could it be expected to believe—that his vote would not be affected by his relationship with his client. A lawyer voting as a legislator on matters affecting the interests of a retained client invites justified criticism, if not distrust, not only of the lawyer but of the legal profession itself.[33]

Malone's analysis is addressed largely to appearances and to the possibility that legislative judgment will be impaired. The point can be carried an important step further—to *actual* as opposed to merely *potential* subordination of the public's interest to clients' interests by lawyers in public service. Senator Borah did this with considerable professional insight when he said:

The relationship of client and attorney is the closest. Consciously or unconsciously he comes to feel that his client's demands are wholly just. Yet men will argue that a lawyer with a thirty or forty thousand dollar retainer from some client is perfectly fitted to shape legislation which his client will argue is all wrong, wholly unjust and vitally injurious to his business interests. I am not speaking now of a conscious corruption which some people assume to take place in legislation more often, perhaps, than it does. There is no occasion for conscious, open, affirmative corruption for which some one may be sent to the penitentiary when the same thing can be accomplished by that unconscious and subtle influence for which there is no punishment and which may even be justified by good people. Suppose every lawyer in the legislatures of the country or in Congress were in the employ of those great business interests engaged in interstate commerce. What do you think would be the necessity of employing lobbyists in order that no laws seriously affecting interests might be passed? A member of Congress is in an indefensible position who is called upon to legislate concerning those matters in which his clients may have an interest and which may concern them vitally.[34]

In both theory and actuality the lawyer-client relationship is such that it is unrealistic to expect lawyers to subordinate their clients' interests when they make decisions as trustees of the public's interest. Temporarily removing the lawyer's hat to put on a public-service hat does not satisfy the ethics of either pursuit.

Accordingly, the New York Special Committee, composed entirely of lawyers, several of whom had notable backgrounds in Washington, concluded unanimously that no member of Congress should practice law except perhaps for a transitional period while phasing out private practice.

33. "The Lawyer and His Professional Responsibilities," *Washington and Lee Law Review,* vol. 17 (Fall 1960), p. 206.
34. "The Lawyer and the Public," pp. 780–81.

It was not recommended that a statute or rule embodying a total prohibition be adopted, but it was recommended that all members voluntarily follow the example of the great majority of their fellow lawyer-members by voluntarily terminating law practice. Since the report relied heavily on disciplinary rule 2-102(B) and implied that most if not all members who continued to practice would be in violation of their profession's state ethical code, it was assumed that there would be widespread voluntary terminations of law practice.

The number of congressional practitioners has been reduced significantly, but the level is still too high and the expectations of the committee have not been fully realized. Congressional financial disclosure reports show that a substantial number are continuing to allow law firms in their home districts to use their names. Common Cause made an effort to induce all practicing members to terminate their practices, but did not pursue this project aggressively. State bar associations have apparently been reluctant to threaten practicing lawyer-members with discipline under rule 2-102(B).

The Senate financial disclosures in the past have not indicated sources of income, so it could not be determined whether any senators were still receiving income from law firms. However, it is believed that senatorial law practice has been virtually eliminated. The only recent instance of a senator's being embarrassed by law practice was when it was revealed that Gulf Oil had Senator Hugh Scott of Pennsylvania on a legal retainer,[35] a disclosure that some believed to be a cause of his failure to seek reelection in 1976.

The rules of the House of Representatives required disclosure of the existence of law practice income in excess of $1,000.[36] In 1969 eighty-one members of the House reported such income.[37] By 1974 the figure had dropped to seventy-six, by 1976 to sixty-five, and by 1977 to thirty-seven. Of the 1976 total, forty-one were not freshmen (many of them were quite senior), who were in compliance with rule 2-102(B) only if they were "actively and regularly practicing law." But if they were in compliance, it is hardly consistent with the claims that congressional service is a full-time job, a major basis for the recent salary increase.

35. "Scott Retires," *Congressional Quarterly,* vol. 33 (December 6, 1975), p. 2657.
36. New rules for calendar year 1978 called for the source and amount of earned income aggregating $100 or more.
37. This and the following disclosure figures are based on *Congressional Quarterly* reports.

Investigation was made in June 1978 of readily available public information on fifteen of the forty-one nonfreshman members of the House who had reported in 1977 receiving legal fees in 1976. It produced some interesting and disturbing results. Ten of the fifteen were allowing their names to be used by law firms and were therefore either violating rule 2-102(B) with impunity or actively and regularly engaging in the practice of law, possibly at the expense of their congressional duties.

There was wide variation among these ten in their firms' open exploitation of congressional office. Two had their district congressional offices and law firms at the same address. In the *Martindale-Hubbell Law Directory,* the principal national directory of lawyers, six were included in the detailed listings that describe a firm's practice and provide biographical sketches of individual partners. The biographical sketches of representatives always included some reference to their congressional positions. Four simply stated that so-and-so had been a congressman since a certain date. Another indicated membership in the House Appropriations Committee. That of the most senior member of the group set forth present and past committee memberships and chairmanships dating back to 1937. Several firms announced specialization in areas of federal law and listed clients who obviously have federal legislative interests.

The limits on outside earned income may alleviate the problem of congressional law practice but do not solve it. Some lawyers have indicated that they will incorporate their practices to convert their earned income to dividends and avoid the new rule. Another possibility is that a firm might pay a House member the total limit of 15 percent of official salary for the use of his name, anticipating possible return to the firm. The Senate's rule is the most effective in countering this. In addition to applying the 15 percent limit to legal fees, it permits senators and employees to practice any profession only if they are not affiliated with any firm and if their work is not carried out during Senate office hours.

Gifts and Unofficial Office Accounts

The new codes for both houses of Congress contain new and tighter restrictions on gifts to members, which vary slightly in terminology. These restrictions may substantially affect the financial situations of some members, such as millionaire Senator Herman E. Talmadge, who has admitted to regularly receiving sums in cash from personal friends in his constituency. However, the impropriety of such gifts is so indisputable, in my opinion, that strict rules against them do not merit extended analysis.

Briefly, the House code prohibits any member, officer, or employee of the House from accepting gifts aggregating $100 or more in value in any one calendar year from any lobbyist or lobbying organization or from foreign nationals or their agents. The Senate adopted the same dollar limit but defined prohibited donors in slightly more detail. Gifts for unofficial office accounts to senators who are not independently wealthy may be more defensible, but for the same reasons they too should be condemned.

The prohibition on such accounts will undoubtedly affect the financial situation of a number of members. The accounts add to the already in-flated financial advantages of incumbents over challengers. Some members have justified unofficial accounts in the past on the grounds that their office allowances were inadequate. Some have spent personal funds to supplement official appropriated allowances. At the same time, however, an undetermined number have been able to employ persons like Elizabeth Ray. She apparently served only as mistress to Congressman Wayne L. Hays, performing few or no official duties, and so could call her book *The Washington Fringe Benefit.*

The Efficacy of Congressional Ethics Codes

The generally low level of public confidence in government officials applies especially to the Congress. Polls show it to be ranked among the lowest in public esteem. The likelihood that the major response of Congress—the adoption of codes of ethics to be enforced by committees in each house—will change this is debatable. The purpose of this section is to assess the efficacy of those codes and to determine whether they may prove to be largely unenforceable. Past congressional experience is the principal basis for prognosis.

The History of Congressional Self-Discipline

The duty and power of Congress to discipline its own members stems from Article I of the Constitution, section 5, clause 1, which states that each house of Congress "shall be the Judge of the Elections, Returns and Qualifications of its own Members," and clause 2, which states: "Each

House may . . . punish its Members for disorderly behavior, and, with the Concurrence of two thirds, expel a Member."

The authority to discipline members for misbehavior was thought by the framers of the Constitution to be essential to the effectiveness of each house as an independent, deliberative lawmaking body. It is one of the provisions that were thought necessary to constitute Congress as a separate and coequal branch of the federal government. Another is the congressional immunity provided by the Speech and Debate Clause, which protects members from being questioned elsewhere about their official conduct. These provisions were intended to free Congress and individual members from possible harassment and usurpations by other branches of the government. However, a member would enjoy total license to abuse this immunity if each house were not given the power and responsibility to deal with a member's conduct. If Congress does not police itself, its members are above the law in the areas protected by congressional immunity, a concept alien to our legal system and never intended by the framers of the Constitution.

The power of the voters to deny reelection to an aberrant member is the most effective form of discipline and has sometimes functioned well. However, it is not foolproof: recent reelections of members who had been reprimanded by the House or indicted or convicted on criminal charges are evidence of this.[38] The continued presence in Congress of an errant legislator was not intended to be a matter solely for his or her constituents, who are often influenced by special favors their district has received. At some point the entire nation, as represented by all the members of the House or of the Senate, has an interest that may override the wishes of a single constituency.

The sanctions used most recently by Congress are innocuous. Those available for congressional self-discipline range from exclusion and expulsion to lesser punishments that allow the member to remain in office.

Expulsion. Each house may expel a duly elected and seated member by two-thirds vote. The Constitution places no express limits or qualifications on this power; its apparent intent is that expulsion can be imposed for any reason a house feels to be sufficient. (Impeachment was not provided for members of Congress, because the plenary power to expel was

38. Subsequent denial of committee chairmanships by the party caucus may help bring about the retirement of a reelected miscreant. Robert L. F. Sikes was reelected to the House in 1976 after a reprimand and then stripped of his chairmanship. He did not run in 1978.

regarded as its equivalent.) Rightly or wrongly, Congress has been extremely reluctant to use this power. Except during the Civil War, when twenty-two senators (all but one from the South) were expelled for disloyalty, the Senate has expelled only one duly elected member: in 1797 Senator William Blount of Tennessee was expelled for scheming with British agents in their dealings with Indians. The House has used the power of expulsion even more guardedly. The three expulsions of representatives were on grounds of treason and occurred at the beginning of the Civil War.

Exclusion. In pronouncing a member-elect to be unqualified and excluding him, both houses have occasionally used this power as the equivalent of expulsion. Exclusion, an exercise of the authority of Congress over its members' elections, was not intended to be a disciplinary measure. The exclusion issue arises most frequently—and most appropriately—in the resolution of election contests, where a house acts as a supreme board of elections, not as a guardian of congressional ethics. On rare occasions, however, both houses have used the power to reject duly elected persons who were found to be unfit to serve. Such exclusions were based on ethical determinations and served obvious disciplinary functions.

The most recent of such exclusions, that of Representative Adam Clayton Powell, produced a Supreme Court decision that conclusively restored exclusion to its proper constitutional and congressional place. By 1967 the accumulated charges against Powell were indiscretion in private life, excessive absenteeism and junketing, contempt of New York courts, misuse of public funds, and erratic behavior as a committee chairman. When Congress convened in 1968, the House rejected a special committee's recommendation that he be seated but censured and fined. Powell was excluded by a vote of 307 to 116, despite express recognition in the resolution of exclusion that he possessed the requisite constitutional qualifications of age, citizenship, and inhabitancy of his district.[39]

Powell brought suit in the U.S. District Court for the District of Columbia, alleging that the House's action was unconstitutional. The district court granted the defendants' motions to dismiss, and the Court of Appeals for the District of Columbia Circuit affirmed. The Supreme Court reversed the decision,[40] agreeing with Powell's contention that the Con-

39. See *Congress and the Public Trust,* pp. 205–11, for a fuller discussion of the Powell case.

40. *Powell* v. *McCormack,* 395 U.S. 486 (1969).

stitution gives the people the right to be represented by whomever they choose, subject only to the mandatory qualifications of age, citizenship, and inhabitancy. These are the sole criteria for judgment by the House when a duly elected candidate appears for membership. The Court's reasoning did not affect the ultimate power of Congress to dissociate itself from an errant member by expelling him or her. It wisely confined itself to this one case and emphasized that it was not ruling on the plenary power of the House to expel a seated member by two-thirds vote.

Other sanctions. Powell was seated when reelected but fined $25,000.[41] This was unprecedented, but he did not challenge it. Although the power to punish has usually taken the form only of censure or reprimand, traditional remedies of criminal law were undoubtedly contemplated by the framers when they used the term "punish." They intended that Congress should exercise essentially adjudicative functions over congressional misconduct that is insulated by the Constitution from the judicial branch. Imprisonment of a member is even possible.

Congress has also used the sanctions of censure and reprimand sparingly. Only eighteen House members have been censured and even fewer reprimanded, three as a result of the recent "Koreagate" scandals. The Senate has used this power against only eight members, the most recent cases being those of Joseph R. McCarthy in 1954, Thomas J. Dodd in 1967, and Herman E. Talmadge in 1979.

The 1968 ethics committees and codes. It was not until 1968 that Congress adopted its first formal codes of conduct, and then it acted reluctantly under public pressure caused by official scandal.

The Senate code had its origins in the case of Robert G. Baker, who resigned as secretary to the Democratic majority in 1963 after it was discovered that he had misused his office for personal financial gain. The Senate then unanimously authorized its Committee on Rules and Administration to investigate the financial interests of Senate employees. Based on its findings, the Rules Committee recommended a rule requiring limited disclosure of assets and income by both employees and senators. The committee divided along party lines on the adequacy of the Baker findings but was unanimous on the disclosure recommendations.

On the floor, Republicans proposed a substitute amendment creating a bipartisan ethics committee. Senator Karl E. Mundt of South Dakota spoke for more of his compatriots than their later voting indicated.

---

41. H. Res. 2, *Congressional Record* (January 3, 1969), pp. 21–22.

I shall be happy to vote for the Cooper substitute, because it is fair and impartial, it is an objective, nonpolitical way of going about the job of snooping on one another, if there exists a prevailing opinion that this should be done to make the U.S. Senate appear decent and honorable and respectable. . . . This is no way to build up mutual respect and amity within a legislative body. If we do not trust each other, let us then adopt the amendment . . . and at least keep the process clean and equitable insofar as politics are concerned.[42]

Mundt then joined thirty-two other senators in an unsuccessful attempt to defeat the substitute.

The Select Committee on Standards and Conduct was authorized in July 1964, but it was not appointed until July 1965 and did not begin to function until October. Although its jurisdiction was considerably broader, the committee at first concerned itself only with Baker's misconduct. This was interrupted by the Dodd case, with which the committee was preoccupied until July 1967. After Dodd had been censured for misuse of campaign funds, the committee resumed its study of ethics and finally recommended a code to the Senate in March 1968. The code was not complete; it dealt mainly with the issues raised by the Dodd and Baker cases. It also did not require the degree of public financial disclosure that had been recommended by the Rules Committee. A proposed amendment calling for fuller disclosure was defeated, 44–40.

In July 1966 the Joint Committee on the Organization of the Congress recommended that the House follow the Senate's example by creating an ethics committee. Influenced by this and the Powell case, the House Rules Committee voted out a resolution to establish such a committee. The resolution met its most vigorous opposition from Representative Wayne Hays, who referred to it as suicidal "self-immolation."[43] House members originally appeared to agree with Hays and quickly tabled the resolution by voice vote. But when a roll-call vote became necessary, the House reversed itself and kept the issue alive by a vote of 238–24. The resolution was then amended to create a study committee charged with recommending a code of ethics. This was approved unanimously. The House Select Committee on Standards and Conduct had only two and one-half months to function, however, and it was able to do nothing more than recommend its reestablishment in the succeeding Congress. This was achieved by a unanimous vote after Powell was excluded.

42. *Congressional Record* (July 24, 1964), pp. 16934–35.
43. *Congressional Record* (October 19, 1966), p. 27717.

The new committee (now called Standards of Official Conduct) proposed in March 1968 that it be made permanent and that the House adopt an incomplete recommended code that contained limited disclosure rules. With one dissenting vote, the resolution was adopted.

Thus by 1968 both houses had created permanent watchdog committees to enforce ethics codes. Almost four years had passed since Senator John Sherman Cooper of Kentucky had first called for such a committee. The Baker and Dodd cases in the Senate and the Powell case in the House were viewed as minimal cosmetic measures designed to satisfy an aroused public. Despite many members' misgivings and objections, new systems of self-discipline, purportedly designed to overcome the historic inertia of Congress, had become parts of the rules and superficial facts of congressional life. However, the fact that Congress had embraced these codes and committees only because of public opinion and its own demonstrated reluctance to use self-discipline were to be major factors in the future effectiveness of the new codes.

It is not possible here to outline in detail the work of the two ethics committees from their conception. But close observers of Congress have agreed that they were virtually useless. Some critics even felt they performed a positive disservice by creating the misleading illusion in some cases that alleged misconduct was being seriously evaluated, by defusing some issues by letting them die in committee, and by perhaps creating the false impression that there was general compliance with a new and higher level of congressional ethical performance. The following is but one example of criticism of the House committee's work and effectiveness:

In April 1975, Rep. Fred Rooney (D., Pa.) asked the Ethics Committee to determine whether there was any impropriety in his having accepted from Bethlehem Steel Corp. free airplane flights to and from his district, or in accepting from TWA free flights for himself and his wife to Málaga, a seaside resort in Spain. It has long been standard operating procedure for House members whose conduct is questioned to put the issue to the House Ethics Committee. Routinely, the committee does little or no investigating and either drops the case for lack of evidence or issues a ruling—carefully worded so as to avoid any embarrassment to the member—on the *kind* of conduct which is questioned. This traditional procedure allows members to tell the press, as Rooney did, "I have been completely vindicated by the (Ethics) committee."

On Rooney's question about free flights, the Ethics Committee issued a ruling saying that it is O.K. for members to accept free flights home on corporate jets if the plane is going their way. The flight Rooney and his wife had taken to Málaga was an inaugural run for a new TWA route, and so the committee also said it is O.K. for members to accept free promotional inaugural flights.

The Ethics Committee overlooked the fact that Rooney was a member of the Commerce Committee, which had jurisdiction over airline regulation, and that shortly after accepting the free flights from TWA, Rooney had voted to approve an airmail rate increase worth $15 million to $20 million to TWA.[44]

The 1977 codes.[45] The national mood following Watergate was seized upon by critics of Congress, who urged it to put itself in order while it was forcing other branches of the government to new and higher standards and tests of levels of ethical behavior. This factor, combined with the severe need for salary increases, provided the opportunity in 1977 to extract from Congress new codes and stronger enforcement mechanisms in exchange for the pay increase recommended by the Peterson Commission.

The purported comprehensiveness and stringency of the new ethics codes even satisfied Common Cause. They included—besides the previously discussed limits on outside earnings, gifts, and unofficial office accounts—new restrictions on foreign travel and the mailing frank, and they required fuller disclosure of personal financial holdings.

Both houses rejected strong recommendations that public representatives or independent enforcement mechanisms be included to ensure that the new codes are actually observed and enforced. Each wanted enforcement to be the responsibility of committees composed of its own members. The Senate, by a vote of 47–26, defeated an amendment sponsored by Senator William V. Roth, Jr., of Delaware for the creation of a three-member commission of private citizens to investigate allegations of misconduct by senators and Senate employees. Roth argued that "history has shown that it is very difficult for any small group to really investigate the conduct of its own Members" and perceptively added that "the ethics problem in Congress has not been a lack of laws or rules, but a lack of enforcement."[46]

The Prognosis for Effective Congressional Enforcement

There is good reason to fear that Congress will continue to be reluctant to discipline itself and to doubt that congressional conduct will be much altered by the 1977 codes. In the opinion of many, Congress acted in 1977

44. Edward Roeder and Alan Berlow, "John Flynt: Fox in the Chicken Coop," *The Nation* (September 10, 1977), p. 203.

45. The new codes are embodied in S. Res. 110 and H. Res. 287.

46. *Congressional Record,* daily edition (March 25, 1977), p. S4880.

primarily because the Peterson Commission had tied its recommendation for congressional salary increases to the adoption of effective codes of conduct. The commission recognized the need for salary increases to attract qualified people to positions throughout the federal government but concluded that Congress dare not increase its own salaries without taking measures to restore public trust in government. Under extreme pressure from the leadership, many members voted for the new codes without believing in their need or efficacy. Senator Gaylord Nelson, the floor manager of the code in the Senate, admitted publicly that many senators voted for the measure only because they feared the political hazards of a negative vote.[47]

There are strong indications that Congress is not really serious about enforcing the new codes, and Common Cause has already accused it of "backsliding" on ethics.[48] In the Senate, the old and largely inactive ethics committee was replaced by a new committee headed by Adlai E. Stevenson III, who seriously and persuasively expressed a determination that the committee would be effective. But Senator Stevenson himself has been quoted as saying that he could not be "enthusiastic about what we are doing," in part because "it is not going to guarantee any more faithful service and it's not going to guarantee that the government is going to be any more innovative or bold." However, he demonstrated a serious commitment to the work of the committee and said at the time of the adoption of the code, "I am determined I am going to make this thing work."[49]

Two of the committee's six members, Harrison H. Schmitt of New Mexico and Lowell P. Weicker of Connecticut, had voted against the code, and a third member, John G. Tower of Texas, missed the final vote but expressed strong opposition to the measure during debate.

There were other grounds for skepticism as the implementation of the 1977 codes got under way. Common Cause reported that several committees in each house began whittling away at different parts of the ethics codes shortly after their adoption. Five senators filed a law suit against the Senate code, attacking its limits on earned outside income. At the time the suit was filed Senator S. I. Hayakawa of California, one of the

47. *Congressional Quarterly Almanac, 1977*, p. 772.
48. "Backsliding on Ethics," *In Common*, vol. 8 (Fall 1977), pp. 3–11.
49. Thomas P. Southwick, "Adlai Stevenson: From Senate Back Benches to Prominent Role as Ethics Panel Chairman," *Congressional Quarterly*, vol. 35 (April 2, 1977), pp. 594–95.

plaintiffs, stated publicly that a majority of the House and Senate members who had voted for the earned income limitation "didn't believe in it" and were "morally bullied" into doing so. Editor and columnist James A. Wechsler of the *New York Post* was moved by Hayakawa's comment to conclude that "Congress might be a better place if those who share his [Hayakawa's] emotions dedicated themselves exclusively to private enterprise." His column was pessimistically headed "Congress and Ethics: A Quiet Farewell to All Reform."[50] The court dismissed the senators' legal action challenging limits on outside income,[51] but it is on appeal and should not be regarded lightly. It raises issues of free speech and privacy that are both novel and serious.

There were also institutional grounds for pessimism, which would have attended the establishment of any new codes. In the debates it was conceded that the old codes had been ineffective, but few members faced up to the underlying causes of this. Analytical review of the history of congressional self-discipline indicates that there are inherent institutional factors at work that may prevent any code from being effective when left to enforcement by internal committees.

The reluctance of Congress to adopt both the 1968 and 1977 ethics codes and its hostility to effective enforcement mechanisms are a strong indication that the new codes may not produce significant change. Institutional considerations perhaps make this both inevitable and understandable. .

First, there is the general difficulty of particularizing rules of ethical conduct for the infinite variety of individual personal situations. To attempt such codification of legally enforceable rules may be quixotic for any group, regardless of enforcement mechanisms and of whether such rules are actual law or self-imposed by a peer group. The late Chief Justice Earl Warren said in a 1962 speech: "Law floats in a sea of Ethics."

Not everything which is wrong can be outlawed, although everything which is outlawed, is, in our Western conception, wrong. *For many years, legislatures and courts have endeavored to define for corporate and Government officials what constitutes a conflict between their public responsibilities and their private interests. None has yet been able to state in legal terms rules that will at the same time afford both freedom of dynamic action by the individual and protection of the public interest.* Every law designed for such purpose has

---

50. *New York Post,* December 15, 1977.
51. *Laxalt* v. *Kimmitt,* No. 77-1230, D.D.C., March 13, 1978.

presumed, and I must necessarily presume, that such laws cannot be effective unless there is law behind the law; i.e., an ethical concept on the part of all who accept public responsibilities.[52]

It is doubtful that developments of the past seventeen years have disproved Warren's wisdom. Also, the chief justice was referring to the difficulty of an *externally imposed* codification of ethics by law. When a peer group attempts self-regulation by codification of its ethical standards, the difficulty is even greater. In evaluating formal rules of congressional ethics, one must bear in mind the many ambiguities of political life and the legislative process, as well as the difficult realities when any such standards are made dependent on group sanctions for enforcement. Some of the limitations inherent in this process were aptly summarized in a 1955 article on the subject by Phillip Monypenny.

Ethics as a system of control also deals with groups, not with isolated individuals. Particular individuals may be capable of very high standards of performance, but it is large groups which must be moved in all social endeavor. Groups impose their own standards on the individuals who join them; they develop their own standards out of their own experience. A man in isolation may change his own conduct radically. It is difficult for a group to develop new standards in relation to the activity which makes it a group.

The standards for groups are therefore likely to be more modest than those which a dedicated individual may embrace. They will also be partial in relation to the whole life of man, covering the aspect of affairs which are common to the group. They must grow out of present practices and standards. They must be capable of relatively easy application to the events of the day: they must not be so general that a long and sophisticated chain of reasoning is necessary to relate the standards and the action required at the moment; in this respect they are the opposite of constitutional law. The standards developed for governmental employment will probably be various, developed separately for the many different kinds of work which is done by governmental employees.[53]

Professor Monypenny's views on the undesirability of detailed codes of peer group ethics are still shared by many, but they are contrary to the trend toward attempting to make detailed codes specifically govern the entire range of professional conduct. The legal profession's Code of Pro-

52. Address at the Jewish Theological Seminary, New York, November 11, 1962; quoted in *Congress and the Public Trust*, p. 221.
53. "The Control of Ethical Standards in the Public Service," *Annals of the American Academy of Political and Social Science*, vol. 297: *Ethical Standards and Professional Conduct* (January 1955), pp. 29, 100–01.

fessional Responsibility is comparable to the new congressional codes. A less professorial view, which accords with that of Monypenny and is based on observation of the Senate Ethics Committee in action, was advanced by Eliot Marshall. He opened a critical column headed "Behavior Modification" with his general views of ethical codes.

A "code of conduct" suggests something imposed by adults on children. The codes I remember all inspired passionate feelings of boredom. The more specific they were, the more they were ridiculed and abused. The really thorough rules, the ones that tried to reach out and grab every nuance of wickedness by the scruff of the neck, were the worst. It was a triumph to break them. Other rules didn't arouse the same vandal spirit. The intimidating ones were vague and absolute and said things like, "Thou shalt not steal."

Many people in Washington are writing codes of conduct today, but few know how to make them intimidating.[54]

There are also unique institutional explanations for the past low level of congressional self-discipline. They are subtle but have some merit when considering the limited potential of congressional self-discipline for uplifting either the quality of Congress or the level of public confidence it enjoys.

Most experts who have reviewed the congressional disciplinary record have reached conclusions unsympathetic to Congress, largely attributing congressional reluctance to discipline itself to a "club spirit" of institutional self-protectionism that generally causes members of Congress either to ignore misconduct or to close ranks in defense of an impugned member. Although this attitude has become less prevalent in recent years, many would still concur with the critical evaluation by Rogow and Lasswell written in 1963.

In the House of Representatives, especially, corrupt behavior owes a good deal to the failure of both the leadership and membership to enforce rectitude standards. Although the leaders of the Senate and the House after the Civil War were not, for the most part, less able or capable than their pre-War predecessors, unlike them they were largely passive in the face of widespread evidence that much legislative business was transacted in a corrupt fashion. Moreover, an indifferent attitude toward corrupt behavior of members remains characteristic of both houses. As George A. Graham has observed, the Senate and House have taken disciplinary action "chiefly when issues have been forced upon them by publicity or other outside pressure, and punishment has been meager." No senator or congressman "has been expelled or disciplined in any way for receiving money, gifts, services, swimming pools,

54. "On the Hill: Behavior Modification," *New Republic,* November 12, 1977, p. 9.

lakes, or anything else from contractors doing business with the government."
In fact, according to Graham, "no member has been expelled for violation of
the law even when indicted, tried, and convicted of crime." The "implication"
of such inaction "is that according to Congressional standards anything goes,
not only everything the law allows, but also what it does not allow."[55]

Although institutional self-protection has undoubtedly played a part
in most of American history, this is not only decreasing but has probably
always been exaggerated. Writing in 1966, Robert Getz criticized the
earlier emphasis on "club spirit" and offered as a more important cause
the historic fact that individual instances of disciplinary powers have often
become too political. He concluded that Congress' long delay in establishing effective codes of ethics resulted partly from many legislators' understandable belief that an objective setting for the enforcement of such codes
cannot be found in the halls of Congress.[56] In support of this doubt, Getz
documented evidence of political partisanship in several disputes over dis-
ciplining members. This was confirmed in 1967 when a much higher proportion of Republicans than Democrats cast anti-Powell votes, with only
11 of 184 Republicans opposing exclusion on the final vote. In the Senate,
both the Rules Committee and the full Senate split along party lines on
confining the Baker investigation to narrow limits, which minimized
possible political damage to the Democratic party, other senators, and
President Lyndon B. Johnson. In several votes Republicans were unanimous in their unsuccessful efforts to broaden the Baker investigation
against Democrats' almost unanimous opposition.

Another motivation for members to move slowly is the fear that repercussions from individual cases may have a harmful rather than a beneficial
effect on the public's confidence in Congress. Many members genuinely
distrust the press and fear that zealous newsmen may mislead the public
into thinking that an aberrant member is typical of the group. They fear
that any praise of Congress for taking disciplinary action will be lost in
the sensational features of a case. This view was expressed in a defense of
Congress once advanced by Representative Emanuel Celler.

There is no doubt that an esprit de corps does exist among members of Congress and they do their best to protect each other. This is not, of course, without its unfortunate aspects, but it must be remembered that members of Congress are assailed more often for their shortcomings than they are praised for

55. Arnold A. Rogow and H. D. Lasswell, *Power, Corruption and Rectitude*
(Prentice-Hall, 1963), pp. 60–62.

56. Robert S. Getz, *Congressional Ethics: The Conflict of Interest Issue* (Van
Nostrand, 1966), pp. 84–116.

their good work. It is natural, therefore, for them to fly to each other's defense. It must be remembered too that very often the whole body is condemned for the misdeeds of one. When one is guilty or allegedly guilty of misconduct, it is not unusual to find that Congressmen generally are assailed. . . . I am not attempting to defend this "esprit de corps"; I am merely explaining it.[57]

A further reason for Congress' reluctance to discipline its members stems from its need for goodwill and cooperation in most of its major functions. In testifying at hearings held on the subject in 1951, Senator J. William Fulbright noted the need for harmony if Congress is to function effectively.

I see this in the press very often: "Why does not the Congress clean its own house? Why do they not discipline their own Members? Why do they not do so-and-so?"

I simply do not agree that is the proper function of the Congress. I think it is extremely difficult to make 96 people from diverse parts of the country get along in some harmony. If we undertake to discipline our own Members and that sort of thing, we will really bog down in recrimination and dissension and will not accomplish anything. The greater purpose of making the Government function far outweighs these individual delinquencies.[58]

Most members agree and regard self-discipline as a diversion from their main business. Members enlisted to serve on an ethics committee may assign low priority to its work. The Dodd case occupied the Senate Select Committee on Standards and Conduct for sixteen months and required four days of public committee hearings, which filled 1,164 printed pages. It was the principal business of the full Senate for nine legislative days, and the debate filled 300 pages of the *Congressional Record*. Senators who were actively involved spent many long, difficult hours in relatively thankless and strife-ridden work.

For many reasons, busy legislators dread repetitions of the sort of experience encountered in the Dodd case. The political fortunes of the senators who were in the vanguard of the ethics movement of the 1960s may be relevant. Most were defeated soon thereafter, including such stalwarts as Senators Joseph S. Clark of Pennsylvania, Paul H. Douglas of Illinois, Wayne L. Morse of Oregon, and A. S. Mike Monroney of Oklahoma, the floor leader for the Dodd disciplinary action. Voters seem to attach little

---

57. H. Hubert Wilson, *Congress: Corruption and Compromise* (Rinehart, 1951), p. 221 (quoting from a letter to Wilson from Celler).

58. *Establishment of a Commission on Ethics in Government,* Hearings before a subcommittee to study Senate Concurrent Resolution 21 of the Senate Committee on Labor and Public Welfare, 82 Cong. 1 sess. (GPO, 1951), p. 259.

value to such service, and members understandably feel that legislative achievements, constituents' casework, and reelection efforts are more important than the policing of each other's ethics.

Before 1977 it was well known that members who were seriously committed to an active program of congressional self-discipline had little chance of being appointed to the two ethics committees. It was less generally known that it was difficult to find willing appointees to these committees among members who were hostile or indifferent to the idea of congressional self-discipline. Several references were made in the hearings on the 1977 codes to the thankless and joyless nature of the work of such committees and its lack of political value with voters. Members were often appointed only after vigorous urging from the leadership, and some reported how difficult it was to get off the committees after reasonable periods of service.

However, the change of mood that produced the 1977 codes was accompanied by a greater sensitivity to the subject, and both the leadership and the membership seem either dedicated or resigned to a new era. The current chairman of the House committee is Charles Bennett, who has long been an activist on this issue. Senator Stevenson's positive attitude has already been discussed.

Other intervening events have shown that the fears expressed by Common Cause and James Wechsler may not have been justified. Efforts in the House to repeal the 1977 codes' limits on outside income failed decisively when it voted 290–97 on September 20, 1978, to retain them.[59] The inclusion of both codes' financial disclosure provisions as statutory law in the comprehensive new ethics bill adopted late in 1978 is an even more positive indicator that a higher level of ethics enforcement may have arrived to stay. The reprimands given by the House to California Democrats Edward R. Roybal, John J. McFall, and Charles H. Wilson for "Koreagate" misconduct offer hope that partisan politics may be diminishing as a negative factor. The Senate committee's action in the Talmadge case, which produced the first formal charges and inquiry since the Dodd case in 1967, is similarly encouraging.

Senator James R. Sasser of Tennessee has provided a valuable and

---

59. However, on March 8, 1979, the Senate, by voice vote, postponed until January 1, 1983, the effectiveness of its new rule on outside earned income, thereby enabling senators to continue earning up to $25,000 a year from honoraria and unlimited amounts from other sources. This action was confirmed on March 28 by a recorded vote of 54–44.

comprehensive history and analysis of the new Senate code. In a recent law review article his conclusions are consistent with my own views of the causes and efficacy of such codes, and he may well place the Senate code in its proper perspective with his final paragraph.

Ultimately, the strength of the Code of Conduct is that it allows the people to judge for themselves the validity of their Senators' actions and to form the basis for an intelligent decision at the polls. This is the sanction upon which the democratic system is based, and it is this sanction which is the most effective and the most feared. The test conducted by the electorate is that which is most likely to improve the quality of Senate membership. If, by the passage of the Code, the Senate has facilitated the public's task, then it will have accomplished its goal of protecting the legislative branch against unethical activity.[60]

This view may be criticized by some as reducing the work of the new committees to little more than providing public disclosure of income and assets and possible misrepresentations thereof. Those who believe disclosure to be a sufficient remedy, without limits or prohibitions, may applaud this view. History has shown, however, that voters will sometimes overlook or forgive notorious conflicts of interest, particularly those of senior members who have delivered well on federal projects or whose personal economic interests coincide with those of a large number of their constituents. If the new codes and committees are to be effective, at least an occasional case must be carried to its conclusion—the imposition of formal disciplinary sanctions.

Conclusion

As Beard and Horn noted in 1975, the past failure of purely internal congressional sanctions is due to considerations that are "rooted in the nation's political institutions."[61] While the best hope may be that the new codes will strengthen the electorate, making it the ultimate sanction, a vigilant press and groups such as Common Cause may well prompt the

---

60. "Learning from the Past: The Senate Code of Conduct in Historical Perspective," *Cumberland Law Review*, vol. 8 (Fall 1977), pp. 357, 384.

61. Edmund Beard and Stephen Horn, *Congressional Ethics: The View from the House* (Brookings Institution, 1975), pp. 82–83. This valuable empirical study is based on information collected from House members, lobbyists, congressional staff and press corps, and executive liaison personnel. The authors' conclusions about the potential for congressional self-discipline without continued public pressure are generally negative.

new ethics codes and committees to function much more effectively than in the past.

Of the conflict of interest regulations discussed above, it appears that only those affecting outside earned income of members of Congress are related to issues of compensation. Here the relationship is real and substantial. One result may be to deter some of those who might otherwise seek congressional office. Nonetheless, these limits should not be repealed or raised. As shown earlier, Congress has merely been brought more nearly in line with the requirements and practices of the other two branches. The substantial pay increases recommended by the Peterson Commission in 1977 were tied to congressional adoption of this and other ethical reforms on the theory that the public would not otherwise accept the increases. Highly publicized outside earnings, particularly those in the form of possibly inflated honoraria paid by interest groups, had contributed substantially to the low level of public confidence. It was justifiable to demand that congressional service become a full-time job free of any appearance that outside employment was an undue influence. The limits should be reviewed in a few years to determine their effects on the composition of Congress.

Although federal conflict of interest regulations in all the branches may well need substantial reform, it is difficult to conceive of any acceptable modification of existing regulations that could be justified on grounds of government compensation. Expanded investment and earnings opportunities for full-time officials, which would mean tolerating conflicts of interest now forbidden, are not the solution to the problem of low government pay. It follows, then, that the 1980 consideration of salary increases need not include major reexamination of the conflict of interest regulations applicable to any of the three branches.

There is one possible exception to this general conclusion. It has been suggested that a study of compensation should include the whole range of disadvantages of government service and evaluate other factors that make recruitment difficult at the higher levels. If so, such matters as the divestitures Senate committees require of presidential appointees and the restrictions on subsequent private employment should be included. These are examples of deterrents to government service that cannot be remedied by realistic compensation proposals but that may well be of greater significance to high-level recruitment.

Robert W. Hartman

The Effects of Top Officials' Pay on Other Federal Employees

WHILE the salaries paid the 2,500 federal employees whose rates are set quadrennially by the procedures of the Commission on Executive, Legislative, and Judicial Salaries are of considerable interest, the salaries of another 30,000 employees of the executive branch, which may also be affected by these procedures, should also be of concern. These employees in the upper reaches of the civil service for the most part occupy career positions and are not simply serving a stint in Washington or capping off an illustrious career in the private sector. As such, they represent the group whose membership, morale, and other characteristics dependent on salary are most likely to be affected by deficiencies in the pay-setting process.

This paper discusses the interaction of the decisions on executive, legislative, and judicial salaries with the rest of the government work force. The recent history of salary changes and the linkages between pay systems are described, and the reasons the linkages are perceived as a problem are briefly reviewed. Recent changes in the present system are discussed, with emphasis on the inadequacy of current comparability procedures for supergrade employees and on the pay provisions of the recently legislated Senior Executive Service.

Recent History of Top Officials' Salary

Perhaps the most astonishing feature of the modern history of top federal officials' pay is that it can all be summarized on one page (table 1). Since 1900 the salary of members of Congress and of cabinet officers has been changed only eight times, or about once every decade. While this record represents an acceleration from the nineteenth century, when cabi-

TABLE 1. *History of Top Officials' Pay, 1900–77*

Dollars

Year	Cabinet officers	Executive level II	Members of Congress	Judges, circuit courts of appeals
1900	8,000	...	5,000	6,000
1903	...	...	...	7,000
1907	12,000	...	7,500	...
1919	...	...	...	8,500
1925	15,000	...	10,000	...
1926	...	...	...	12,500
1946	...	...	...	17,500
1947	...	...	12,500	...
1949	22,500	...	...	...
1955	...	...	22,500	25,500
1956	25,000	...	...	...
1964	35,000	30,000	...	33,000
1965	...	...	30,000	...
1969	60,000	42,500	42,500	42,500
1975	63,000	44,600	44,600	44,600
1977	66,000	57,500	57,500	57,500

Sources: 1900–74, *Documentary History of Federal Pay Legislation, 1975*, Committee Print, Senate Committee on Post Office and Civil Service, 94 Cong. 2 sess. (Government Printing Office, 1976), pp. 29–33; after 1974, *The Budget of the United States Government—Appendix*, pt. 2: "Schedules of Permanent Positions," various years.

net members' pay was changed only four times, the historical stickiness of top officials' salaries is the single most important fact to be considered in appraising the effect on other federal workers.

The infrequency of pay changes does not necessarily imply that they were too low at any time or that contemporary officials are underpaid relative to those in the past. Alexander Hamilton, when he was secretary of the treasury, could have bought about 1,900 bushels of wheat with his $3,500 salary; in 1978 Michael Blumenthal could have taken home about 23,000 bushels on his $66,000 salary. By contrast, in 1932 the secretary of the treasury in Herbert Hoover's administration was earning over $70,000 in today's prices. By choosing the appropriate base year one can prove almost anything about the level of top officials' pay.

Before 1967 their pay was set by statute according to no particular schedule. In 1967 Public Law 90-206 was enacted, authorizing the appointment of a Commission on Executive, Legislative, and Judicial Salaries. The quadrennial commission reviews top officials' pay and recommends revisions to the President. Commissions served in 1968, 1972, and 1976.

The Quadrennial Commission

A number of important changes have occurred in leading officials' remuneration since the quadrennial commission apparatus was set up, among them a rigid set of internal linkages. Since 1969, when the first commission report was transmitted to Congress (after some modification) by the President, the salaries of members of Congress, executive level II officers in the executive branch (deputy secretaries of major departments, chairman of the Council of Economic Advisers, and so forth), and judges of circuit courts of appeals (of whom there are ninety-seven) have been identical (see table 1). These three salaries form the crosspiece of the federal pay abacus. Each quadrennial commission has set pay in the executive branch by establishing a rate for executive level II, then making executive level I a little higher and levels III–V a little lower. The House and Senate leaders get an amount between executive levels I and II (except the Speaker of the House, who is paid the same as the vice-president), and the pay of the heads of congressional offices such as the Library of Congress, the Congressional Budget Office, and the architect of the Capitol is scaled down from members' pay. In the judiciary, associate justices of the Supreme Court are somewhat higher than executive level I, and district court judges are just below the court of appeals judges' level. It is not too much of an exaggeration to say that since 1969 the salary of members of Congress has set the pay for the other 2,000 slots covered by the quadrennial commission.[1] It is important to note that this linkage of branches occurs even though it has no statutory basis.[2]

The quadrennial commission procedure has proved to be a failure in providing timely salary adjustments in a period of inflation. In January 1969 President Johnson submitted his recommendations for pay changes based on (but not identical to) the 1968 quadrennial commission's re-

---

1. The commission's domain in 1976 included 856 jobs in the executive schedule, 550 legislative positions, and 1,052 judicial slots. The executive schedule positions included 83 at levels I and II, 118 at level III, and 654 at levels IV and V. See *Staff Report to the Commission on Executive, Legislative, and Judicial Salaries, February 1977* (Government Printing Office, 1977), p. 117.

2. The 1976 quadrennial commission proposed to unlink salaries in the three branches by raising pay more for executive level II and judges of circuit courts of appeals than for members of Congress. By the time the increases were submitted to Congress by President Ford (with the concurrence of President-elect Carter and Chief Justice Burger) in January of 1977, the rates had been equalized. See *Report of the Commission on Executive, Legislative, and Judicial Salaries, December 1976* (GPO, 1977), p. 133.

port. The Senate defeated a proposal to disapprove the President's recommendations, and a similar motion was tabled before it reached the House floor. As a result, the pay increases went into effect in 1969. After this success, the history is all downhill.

In 1972 the commission was not appointed until after the presidential election, and the President's recommended salary adjustments were not submitted to Congress until February 1974. Although Congress was aware that consumer prices had risen by more than 30 percent since the 1969 pay raise, Watergate-related factors and the fact that 1974 was an election year led the Senate to turn down President Nixon's proposal by a vote of 71–26.[3] Thus top officials' salaries remained frozen until 1975.

In 1975, apparently recognizing that there would be at least two more years of pay freeze before the next quadrennial commission report, Congress passed Public Law 94-82, the misnamed Executive Salary Cost-of-Living Adjustment Act, which stipulates that whenever general schedule (GS) pay is increased (annually under Public Law 91-656) executive, congressional, and judicial salaries shall be increased by an equal percentage.[4] This law was designed to fill a gap by providing a basis both for making the job of the 1976 quadrennial commission easier (automatic increases in 1975 and 1976 would reduce the increases to be requested in 1977) and for putting pay on automatic pilot in between future quadrennial recommendations.

It has not worked out that way at all. In October 1975 executive salaries were raised by 5 percent, the same as the GS pay increase. But in 1976 Congress voted not to apply the average 5 percent GS increase to top officials' salaries. With only one 5 percent raise since 1969, the commission that reported to President Ford in late 1976 was forced to recommend huge increases in salaries for the federal leadership. Table 2 shows the recommended increases and the modifications made by President Ford in his ultimate recommendation after conferring with congressional leaders and the incoming administration. It does not take much inside information to infer that the sentiment "the people won't stand for more than about a 25 percent increase" ruled the day.[5]

---

3. The proposal was for a 7.5 percent increase for executive level I in 1975 and phased-in increases for levels II–V in 1974, 1975, and 1976 of about 7.5 percent a year.

4. Since GS pay is supposed to be adjusted annually to be comparable to *wages* in the private sector, the adjustment for top officials provided for in the 1975 law is not a "cost-of-living adjustment" in the ordinary (*price* level) use of the term.

5. Between mid-1969 and early 1977 the consumer price index had risen by 60 percent and the general schedule had risen by 52 percent.

TABLE 2. *Salaries of Selected Federal Officials for 1977 Recommended by the Quadrennial Commission and by the President*

Position	1976 salary (dollars)	Commission's proposal for 1977		President's proposal for 1977	
		Dollars	Percent increase from 1976	Dollars	Percent increase from 1976
Member of Congress	44,600	57,500	28.9	57,500	28.9
Executive level II	44,600	60,000	34.5	57,500	28.9
Circuit court judge	44,600	65,000	45.7	57,500	28.9
Executive level I	63,000	67,500	7.1	66,000	4.8
Executive level III	42,000	57,000	35.7	52,500	25.0
Executive level IV	39,900	53,000	32.8	50,000	25.3
Executive level V	37,800	49,000	29.6	47,500	25.7

Sources: *Report of the Commission on Executive, Legislative, and Judicial Salaries, December 1976* (GPO, 1977), p. 53; and *The Budget of the United States Government, Fiscal Year 1978—Supplement: Executive, Legislative, and Judicial Salary Recommendations.*

The presidential recommendation for 1977 made it through Congress but not without significant controversy. Attempts to bring resolutions of disapproval to the floor of both houses in January and February were blocked by an assortment of parliamentary tactics.[6] In March the salary boost went into effect, but several attempts were made later in 1977 to rescind the increase. Although no rescission was passed, two laws affecting pay were enacted in 1977. In April the law was changed so that future quadrennial salary proposals of the President (but not interim annual adjustments) would have to be approved by each house within sixty days to become effective. Separate votes would be taken on proposed pay changes for each branch of government.[7] In July Congress approved a law stipulating that the "automatic" adjustment due in October 1977 would not take effect. This stipulation was introduced in the Senate by the majority and minority leaders at 9:45 A.M. on March 10; it passed, 93–1, before dinner the same day.[8]

In 1978 President Carter's anti-inflation program included provisions not only to limit the increase in the general schedule to 5.5 percent, but also to freeze executive-level employees' pay. Both actions were accepted by Congress.

6. See "Congress Votes Controversial Pay Raise," *Congressional Quarterly Almanac, 1977*, pp. 751–55.

7. Public Law 95-19, approved April 12, 1977.

8. *Congressional Record*, daily edition (March 10, 1977), p. S3879. The law is Public Law 95-66.

The upshot of all these recent maneuverings is that the state of the legislation governing top officials' pay, which had evolved by mid-decade into automatic-annual-increases-supplemented-every-four-years-by-a-major-review-on-none-of-which-did-Congress-have-to-vote (a textbook example of creative legislative avoidance of a thorny issue), was chaotic. One out of three quadrennial commissions had resulted in failure. Three out of four "automatic" annual adjustments had not taken place. The next quadrennial commission will almost certainly have to deal with studies calling for large salary increases as a result of the breakdown of the adjustment system, and both houses of Congress will have to take a recorded vote on any recommendations the President makes based on the quadrennial commission's report.

The Linkage to General Schedule Pay

Two pertinent provisions of law connect top executive, legislative, and judicial salaries to the salaries received by other government workers. The first of these is that the annual salary of a federal general schedule employee (and related statutory salary systems such as the foreign service, the Veterans Administration Department of Medicine and Surgery, and the military) may not exceed that of executive level V.[9] Thus, for example, the rate of $47,500 set in 1977 for level V became the ceiling for virtually all other employees of the government.

The second provision is that general schedule employees' pay be adjusted annually so as to maintain comparability with pay rates for similar jobs in the private sector. In practice, comparability is based on making a yearly survey of salaries in matched jobs in the private sector and then, through a complicated procedure to be described later, adjusting GS pay rates to the survey findings.[10]

The interaction of these two provisions of law is what causes the problem of pay compression. As the annual survey results roll in and are implemented fully (or even partially) while the ceiling is adjusted very infrequently, an increasing share of the federal work force finds that its pay is governed by the ceiling rather than by comparability. Anyone who has ever lived in Washington is familiar with "asterisked salaries," which

9. 5 U.S.C. 5308.

10. Under other laws, the average GS increase is also applied to many other federal pay systems, the largest of which is the military.

TABLE 3. *General Schedule Salaries for Grades 15–18,*
Effective October 1978

	GS level			
Pay step	15	16	17	18
1	38,160	44,756	52,429*	61,449*
2	39,432	46,248	54,177*	...
3	40,704	47,740*	55,925*	...
4	41,976	49,232*	57,673*	...
5	43,248	50,724*	59,421*	...
6	44,520	52,216*	...	...
7	45,792	53,708*	...	...
8	47,064	55,200*	...	...
9	48,336*	56,692*	...	...
10	49,608*	...	...	...

Source: "Adjustments of Certain Pay and Allowances," Executive Order 12087, *Federal Register*, vol. 43 (October 11, 1978), p. 46824.
* Annual salary limited by law to $47,500.

show how much federal workers would receive but for the executive level V ceiling.

An illustration of the effect of the ceiling is given in table 3, which shows federal salary levels for GS-15–18 employees, effective in October 1978. These salary rates take into account the 5.5 percent salary rise limitation for 1978 as well as the freeze on executive salaries.

All federal employees at the GS-17 and -18 (supergrade) levels received the same rate of pay under the 1978 salary schedule. Similarly stuck at $47,500 were the salaries of GS-16 employees at steps 3 and above and GS-15 employees at steps 9 and 10.[11] All told, some 4,520 supergrades and 3,500 GS-15s were compressed at a single salary level as a result of the interplay of comparability and salary ceilings.

The population frozen at a single salary level has varied. When President Carter took office, about 13,200 GS employees were at the $39,600 ceiling. After the February 1977 hike in executive salaries this number was reduced to 2,200 at $47,500. The October 1977 GS pay raise pushed the number of those at the ceiling to 3,300. In 1978, with the $47,500 salary frozen and GS workers semithawed at 5.5 percent, there were 8,000 victims of compression. The 1978 "ceiling" cut through the GS schedule

11. Ordinarily an employee spends one year for each advance to steps 2, 3, and 4 within grade, two years for each move to steps 5, 6, and 7, and three years for each advance to steps 8, 9, and 10.

at a point with a high density of workers: each of the next two 6 percent GS pay increases would add about 7,000 employees to the frozen GS ranks unless the executive ceiling was raised. Without the establishment of the new Senior Executive Service (see below), the 1980 quadrennial commission would have faced at least as great a compression problem as its predecessor, and it may still have to deal with some compression.[12]

The Effect of Pay Compression

The effect of pay compression on the federal work force has been analyzed recently in a number of studies.[13] What follows is a summary of these studies' findings on hiring, retention, and morale.

When jobs at several levels of responsibility carry the same salary, it is difficult for any organization to hire externally and promote internally. One aspect of this problem is that many employees are unwilling to accept the greater responsibilities that come with a promotion when the new job carries the same salary as the old, reasoning that with the increased pressure and longer hours the new job is not worth it. Moreover, in the federal government, a promotion to greater responsibility may involve relocation, often to the Washington, D.C., area. Since Washington has a higher cost of living than most of the rest of the country, the compressed pay scale means that the employee is being asked to take a cut in real income to assume a higher position. During the severe 1969–76 compression, these and related horror stories were emphasized by federal executives.[14]

The interplay of pay compression and the provisions of the civil service retirement system has also made it difficult to retain experienced employees. Under the retirement plan, an employee may normally retire at

12. As noted, the total compressed population extends beyond the general schedule. In 1976, 7,000 employees in the military, foreign service, Veterans Administration, and other systems also had their salaries determined by the executive level V ceiling.

13. See *Report of the Commission on Executive, Legislative, and Judicial Salaries, December 1976;* U.S. Comptroller General, General Accounting Office, *Critical Need for a Better System for Adjusting Top Executive, Legislative and Judicial Salaries,* report to the Congress, FPCD-75-140 (GAO, 1975); Department of the Army, *Civilian Pay Compression–Pay Inversion Survey, November 1976* (Department of the Army, 1976).

14. See especially *Report of the Commission on Executive, Legislative, and Judicial Salaries, December 1976,* pp. 16–20; and Department of the Army, *Civilian Pay Compression,* p. 16.

the age of fifty-five with thirty years of service, at sixty with twenty years of service, or at sixty-two with five years of service. After an employee has had ten years of service, for each additional year that he works the annuity is increased by 2 percent of his "high-3" average salary. This is the average of the annual pay for the three consecutive years in which pay was highest. Once an employee retires, his annuity is increased twice a year to reflect cost-of-living increases.

The incentive for a federal employee to continue working for the government once he is eligible for retirement, therefore, is that his service increment (2 percent of average salary) and his high-3 average will rise more than the cost-of-living adjustment in the annuity that would be received if he retired early.[15] During periods of pay compression, employees stuck at the pay ceiling are unable to increase their high-3 average at all. If during such a period cost-of-living adjustments are adding substantially to the annuities of those who retire, all the incentives are for early retirement.[16] Moreover, when the pay ceiling is lifted (or when it is anticipated that it will be lifted), there is a strong incentive for those eligible for retirement to continue in their jobs in order to drive up their high-3 pay.

The attitude of federal employees toward retirement seems to be sensitive to economic incentives. Retirement rates are much higher for employees with frozen salaries than for others eligible for retirement. For example, in 1975 the retirement rate of those eligible was about 40 percent for those at the frozen levels and less than 20 percent for others. About half of the frozen salary retirees were under sixty years old, implying that the government was losing valuable people at their career peak.[17] The executive vacancies resulting from retirement closely accord with changes in the pay ceiling. In 1973, after a freeze of four years, nearly 10 percent of all executive positions became vacant because of retirements; in 1976, in anticipation of a rise in the pay ceiling, less than 3 percent of

15. The maximum retirement benefit is 80 percent of the high-3 average. A person who has accumulated enough service to be at this maximum increases his annuity by working only to the extent that the high-3 average is increased.

16. The ultimate example was given by the Civil Service Commission in 1975 when it reported seven cases of employees who had retired in the early 1970s and were receiving an annuity that exceeded the current salary for their positions. This resulted from the 80 percent of salary ceiling being raised by cost-of-living increases to over 100 percent of salary while the salary of the position remained frozen. See Civil Service Commission, *Executive Manpower in the Federal Service, September 1975* (GPO, 1976), p. 9.

17. Civil Service Commission, *Executive Personnel in the Federal Service, October 1976* (GPO, 1977), p. 25.

the slots were vacated by retirement. These swings in retirement are the most volatile cause of vacancies in executive positions and contribute to a feast or famine pattern of hiring for top jobs.[18]

The final complaint about pay compression concerns its detrimental effect on employee morale. Government executives read pay tables extremely well. When they repeatedly see wage schedules showing that they should be receiving comparability salaries that are many thousands of dollars above what they are paid, they say such things as this GS-18 did: "Congressional/Administration treatment of Compensation for Senior Career Executive (Grades 16–18) has been, and is, uncalled for, patently unfair, and manifestly stupid. A breach of faith, shabby, and demeaning of public career service. I will separate when first eligible for annuity."[19] Getting out is not the only consequence of low morale. Another federal executive referred to pay compression as "the single most important factor in 'retirement on the job' syndrome."[20]

Comparability

One appealing approach to removing the inequities in supergrade employees' pay is to simply remove the pay ceiling and let salaries be governed by the regular pay comparability process. Ostensibly this would put all general schedule employees on a market-related pay scale, which seems like a desirable change.[21]

Unfortunately, existing procedures for carrying out the comparability principle are totally inadequate to replace the pay ceiling. Published rates for the supergrades bear no necessary relation to market salaries for comparable jobs. In fact, such market salaries are not even surveyed. Also, the pay raises proposed under the present methodology are unaffected by the pay raises recently granted the supergrade workers. Finally, there is

18. For data on executive vacancies by cause, see Civil Service Commission, *Executive Personnel in the Federal Service, November 1977* (GPO, 1978), pp. 11–13.

19. Department of the Army, *Civilian Pay Compression,* p. C-13.

20. Ibid., p. C-12.

21. What might be deemed undesirable about the change is that some supergrade employees would be earning more than their executive schedule bosses. This did happen in late 1976 as a result of a quirk in the law (from October 1976 to February 1977, GS-18s were paid $39,600 and executive level V employees received $37,800) and the world did not end.

reason to believe that the statistical methods employed in the comparability process (combined with the tendency of recent administrations to grant constant, "across-the-board" percentage pay raises) leads to an upward bias in the comparability pay increases proposed for the upper grade levels. To understand these dicta requires some detailed explanation of how comparability works. The reader who is not interested in the technical methods used in determining comparability should skip the next two sections.

How Comparability Works

Each year the Bureau of Labor Statistics (BLS) conducts a survey of private sector pay rates for professional, administrative, technical, and clerical jobs (the PATC survey).[22] At each federal GS level certain jobs are singled out and matched with private sector jobs that experts have judged to be comparable in duties and responsibilities. Average salaries are then computed for these private sector jobs at each federal GS level using the survey data on the matched jobs.[23] These averages are next used to determine the pay agent's recommended comparability pay increases to the President.[24]

The single most important fact about the survey is that only jobs at GS-1 to GS-15 are surveyed and matched. No private sector data on the supergrade type of job are currently considered in the comparability procedures. Instead, statistical methods are used to extrapolate GS-1 to GS-15 results into the supergrade range. The methods amount to adjusting supergrade pay by analogue to the rest of the general schedule.

The technique for determining comparability increases for the fifteen matched-job grades is as follows. A smooth curve is first fitted through the

22. The survey is described and reported annually by the Bureau of Labor Statistics as *National Survey of Professional, Administrative, Technical, and Clerical Pay*. For further details on comparability techniques, see Congressional Budget Office, *The Federal Government's Pay Systems: Adjustment Procedures and Impacts of Proposed Changes,* Background Paper 19 (GPO, 1977).

23. The weights used to determine averages are the numbers of federal employees in the occupational categories represented by matched jobs in the survey. In 1977 about 92 percent of all federal jobs up to GS-15 were so represented.

24. The President's pay agent consists of the secretary of labor, the chairman of the Office of Personnel Management, and the director of the Office of Management and Budget. They issue an annual report, *Comparability of the Federal Statutory Pay Systems with Private Enterprise Pay Rates: Annual Report of the President's Pay Agent.*

average-salary-by-grade points derived from the BLS survey. This "survey pay-line" curve is estimated by regression techniques that place the greatest weight on GS grades with the largest number of employees. Because of this weighting, the curve may deviate from the actual survey averages by a considerable margin in GS categories containing few represented employees.[25] The mathematical form of the curve used—out of many possible forms—is one in which intergrade percentage differences gradually diminish.[26]

A curve of identical mathematical form is then fitted through the data on actual average GS salaries in each grade. This "reference line" also is based on the principle of making the curve fit the heavily populated GS levels most closely and has the characteristic of diminishing intergrade percentage differences.

The percentage pay increase is then found, in the pay agent's exercise, by calculating the percentage difference between the survey pay line and the reference line at each GS level. Table 4 illustrates this, using 1978 data. For example, the GS-15 pay increase in 1978 under comparability is 13.27 percent, the difference between \$45,757, the GS-15 salary computed from the survey pay line, and \$40,396, the GS-15 salary computed from the reference line.[27] This comparability increase, it should be noted, may differ considerably from a pay adjustment based on simply observing the difference between the survey average (in this example, \$45,436 at GS-15) and the actual average GS pay (\$41,800 in this example). (If this method were used, the comparability increase for GS-15 would be 8.70 percent in 1978. President Carter's pay increase cap of 5.5 percent

25. In the 1978 survey about three-fourths of the employment weights were between GS-4 and GS-12.

26. The form of the equation is $W_g = ab^i c^{i^2}$, where W_g is average salary in grade g; a, b, c are constants to be estimated; and i is a grade index. (Since promotions up to GS-11 are typically "double grade"—that is, from GS-5 to GS-7—and each GS level above grade 11 represents a promotion, the grade index used in the computation is $i = g$ for $g = 1, 2, 3, \ldots, 11$; $i = 13, 15, 17, 19$ for $g = 12, 13, 14, 15$.) In each of the last three years the estimate of the parameter b has been slightly above one and that of c slightly below one. Since the percentage difference between grades 1 and 2 in the equation is equal to $bc^3 - 1$ and that between grades 2 and 3 is equal to $bc^5 - 1$, and so on, the intergrade percentage difference diminishes as long as c is less than one. The regression technique used to estimate the parameters amounts to first rewriting the equation in logarithmic form and then finding (by standard regression methods) the parameters that minimize the weighted sum of the squared logarithms of the deviations of the data from the curve.

27. The parameters $a, b,$ and c defined above for 1978 are: for the survey pay line, \$6,389, 1.1385, and 0.9986, respectively; for the reference line, \$6,015, 1.1393, and 0.9984, respectively.

TABLE 4. *Computation of 1978 Pay Increases with Comparability Method, Selected General Schedule Levels*
Dollars unless otherwise specified

GS level	General schedule		Survey		Percentage increase	
	Average salary	Reference line	Average salary	Pay line	Between averages	Between lines
1	6,405	6,842	7,036	7,263	9.85	6.15
3	8,524	8,769	9,620	9,311	12.86	6.18
5	11,321	11,096	11,418	11,806	0.86	6.40
7	13,946	13,864	15,356	14,807	10.11	6.80
9	16,924	17,104	19,050	18,367	12.56	7.39
11	20,563	20,834	23,150	22,535	12.58	8.17
13	29,755	29,757	32,363	32,824	8.76	10.31
15	41,800	40,396	45,436	45,757	8.70	13.27
16	46,618[a]	46,178	...	53,142	...	15.08
17	47,500[a]	52,122	...	61,046	...	17.12
18	47,500[a]	58,088	...	69,359	...	19.40

Source: *Comparability of the Federal Statutory Pay Systems with Private Enterprise Pay Rates: Annua Report of the President's Pay Agent, 1978*, p. 23.
   a. Not used in computing reference pay line.

comes closer to the data for this grade than does the existing methodology.)

The last step in the comparability methodology is to apply the percentage increases derived from the curves (last column in table 4) to the step 1 salary rates of the previous period in each grade. This is illustrated for 1978 in table 5. The 13.27 percent pay increase for GS-15 under the comparability methodology is applied to the prevailing rate for step 1 of GS-15 ($36,171) to determine the new step 1 rate ($40,971).[28]

In sum, the comparability procedure for the first fifteen general schedule grades involves, first, deriving a percentage pay increase for each grade from the relation between statistically estimated curves *based on actual private market and government pay data*. The second step is to apply the percentage increases to *the actual prevailing pay schedule*.

Supergrade Pay

The procedure for adjusting the supergrade pay scale is exactly the same, except that the italicized clauses in the last paragraph do not apply in most cases.

28. Within-grade increases are constant dollar amounts equal to 3.33 percent of the step 1 rate in each grade.

TABLE 5. *Computation of Step 1 Salary Level for October 1978 Based on Comparability Method, Selected General Schedule Levels*

GS level	Old step 1 (1977–78) rate (dollars)	Percent adjustment	New step 1 (1978–79) rate (dollars)
13	26,022	10.31	28,704
15	36,171	13.27	40,971
16	42,423	15.08	48,821*
17	49,696*	17.12	58,204*
18	58,245*	19.40	69,547*

Source: Same as table 4.
* Theoretical rate.

In computing the percentage increase for the supergrades, the procedure is to calculate the difference between the points on the estimated curves (see table 4). Since no data on supergrade pay are used in estimating the curves, this procedure, as noted, amounts to a pure extrapolation of the data for the GS-1 to GS-15 employees surveyed. The implicit logic is that, if the survey pay line faithfully depicts the wage structure in the private sector and if the reference pay line embodies desired intergrade differences, such extrapolation is warranted.

The percentage increase for each supergrade level should then be applied, by analogy with the procedure for lower grades, to the prevailing step 1 rate. But the prevailing rates for GS-18, GS-17, and some steps of GS-16 in 1978 were subject to the executive level V ceiling. Thus the President's pay agent applies the pay boost to the prevailing theoretical (asterisked) rate (see table 5).[29] This theoretical rate has virtually no meaning; it was derived from the accretion of a variety of past pay decisions, including differently defined across-the-board raises. Unlike the case for the lower grades, application of the comparability increases to the asterisked rates does not necessarily bring supergrade pay to the level implied by the survey pay line. As a result, the salary rate reported as full comparability for supergrades defies definition and may even be inconsistent with the underlying assumptions.[30]

29. The old step 1 salary of $58,245 in table 5 was the asterisked rate for GS-18s in 1978.

30. For example, the 1978 full comparability salaries for the supergrades (table 5) shows an *increasing* percentage difference between grades 16 and 17 and between 17 and 18, although the underlying salary curves show diminishing differences. To explain why this occurs requires a complete review of pay changes over the last three years. After making such a review, one knows a lot more numbers, but it all makes no more sense.

TABLE 6. *Comparison of Pay Increases for GS-15 Based on Actual Data and on the Comparability Method, 1976–78*

Percent

Basis for increase	1976	1977	1978	1976–78
Actual data[a]	8.59	5.52	8.70	24.6
Comparability[b]	7.92	9.85	13.27	34.3

Source: *Annual Report of the President's Pay Agent* for years shown, app. A, table 2.
a. PATC survey average divided by actual GS average.
b. PATC survey pay line divided by GS reference line.

The Inadequacy of Current Procedures

Current comparability procedures are woefully inadequate for setting supergrade salaries. The percentage pay increases under the comparability process for these employees are based entirely on an extrapolation of data collected on employees at lower grades. Any biases in the procedures for the upper portion of the general schedule employees will tend to become more pronounced at the supergrade level.

Such a bias seems to have crept into the comparability procedure for determining GS-15 pay. Table 6 shows that the pay increases for that level computed directly from the data would have aggregated to less than 25 percent from 1976 to 1978, but the comparability procedures would have led to an increase of over 34 percent in the same period.[31]

This discrepancy is due entirely to the statistical procedures used in the comparability process. Although one cannot rule out the possibility that the apparent upward bias in the statistical procedure is a chance occurrence, soon to be reversed, examination of other evidence in the comparability method points toward a systematic bias. The way the curve currently employed fits the GS-15 data does not seem to be free of bias.[32]

31. Actually, the pay increase for GS-15 amounted to only 22 percent as a result of an across-the-board rise in 1977 and the pay cap in 1978. Had the 1977 comparability increase been granted to GS-15s, both entries in the 1978 column of table 6 would have been lower by about the same amount.

32. The pay increases under comparability procedures for GS-15 are higher than the increases derived from the underlying data for 1977 and 1978 because the survey pay-line curve exceeds the survey average and because the reference curve is below actual GS pay in both years. An examination of residuals (deviations of curves from data points) at all grade levels for 1976, 1977, and 1978 discloses a consistent pattern whereby current procedures lead to an upwardly biased wage increase in some grades (5, 6, 8) and a downward bias in others (3, 9, 11). The pattern of the arithmetic signs of the residuals is remarkably similar at each grade from year to year, both in the survey pay line and in the reference line, suggesting that the curves to which the data are fitted may not accurately capture the salary structure.

If such a bias exists at the GS-15 level, the determination of the GS-16 to GS-18 percentage pay increases by the same statistical procedures will be subject to the same biases in even more pronounced form.

Aside from the purely statistical problem in setting supergrade pay is the implication (for subsequent comparability calculations) of the practice of giving across-the-board increases. In recent years, only in 1976 were full comparability pay raises granted for grades 1–15.[33] In both 1977 and 1978 flat increases of 7.05 and 5.5 percent, respectively, were granted at all grades. Such increases keep the pattern of intergrade differentials constant. In these two years, however, the private sector data showed that pay increases for the matched jobs in the upper part of the pay scale exceeded those of the lower part.[34] This implies that the slope of the survey pay line is rising.

The effect of a GS reference line that remains flat as the survey pay line becomes steeper is that percentage pay raises at the upper end of the scale become larger and larger. For GS-11 to GS-15 this simply means that a larger raise is necessary to make up for the losses suffered when the across-the-board raises were granted. The only issue for these employees is the political difficulty of implementing comparability increases that are much larger at the higher grades than at the bottom.

For the supergrades, however, the progressive widening of the spread between survey results and the extrapolated GS data is confusing and misleading on all counts. The comparability pay raises get larger and larger at the supergrade levels irrespective of what actually happens to supergrade pay. Thus in late February 1977 virtually all supergrade employees received an increase in pay of up to 19.9 percent (from $39,600 to as much as $47,500). However, this pay increase did not significantly affect the comparability calculation for October 1977, which called for further increases of 11 to 14 percent, a result of the widening spread between the extrapolated pay lines. Because supergrade data are excluded from the pay-line procedures, changes in the ceiling (and in actual salary received) play no part in the comparability calculation.

Naturally, comparability pay increases for the supergrades have been irrelevant to actual pay in recent years because of the ceiling. Perhaps

33. In 1976 pay increases ranged from a little over 4 percent in the lower grades to nearly 8 percent at grade 15.
34. The main reason for this seems to be more rapid salary advances in professional and administrative positions (heavily represented in the upper part of the pay scale) than in clerical jobs. See "White Collar Salaries, March 1978," Department of Labor *News,* July 3, 1978.

knowledge that the calculations would not really affect anyone's paycheck contributed to a lack of concern about comparability. However, should the pay ceiling be removed, the procedures governing comparability for the supergrades would become more important.[35]

The Survey Alternative

There are two alternatives to the present procedures for adjusting supergrade pay without a pay ceiling. One is to collect data on nonfederal salaries for comparable positions, and the other is simply to set pay rates, more or less arbitrarily, so that desirable intergrade differences obtain.

Collecting data on compensation for jobs comparable to federal supergrade positions would be the most satisfactory substitute. Some doubts have been voiced about the feasibility of finding job matches and of comparing all the elements of compensation (bonuses, in particular) in the nonfederal sector to the compensation for federal jobs. Evaluating such doubts is beyond my competence, but two developments that may dispel them should be cited.

First, what appears to be a careful attempt to survey private industry practices in compensating executives was completed by the Civil Service Commission in 1974.[36] The study was able to identify eight occupations in which there were over 300 jobs comparable to ones in the supergrade range. Data were obtained from 144 companies representing all industries. The results of this survey, which showed federal supergrade salaries to be way below private sector jobs, are less important than that it demonstrated the technical feasibility of surveying supergrade-equivalent positions.[37]

35. A good case can be made that as long as the ceiling determines pay in any grade the government would be well advised not to publish or even calculate theoretical pay rates. The contrary view is that as long as the theoretical pay rates are conservative estimates of private sector pay (see the next section) they are a reminder of the unfortunate effects of the ceiling.

36. Civil Service Commission, *Staff Report, Study of Private Enterprise Pay Rates for Positions Equivalent to GS-14/18* (CSC, 1974).

37. The 1974 survey showed average compensation (salary plus bonus, in dollars) as follows:

GS equivalent	Employees receiving no bonus	Employees receiving bonus
16	47,615	48,789
17	57,773	70,277
18	74,383	86,124

The supergrade pay ceiling at that time was $36,000. The private sector survey averages exceeded the asterisked rates as well. See ibid., p. 30.

Second, if a survey of supergrade-equivalent jobs were undertaken, the task of job matching might be greatly eased by extending the survey to state and local governments. President Carter's personnel management project contained a proposal that the survey of all GS levels be so extended.[38] If such extension is a good idea for the position of entry-level file clerk, it must be an even better one for a "director of the Bureau of Vocational Education" and other jobs unique to government.

A Simple Alternative

The alternative to a survey of comparable nonfederal jobs, though arbitrary, would be more straightforward than present procedures. First, the annual comparability exercise should be strictly limited to GS levels 1 to 15. Second, the President would make recommendations for supergrade pay based on some set of "desirable" intergrade differences. For example, if studies of private industry showed fairly high differentials—say, 25 percent—for supergrade-equivalent jobs,[39] the President could simply promulgate a schedule consistent with this finding. Alternatively, if the President deemed it essential only that there be some difference, he might recommend a schedule with small differences between jobs. Such a procedure is contained in the new Senior Executive Service and will be discussed in the next section. Let me simply note here that the important point of an admittedly arbitrary schedule is that it unlinks the determinants of executive (supergrade) pay from that of a system designed for GS-1 to GS-15. Such a separation has heretofore taken place anyway through the pay ceiling; it is high time to abandon the myth that supergrade pay is based in any way on comparability.

The Senior Executive Service

The Civil Service Reform Act of 1978 promises major changes in the compensation of federal executives, the most important being the creation

38. President's Reorganization Project, Personnel Management Project, *Final Staff Report* (PMP, 1977), vol. 1, pp. 155–56.

39. This was the finding of the 1974 Civil Service study; see *Staff Report, Study of Private Enterprise Pay Rates,* p. 31. See also the Liebtag paper, this volume.

of the Senior Executive Service.[40] Much of the debate over this new managerial cadre questioned whether the alleged gains in management efficiency were worth the potential politicization of the career service.[41] Less attention was paid to the pay aspects of the Senior Executive Service, whose implications are far-reaching.

Pay Structure

The Senior Executive Service (SES) features an entirely new compensation system for about 8,500 federal positions previously classified as GS-16 to GS-18 through executive level IV (or equivalent positions in other salary systems). Executives in these positions will be compensated by a system of basic pay, incentive awards, and performance awards.

Basic pay is analogous to the previous salary system for federal executives. The legislation stipulates that there shall be at least five rates of basic pay in the SES. The maximum rate may not exceed that for level IV of the executive schedule, and the minimum rate cannot be lower than that for GS-16, step 1. No automatic steps, as such, are contemplated for the SES.

In addition to basic pay, a limited number of members of the SES will be eligible for special ranks. Up to 5 percent of the SES in any year may be designated "meritorious executives" (for what the act calls "sustained accomplishment"). Another 1 percent may become "distinguished executives" (for "sustained extraordinary accomplishment"). These ranks are conferred by the President and entitle the meritorious executives to a lump-sum payment of $10,000 and the distinguished executives to one of $20,000. These "incentive awards" do not affect retirement benefits or deductions. A person may be awarded the same rank only once in a five-year period.

Most important, SES members will be eligible for "performance awards," which are intended to "encourage excellence in performance." Performance awards may be given to no more than 50 percent of the SES members in any agency. The amount of the award can be no more than 20 percent of basic pay. For any one person, the combination of basic pay,

---

40. Title IV of Public Law 95-454.

41. On this subject, see Bernard Rosen, "Merit and the President's Plan for Changing the Civil Service System," *Public Administration Review,* vol. 38 (July–August 1978), pp. 301–04.

incentive award, and performance award cannot exceed the salary for executive level I.[42]

The provision for adjusting pay for the SES should also be noted. The President is directed by the legislation to adjust both the minimum and the maximum rates of pay for the SES at the time he submits his annual recommendation for general schedule increases. While the minimum and maximum are changed by this procedure, the salary of any particular SES employee (except those below the new minimum) is not necessarily changed—there is no automatic adjustment in a person's pay.

Implications of the Pay Structure

The establishment of the Senior Executive Service in 1979 illustrates both the promises and the problems of the new pay structure. When the SES was inaugurated on July 13, 1979, the salaries of those transferred to the new service were maintained at the then-current rates (table 7). The rate structure was severely compressed, with six pay levels squeezed into a pay range of less than 12 percent. In October 1979 it became possible to broaden this basic pay range considerably. President Carter's proposed 7 percent pay increase for general schedule workers raised the SES minimum pay by a like amount. However, the maximum SES basic salary would have risen by an even greater percentage because level IV of the executive schedule was due for two years' worth of increases in October.[43] Had these permissible rates gone into effect in October, the basic pay range would have widened to about 18 percent, and there would have been six distinct pay levels in the SES (see the second column in table 7). Instead, the Congress, after a blistering fight over members'

---

42. Incentive and performance awards will be available only to career employees in the SES. Noncareer ("political") and limited (short-term) appointees—up to 15 percent of the SES work force—will not be eligible for these awards. Since the 50 percent limitation on performance awards applies to all SES members, more than 50 percent of the career employees may be eligible to receive a bonus in any year. In addition to direct monetary rewards, the SES also contains two new fringe benefits. First, employees will be eligible for an eleven-month sabbatical at full pay once every ten years. Second, SES members will be allowed to accumulate unlimited amounts of unused annual leave—in the past, leave was forfeited once thirty days had been accumulated.

43. The large increase in executive level pay (12.9 percent) was the result of combining the postponed "automatic" 5.5 percent pay increase for 1978 and the 7 percent increase for 1979.

TABLE 7. *Pay Rates for the Senior Executive Service, 1979*
Dollars

Pay rate category	Basic pay			Payable rate[b] plus maximum performance award[c]
	Initial rate[a]	Scheduled rate[b]	Payable rate[b]	
ES-1	44,756	47,889	47,889	57,467
ES-2	46,470	49,499	49,499	59,399
ES-3	47,500	51,164	50,112.50	60,135
ES-4	47,500	52,884	50,112.50	60,135
ES-5	47,500	54,662	50,112.50	60,135
ES-6	⎰47,500 ⎱50,000[d]	56,500	⎰50,112.50 ⎱52,750[d]	⎰60,135 ⎱63,300[d]

Source: Office of Personnel Management, "Adjusting Pay for the Senior Executive Service," FPM bulletin 920-31 (November 15, 1979).
  a. Effective July 1979.
  b. Effective October 1979.
  c. Maximum performance award equals 20 percent of basic pay in each pay rate category.
  d. The higher rate for ES-6 was initially payable only to those in offices or positions that were in level IV of the executive schedule before conversion to the SES; in October these persons received the 5.5 percent pay raise shown. Others who were classified as ES-6 were limited to the lower rate of pay shown in the line above.

pay, voted to limit the basic pay rates to only 5.5 percent more than those paid before October 1979. As a result, the SES entered its first full year with two pay rates: the "scheduled rate" and the "payable rate."[44] The payable rates, which are the amounts actually received by those in the SES, exhibit all the faults of the past pay system. There is even more compression, with six basic pay levels squeezed into a 10 percent range. Four levels of pay are identical. The only real differentiation in basic pay for the SES is in the scheduled rates, which, like the asterisked rates of the supergrade pay system, probably induce more anger than comfort.

The performance award system—to be implemented for the first time in 1980—may change this picture somewhat, but at considerable cost. If performance awards of 20 percent are made available, pay in the SES will range from $47,889 to $63,300, a difference of over 30 percent. A few members of the SES may even take home a total (basic pay plus performance award) higher than the salary of members of Congress.[45]

44. This two-track system is analogous to the asterisked rate–pay ceiling rate system described previously for the supergrades.
45. Members' pay after October 1979 is $60,662.50. Note that, except for some individuals at ES-6, most members of the SES, even with a maximum performance award, will receive about $500 less than members of Congress.

But most of the differentiation in pay will result from the annual performance awards, not the basic pay structure. This places a heavy burden on the untried system of performance awards. Inevitably, there will be an attempt to use some of the bonus money to redress inequities in the highly compressed basic pay structure. But if the distribution of this money is based on criteria other than performance, its usefulness as an incentive to encourage excellence will be diluted.

In the future the compressed basic pay structure of the SES may become an even greater problem because minimum and maximum pay may change at different rates. Changes in the minimum will be based on the GS-16, step 1, rate, which is governed by the comparability procedures previously described. Increases in the maximum pay rate, limited to level IV of the executive schedule, will be based on the *average* increase in the general schedule. The imposition of flat across-the-board pay increases in 1977, 1978, and 1979 has placed GS-16 pay as much as 11 percent below the comparability standard.[46] Any comparability pay increase for GS-16s in the next couple of years will drive up the minimum pay rate of the SES by much more than the maximum rate increases.[47] Should such a narrowing of the basic pay range occur, the performance award process would have to play an even larger part in differentiating among employees.

In the next few years, it is more likely that across-the-board increases will be granted to all general schedule employees. Under these circumstances, the minimum and maximum rates of SES base pay would rise in tandem, provided the automatic increases in the salaries for the executive schedule were allowed to take effect, and would at best maintain the compressed pay structure established in 1979.[48] However, in 1980 (an election year) it is unlikely that the automatic increase for the executive schedule will be allowed, which means that SES basic pay will be further compressed.

46. In the March 1979 pay survey GS-16 salary was found to be 17.8 percent below that for similar jobs in the private sector. The October 1979 pay raise for GS-16 was only 7 percent. See *Annual Report of the President's Pay Agent, 1979*, table 2, p. 17.

47. The minimum level of base pay for the SES fortunately cannot exceed the maximum since the GS-16, step 1, rate can never exceed that of level V of the executive schedule, and level IV must be higher than level V. The rate range could, however, shrink to a few hundred dollars covering six ranks.

48. The adverse effects of failing to raise executive salaries are spelled out in U.S. Comptroller General, *Annual Adjustments: The Key to Federal Executive Pay*, Report to the Congress, FPCD-79-31 (GAO, 1979).

Implications for the 1980 Quadrennial Commission

No matter what the situation in 1980, in the future the dog may wag the tail in top-level federal pay. In the past decade, once pay for members of Congress was set, the effective pay rates for most supergrades and higher officers in the executive fell into place like dominoes. The next quadrennial commission may find its problems considerably different.

If the 1980 quadrennial commission considers the need for maintaining a viable Senior Executive Service to be part of its charter, it will find its decisions on the executive schedule quite constrained. To maintain a reasonable range of basic pay in the SES, salaries for executive level IV will have to exceed pay for GS-16, step 1, by, say, 25 percent.[49] But to provide room for the maximum performance bonus for the top people in the SES, the salary for executive level I must be at least 20 percent higher than the salary for executive level IV. What these constraints amount to is that the pay for a GS-16 becomes the driving force behind the salaries of the highest political appointees in the executive branch. Since the 1980 quadrennial commission will inherit a GS-16 pay rate and the commission's purview does not include reviewing that pay rate, the agenda for the quadrennial commission looks pretty cut and dried.[50]

The only problem with this is the present linkage of executive level II pay to congressional salaries. If this continues and if there is pressure to hold down congressional pay, the entire pay structure of the SES could be undermined indefinitely. Linking low congressional pay to the executive schedule will continue to create the same kind of compression in basic pay rates for the SES as in its first year.

There is reason for cautious optimism that the SES will reduce compression once the transitional problems are overcome. In creating the SES, Congress clearly recognized that the career civil service should be remunerated under a separate system not hierarchically linked to the pay of political appointees. This recognition is reflected in the Civil Service Reform Act provisions that do not allow noncareer employees to earn bonuses or to be granted special ranks and that do allow career employees to earn more than all executive level appointees except cabinet secre-

49. This would permit 5 percent pay differences between the six levels in the SES, or about $2,500 for each level at 1980 rates.

50. For those who treasure famous last words, the implication here is that the commission will observe a 1980 GS-16 pay level of about $50,000 and will then set executive level IV pay at about $62,500 and executive level I pay at about $75,000.

taries. The "workers," in other words, can make more than the "bosses." If Congress can deliberately vote for such a system, this would seem to encourage the next quadrennial commission to break the remaining links. Specifically, the commission could openly recognize that political appointees in the executive schedule and members of Congress hold entirely different positions from career employees and that these warrant different pay systems. Also, the commission could recommend that Congress finish what it started by eliminating the ceilings on basic salary and total compensation in the SES. These moves would simply extend the principle started by the creation of the SES: that all the positions at the top of the federal pay structure need not be inextricably linked to one another in a hierarchical way, but rather that a separate pay plan should be designed for each group of employees.

Implications of Comparability and Annual Adjustments of Salary

Limitations on the basic pay band of the SES are set by comparability increases for GS-16 and by the overall average increase for the general schedule. If either of these pay changes are suspect, the new pay system may be discredited. At present, there are enough problems with each of these concepts to warrant further study.

As noted earlier, the pay curves used to fit the survey and employment data may not perform well at the top of the surveyed jobs, making the extrapolation at the GS-16 level somewhat suspect. Some consideration should therefore be given to trying an independent survey of GS-16 level jobs in state and local governments to establish a floor for the SES. If such a survey breaks the link with the lower part of the general schedule, so be it. At least the survey would supply some market data where none now exists.

Current law emphasizes the "average" increase in general schedule pay. This average determines the automatic rise in the pay of executive schedule employees and thereby determines the increase in the maximum basic pay for the SES. The average increase in the general schedule is, however, an elusive concept.

When comparability increases are granted, there are ordinarily different rates of increase at each level of the general schedule. In recent years it has been the practice of the President's pay agent to weight these different percentage changes by the salary bill in each GS grade to compute an average pay raise. Thus, for example, in the 1978 comparability calculation, the average so computed was 8.4 percent. If the percentage increases at each grade had been weighted by total employment in each grade (rather than by salary), the average would have been 7.6 percent.[51] If the current law's intent is to provide executive level pay increases equivalent to those granted other federal workers, it is not at all clear why a salary-bill weighted average is the correct concept. If a comparability increase is ever again implemented, some attention ought to be paid to the various concepts used in determining the average GS salary increase.

The practice of granting across-the-board increases removes most of the ambiguity from the average general schedule increase. All job slots (for example, GS-5, step 2, or GS-9, step 5) are raised by approximately the same percentage, and it therefore seems reasonable to raise pay in an executive level slot (for example, secretary of HEW) by the same percentage. In the case of the Senior Executive Service an ambiguity arises, however. The SES is supposed to embody the idea of rank in a person rather than rank in a job slot. Thus a person with a relatively low SES rank could be assigned to a highly responsible post without any pay adjustment, since the rank and basic pay rate are determined by his or her qualifications, not by the job actually performed. The question is why a rank-in-person pay rate should be adjusted by a job-slot-specific pay increase rather than by pay increases for a continuing employee. A continuing employee in the general schedule receives not only the schedule increase but also periodic step increases, which average between 1 and 2 percent annually. If the basic salary of an SES member is intended to keep pace with that of an average continuing employee, use of a fixed-job index (the average general schedule increase) appears inappropriate. In any event, the underlying theory that establishes a link between a job-slot-specific pay increase and a rank-in-person pay system has yet to be clearly defined.

Coda

If one reads through enough reports of past commissions, congressional hearings, and special studies on top officials' pay, a consensus does emerge. The standard for top political appointees, judges, and members of

---

51. Employment weights yield a smaller average increase than salary-bill weights because the latter are greater than employment weights at the upper end of the pay scale where the comparability increases were highest.

Congress goes like this: the government should pay enough so that people of modest independent means are attracted to public service, but not so much that general public resentment will be aroused. Since high government officials are expected to maintain the same standard of living as the professional and business elite while public opinion polls currently suggest resentment of almost any pay increase, the standard cannot produce a number to meet both objectives. For this reason, the process by which the salaries of our highest officials are set must be chosen carefully, in the hope that a well-received process may legitimate the necessarily compromised results.

No matter what procedure is adopted for the executive, judicial, and legislative branches, pay for career civil servants should be set by some other procedure. The important consideration for this group is that federal pay—including nonsalary benefits—be sufficient to make a career in public service attractive, facilitating the recruitment and retention of people whose quality and performance are commensurate with the responsibilities of their jobs. Meeting this criterion requires a long perspective. For example, even if the problems of pay compression discussed earlier had little discernible short-run effect, they could be severely damaging if they discouraged able young people from entering the federal pipeline. Pay for high-ranking career officials, in this view, is one element in shaping the career choice of future government managers. Along with working conditions, the prestige accorded public service, promotion rates, the perception of whether merit is rewarded, and so on, federal pay policy will help determine whether future executives can meet the challenge of running the nation's biggest enterprise.

The pay aspect of federal careers in recent years cannot have helped attract quality people. Even if the average level of pay for career managers in the last decade was in the right ball park, the structure of pay was daunting. A pattern of long pay freezes followed by abrupt jumps in pay (with only the latter featured in the headlines) is not likely to lure people into a career. Nor is the compression of several levels of responsibility at one rate of pay. Nor is the lockstep of longevity raises unrelated to merit or the common classification given to different jobs that span a wide range of responsibility.

The reform of the civil service that passed in 1978 has therefore created substantial hope for a break with the past. The Senior Executive Service, on paper at least, could remedy many of the previous shortcomings. Not the least of its virtues is that it seems to separate pay for career public servants from pay for other officials.

This paper has emphasized some of the narrower aspects of the SES—its effects on compression and on rewarding exemplary service. In these respects, the SES has the potential to be a clear improvement over past practices.

How the SES will affect the long-term attractiveness of federal service is more open to conjecture. If the merit-based pay aspects are handled improperly[52] or if reassignments or pay reductions for members of the SES are perceived to be political or capricious in its early years, the SES could damage the chances for attracting a quality work force in the future. Designing the pay structure for the SES is no easy task: it must simultaneously appear to be a stable system for rewarding experience and a flexible system for improving management. It must institute sufficient checks on merit-based awards to avoid the charge of political favoritism, and in general convince aspirants that public service is a reasonable choice over other possible careers. Carrying out such a task in a society that distrusts government employees and in a government that stresses budgetary stringency will be a formidable challenge.

---

52. Will agencies simply offer each manager a bonus (performance award) every other year to get around the 50 percent rule? Will these awards be subject to affirmative action tests?

Conference Participants

with their affiliations at the time of the conference

Joel D. Aberbach *Brookings Institution*

Alan K. Campbell *U.S. Office of Personnel Management*

Mark W. Cannon *U.S. Supreme Court*

Mortimer Caplin *Caplin and Drysdale*

W. D. Conley *Honeywell Incorporated*

Roger H. Davidson *University of California, Santa Barbara*

Louis Fisher *Library of Congress*

Robert J. Flanagan *Council of Economic Advisers*

William E. Foley *Administrative Office of the U.S. Courts*

Bernard L. Gladieux *Committee for Economic Development*

Arthur A. Handy *Kaiser Steel Corporation*

Robert W. Hartman *Brookings Institution*

Hugh Heclo *Harvard University*

Walter G. Held *Brookings Institution*

James Hodgson *Pathfinder Mines Corporation*

Stephen Horn *California State University, Long Beach*

Roger W. Jones *New Hartford, Connecticut*

James C. Kirby, Jr. *New York University Law School and University of Tennessee College of Law*

Frederick A. Kistler *U.S. Office of Personnel Management*

Edward Lazear *University of Chicago*

Martin Lefkowitz *U.S. Chamber of Commerce*

Wesley R. Liebtag *International Business Machines Corporation*

Frederick R. Livingston *Kaye, Scholer, Fierman, Hays and Handler*

Ross A. Marcou *U.S. Office of Personnel Management and Brookings Institution*

231

Robert B. McKersie *Cornell University*

Daniel J. B. Mitchell *Brookings Institution*

James M. Mitchell *Brookings Institution*

Norman J. Ornstein *Catholic University of America*

Arch A. Patton *McKinsey and Company*

Joseph A. Pechman *Brookings Institution*

Nelson Polsby *University of California, Berkeley*

Edward F. Preston *U.S. Office of Management and Budget*

Melvin Reder *University of Chicago*

Albert Rees *Princeton University and National Bureau of Economic Research*

Bernard Rosen *American University*

Sherwin Rosen *University of Chicago*

Jerome M. Rosow *Work in America Institute*

Laurence H. Silberman *American Enterprise Institute for Public Policy Research*

Sharon P. Smith *Federal Reserve Bank of New York*

Elmer B. Staats *U.S. General Accounting Office*

James L. Sundquist *Brookings Institution*

David P. Taylor *Hay Associates*

Arnold R. Weber *Carnegie-Mellon University*

Index

Adams, Charles Francis, 172n
Adams, John Quincy, 171
Agency theory, 119
Alexander, John, 48
Allen, James B., 83–84
American Bar Association, 8, 168n, 181–82
Anderson, Jack, 174
Army, Department of the, 210n
Association of the Bar of the City of New York, 166, 172n
Average hourly earnings, index of, 10, 150, 159

Backdating. *See* Retroactivity
Baer, George, Jr., 49
Bailey, Joseph W., 173
Baker, Robert G., Senate action against, 189, 190, 191
Barkley, Alben W., 50
Barro, Robert J., 119n
Bartlett, Dewey F., 85, 86
Beard, Edmund, 200
Becker, Gary S., 110n, 119n, 122n
Bell, John, 50
Bennett, Charles, 199
Berlow, Alan, 192n
Biddle, Nicholas, 171
Blaustein, Albert P., 179n
Blount, William, 188
Bolling, Richard, 73, 74
Bonuses: Civil Service Reform Act and, 225; for Senior Executive Service, 11, 16, 160, 222–23, 224
Borah, William E., 173, 180, 183
Boyd, Julian P., 27n
Bright, John M., 50n
Bulwinkel, Alfred L., 42n
Burdick, Quentin N., 74, 75
Bureau of Labor Statistics, 213–14
Burman, George R., 106, 108, 109, 113, 145n

Byrd, Robert C., 78, 84
Byrns, Joseph W., 30

Cabinet officers, 8, 155, 203–04. *See also* Executives; Executive schedule
Calhoun, John C., 44, 49
Cannon, Clarence, 30
Careers, remuneration effect on choice of, 104, 109
Carter, Jimmy: civil service reform, 65, 69, 75, 90, 94; and federal salaries, 83, 92, 207, 214–15, 222; personnel management project, 220; staff salaries, 67
Cass, Lewis, 50
Celler, Emanuel, 43, 197–98
Chamber of Commerce of the United States of America, 157
Champion, Hale, 8
Chappell, John L., 49
Chipman, Daniel, 48
Church, Frank, 79, 92
Citizens' Committee for Restoring Public Trust in Government, 12, 96
Civil service: congressional committees and, 72–75; reform proposals for, 65, 69, 75, 90, 94. *See also* Civil Service Reform Act of *1978;* Executive schedule; General schedule; Senior Executive Service; Supergrade compensation
Civil Service Commission, 219
Civil Service Reform Act of *1978,* 149, 228; and linkage principle, 97; merit pay system, 143, 156, 159–60
Clark, Joseph S., 198
Clay, Henry, 44; on constituency reaction, 49; on Salary Act of *1816,* 37
Clayton, Thomas, 46n, 48
Clendenin, David, 48
Code of ethics, 5, 97; actions resulting from, 189–91; and compensation, 115; effectiveness of, 191–92; enforcement prognosis for, 192–200; on gifts, 185–

233